VISUAL METHODS
IN SOCIAL RESEARCH

D0104375

VISUAL METHODS
IN SOCIAL RESEARCH

Marcus Banks

SAGE Publications
London ● Thousand Oaks ● New Delhi

ISBN-10 0-7619-6363-4
ISBN-10 0-7619-6364-2 (pbk)

ISBN-13 978-0-7619-6363-9
ISBN-13 978-0-7619-6364-6 (pbk)

© Marcus Banks 2001
First published 2001
Reprinted 2003, 2005, 2006

SAGE Publications Ltd
1 Oliver's Yard
55 City Road
London EC1Y 1SP

SAGE Publications Inc
2455 Teller Road
Thousand Oaks
California 91320

SAGE Publications India Pvt. Ltd
B–42 Panchsheel Enclave
PO Box 4109
New Delhi 110 017

British Library Cataloguing in Publication data

A catalogue record for this book is available from the British Library

Printed on paper from sustainable sources

Typeset by Photoprint Ltd., Torquay, Devon
Printed and bound in Great Britain by
Athenæum Press Limited, Gateshead, Tyne & Wear

Contents

Preface

This book aims to provide a brief account of some of the ways in which social scientists can incorporate visual images (of various kinds) into their research, together with a discussion of why they might wish to. The emphasis is very much on the use of visual materials as one among several research methods that may be employed by a social researcher during the course of an investigation, rather than a focus on the visual for its own sake. I assume that readers already have or are acquiring the skills to devise a research project that is valid within the context of their discipline, but may not have thought of adding a visual dimension. Those who are already experienced visual researchers and are seeking to add a sociological dimension to their work should probably look elsewhere, as they will probably find what I have to say basic or naive with regard to the visual and opaque or elliptical with regard to the sociological.

While basic, and intended as a simple and practical guide for students, academic and non-academic researchers new to the fields of visual anthropology and visual sociology, this is not a technical guide to button-pressing on video cameras and the like. For that, readers should consult the technical manuals readily available in any large bookshop, in conjunction with a more specialist text written by and for social scientists. For film and video, Ilisa Barbash and Lucien Taylor's *Cross-Cultural Filmmaking* (1997) is both encyclopaedic in its detail and authoritative in its commentary. For still photography, Terence Wright's *Photography handbook* (1999) is a relatively short but practical text, shot through with historical, psychological and anthropological insight (Wright was a professional photographer before becoming an academic). Other relevant works are mentioned at various points in what follows. For computer-based multimedia, which I touch on in some places, there is no comparable text to Barbash and Taylor's or Wright's books, but I reference the few articles and other sources I have found useful where appropriate.

A few more qualifications before going on. First, although I have tried to write this book for the generic social scientist I cannot hide the fact that I am trained as a social anthropologist and that to a large extent I write as one, certainly in terms of the material I reference. There is some justification for this, as I hope that most academics would acknowledge that of all the social science disciplines it is anthropology, in the form of visual anthropology, that has made most use of visual materials in the course of research. There is now a growing tendency to involve visual materials in sociological and psychological research (see Prosser 1998a for some examples), as well as to invoke sociological perspectives in well-established visual disciplines such as art history and film studies. I hope scholars from these and other disciplines, such as educational studies and human geography, will still find something of use in what follows and be able to read across the anthropological bias of the material. Secondly, although I set out to write a book that dealt with a range of visual materials in a relatively even-handed way, I discovered once I had finished that there was a heavy emphasis on still photography. I'm not quite sure why this happened (my own background is in film, not photography), but I'm not unhappy with it. Still photography is a medium available to almost everyone in the world as either producer or consumer, and examples from the use of still photography can often serve to make points arising from the use of all or most visual media (exceptions are noted where appropriate).

The final qualification concerns my own qualifications. My initial exposure to visual techniques was a year that I spent as a Royal Anthropological Institute/Leverhulme Film Fellow at the (British) National Film and Television School in 1986–7; I am profoundly grateful to both institutions for affording me this opportunity. Since then, I have used film, video and still photography in the course of relatively mainstream anthropological fieldwork. My field research has largely been confined to India, as has my archival research, and hence material from India – both of my own collecting and that of others – figures prominently in this book. In particular, I have worked on the social organization of a minority religious group – the Jains – in a small city in western India. More recently I have begun to research the history of this city, in which the Jains as group of merchants and traders have played an important part, from a visual perspective.[1] I have also worked on the history of ethnographic film generally, compiling an online catalogue of early film sources (the HADDON catalogue, discussed in Chapter 6.4.2), subsequently drawing on this material to examine the visual representation of India in colonial period documentary film. I list these activities not in order to promote them or myself, but rather to give the reader a sense of my background and hence the gravitational centres around which my thinking on visual methods revolves.

The other source of ideas for this book, and certainly the incentive and stimulus for writing it, has been the students I have taught over the last decade or so. Several have been contributors to a class on visual anthropology that I run, others have been doctoral or other research students working on projects with a visual emphasis. As a result of this teaching activity I wrote a short piece on visual methodology (Banks 1995), followed by a longer article (Banks 1998). This book seeks to expand the ideas presented in the two articles, and the diligent reader may spot some overlap.

The book is divided into seven chapters. Chapters 1–3 introduce a variety of general and introductory issues concerning images, including a discussion of the physical materiality of many visual forms and the need for this to be considered in research and analysis (Chapter 3). Chapters 4 and 5 form the book's core and deal most directly with visual research methods in practice. Chapter 6 deals with the presentation of visual research results, and Chapter 7 offers a few more abstract thoughts by way of conclusion.

I have also set up a Web site to complement the book:

< v ww.rsl.ox.ac.uk/isca/vismeth >

The Web site is intended to keep the information given in the book up to date, and includes a list of useful addresses, details of the main journals in the field and links to various electronic resources.

Note

1 My overview work on the Jains is Banks 1992, but those who wish to go further should consult both Dundas 1992 and Laidlaw 1995; see also John Cort's programmatic article on the value of visual approaches to religious studies, based on his own and other published Jain material (Cort 1997). Until recently I have kept my Indian and Jain studies fairly distinct from my visual studies while I sought to come to grips with both; Banks 1989a is an early and not terribly satisfactory attempt at a photographic essay using my Jain material (based originally on a photographic exhibition at the Cambridge University Museum of Archaeology and Anthropology), while Banks 2000 is a more recent attempt to adopt a visualist perspective – as opposed to the explicit use of visual materials – in my analysis of the Jain social history, inspired by the work of Grimshaw (1997) among others.

Acknowledgements

The production of this book would not have been possible without the help and advice of a great many colleagues, friends and skilled professionals. There are too many to name them all, but I would like to thank some individually for their particular help. Elizabeth Edwards, Alison Kyst, Olwen Terris, and Chris Wright all agreed to be interviewed at length and to be endlessly pestered with trivial questions thereafter. Staff at the National Film and Television Archive in London, the Indian National Film and Television Archive, the Cambridge Centre of South Asian Studies, the Imperial War Museum Film and Video Department, and Christie's and Phillips auction houses provided information in the course of brief interviews as well as their professional assistance. Beth Crockett, Vanessa Harwood, and Simon Ross at Sage, and Jane Holden of Elliott-Holden Editing, all helped turn a jumble of text, images and questions into a book.

In Oxford, staff and colleagues at ISCA and at the Pitt Rivers Museum were endlessly patient when dealing with my many requests, while Mike Morris and Mark Dickerson tracked down many publications for me. Jonathan Miller, Malcolm Osman and Conrad Weiskrantz were all invaluable in helping me to produce the scans and frame-grabs that make up many of the illustrations used.

I also owe a debt of thanks to all the individuals and organizations named in the list of image credits, but particularly to Patsy Asch, Linda Connor, Paul Henley, and David MacDougall who were more than generous in providing images and background information. More generally, those who provided references, feedback and intellectual stimulus include Elizabeth Edwards, Howard Morphy, Laura Peers, Terry Wright and David Zeitlyn, as well as the many students who have contributed to visual anthropology courses over the years.

Finally, Barrie Thomas, David Zeitlyn and Anna Rayne all helped me to see things in perspective.

Image credits

Those named below supplied images and/or own the copyright in them, but are not necessarily the image-makers. All images are copyright and every effort has been made to trace the copyright holders. If any have been overlooked, or if any additional information can be given, amendments will be made at the first opportunity. The lines from 'Picture This' (words and music by Deborah Harry, Chris Stein and Jimmy Destri) © 1978, Monster Island Music/Chrysalis Music and are used by permission, all rights reserved.

1

Reading pictures

Figure 1.1   Layers of Gujarati and Hindi film posters on the wall of a busy street in Ahmedabad, India, 1984.

1.1 The trouble with pictures

Anthropology has had no lack of interest in the visual; its problem has always been what to do with it. (MacDougall 1997: 276)

It is quite common for visual researchers in the social sciences to claim that they work in a minority field that is neither understood, nor properly appreciated by their colleagues (e.g. Grady 1991; Prosser 1998b;

cf. MacDougall 1997). The reason, the argument goes, is that the social sciences are 'disciplines of words' (Mead 1995) in which there is no room for pictures, except as supporting characters. Yet at the same time visual anthropology, my own field, has never seemed more popular. Student demand is growing, and in response a number of masters degrees in visual anthropology have been developed in Britain and elsewhere, while visual options are increasingly being offered on undergraduate degree programmes. Visual anthropology leads the way in this, although visual sociology is also a relatively well-established sub-discipline, and visual approaches can be found in other research areas such as social psychology, educational studies and the like.[1]

There is now an abundant research literature from within cultural studies and most social science disciplines that specifically addresses visual forms and their place in mediating and constituting human social relationships, as well as discussing the visual presentation of research findings through film and photography. Methodological insight is, however, scattered or confined to quite specific areas, such as the production of ethnographic film. Paradoxically, while social researchers encounter images constantly, not merely in their own daily lives but as part of the texture of life of those they work with, they sometimes seem at a loss when it comes to incorporating images into their professional practice.

1.2   An introductory example

Figure 1.2   Early to mid twentieth-century postcard. Photographer unknown

So, what can social researchers do with pictures? Take Figure 1.2. It is a photograph, clearly. Eight men sit in a rough line, cross-legged, on the ground about 2 metres or so from the camera. Behind them are some trees, a cart with an ox yoked to it and on the far left of the picture some sort of small structure in front of which sit two other men. The men in the central line are oddly attired – some have white cloths draped across their shoulders but otherwise appear naked except for loin cloths. The faces of some are whitened with paint or ash; they are all bearded and some appear to have long hair gathered up on top of their heads. Several of the men are looking at the camera, and one holds something up to his mouth.

So far, assessing the content of the image has been a matter of applying labels – 'man', 'cart', 'cloth' – which lie within most people's perceptual and cognitive repertoire, as does the assessment of spatial arrangements: 'in a line', 'to the left of', 'behind'. To go much further in a reading of the image requires more precise information. The ox cart, for example, indicates that the scene is probably somewhere in South Asia, while anyone with a familiarity with India will probably guess that these are some kind of Indian 'holy men'. More specifically, they seem to be Hindu sadhus or ascetics. The man second from the left is actually not attired like the rest – he wears some kind of shirt or coat, and a turban. He is perhaps a villager who has come to talk to them or a patron who gives them alms. Those with more knowledge of Hindu practice may be able to highlight further detail, relating to the patterns of white markings on their faces, the just visible strings of beads some of them wear. Other areas of knowledge might enable us to identify the particular species of trees in the background or the specific construction type of the cart, helping us to guess at the altitude or region. Clearly it is not merely a question of looking closely but a question of bringing knowledges to bear upon the image.

While such a reading may help us towards understanding what the image is of, it still tells us nothing about why the image exists. To do that, we must move beyond the content and consider the image as an object. It is in fact a postcard, printed upon relatively thick and rather coarse card. The image itself is a photomechanical reproduction, not a true photograph, and although apparently composed of a range of sepia tones, this is an illusion, with only brown ink – in dots of varying size – having been used.

The reverse is marked in two ways (see Figure 1.3). First, the words 'Post Card', 'Correspondence' and 'Address' are printed lightly along the long edge. Secondly, these words are almost completely obscured by handwriting, which reads:

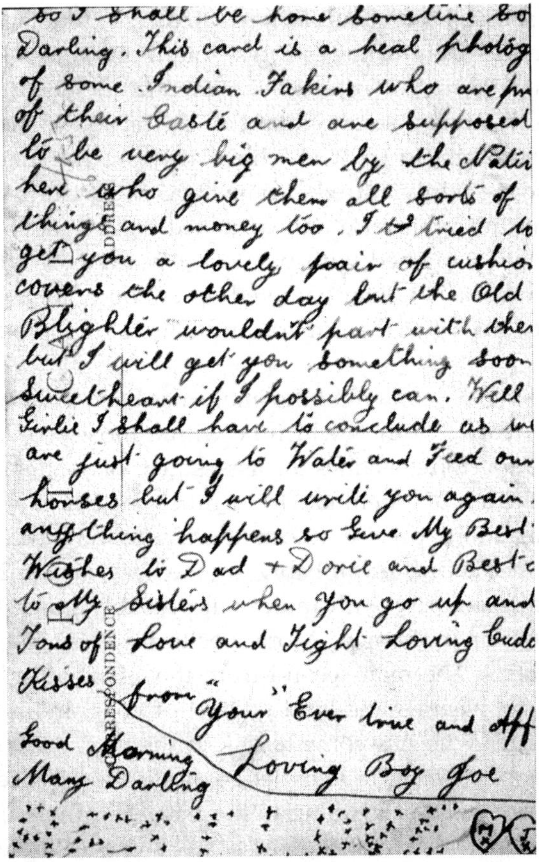

Figure 1.3   Reverse of postcard reproduced in Figure 1.2

so I shall be home sometime soon
Darling. This card is a real photograph
of some Indian Fakirs who are priests
of their Caste and are supposed
to be very big men by the Natives
here who give them all sorts of
things and money too. I tried to
get you a lovely pair of cushion
covers the other day but the Old
Blighter wouldn't part with them
but I will get you something soon
Sweetheart if I possibly can. Well
Girlie I shall have to conclude as we

are just going to Water and Feed our
horses but I will write you again if
anything happens so Give My Best
Wishes to Dad + Doris and Best Love
to My Sisters when you go up and
Tons of love and Tight Loving Cuddly
Kisses
   from
      "Your" Ever true and Afft
         Loving Boy Joe
Good Morning
Mary Darling
B E S T   L O V E
I will give you that ([pointer to the words 'best love']) when I come home
Sweetheart

So, it is a postcard from Joe to his wife or fiancée Mary. There is no
address or stamp and indeed the message appears to be only partial ('so
I shall be home sometime soon . . .' seems to follow on from some
previous statement) and perhaps the letter was begun on ordinary paper
and the whole posted in an envelope. But there is now a completely
different reading, one that ties the image's narrative to Joe's narrative.
Joe's 'real photograph' is a print, not a real photograph, but by 'real'
he seems to mean 'there really are people and places that look like this':
he knows what he has seen. He is less sure about what it means – the
men are called 'Fakirs' and are priests, but they are only 'supposed' to be
big men. He knows they are given money, which reminds him that he
tried to give someone money but the 'Old Blighter' wouldn't accept it,
and so on. My own guess is that Joe was a soldier, serving in India
towards the end of the Second World War – his mention of the cushion
covers reminds me of a crewel work bag that my own father brought
back from Bengal for his mother, subsequently passed on to my mother,
when he was stationed there with the RAF in the late 1940s.
   Now that we have a (partial) reading of the image it remains to
sociologize it, to place that reading within the context of a particular
social research project. To follow up the story of the 'Indian Fakirs'
would require some detailed research in picture archives and museums,
perhaps trying to trace the company that produced the postcard and
then using ethnological and Indological research to identify the sadhus,
or at least their sect. By the end, one might have uncovered enough
information possibly to locate the sadhus – or at least people who knew
them. One could then use the image, and any others if the postcard were

part of a series, in the course of an anthropological or religious studies research project. In the course of fieldwork in India with contemporary Hindu sadhus one could produce the postcard during interviews to prompt memories and reflections on the part of the sadhus about changes in Hindu asceticism over the last half century.

Alternatively, there is another story to follow: that of Mary and Joe. Initially the research might follow similar lines: use archival resources to trace the postcard, and to establish where and when it might have been sold. Then Army records may be used to try and establish which regiments might have been in that area at that time, and so on to try and locate Joe. (In truth, identifying the individual sadhus is probably easier than trying to identify Joe.) The image could then be used as part of a research project in British social history – together with other images and letters sent by soldiers overseas to family and loved ones – to assess the role of British women and how they lived their lives at home while their menfolk were away. Did new brides and fiancées maintain closer ties than normal to their female affines or affines-to-be, for example ('Best love to my Sisters when you go up')?

A third line of enquiry also presents itself. I bought the postcard at a sale of postcards, cigarette cards, telephone cards and other collectable ephemera in a village hall near my home in Oxford about three years ago. It had travelled half way around the world, passed through many people's hands, and is now in Australia, where I sent it as a gift to a friend.[2] I was attracted partly because I like old postcards of ethnographic subjects, but especially because it was of India, my own area of ethnographic interest. It cost me £1.50, a price at the lower end of the scale in such sales: a seller I interviewed told me that serious postcard collectors prefer mint condition cards, without writing, stamps or franking. Clearly, I am not the only one interested in old postcards – there were thousands on the one stall, all sorted by geography (this was in 'Ethnic', but postcards of the British Isles are meticulously subdivided by county and town) or types ('Animals', 'Flowers', 'Famous People'). Nor am I the only one interested in antiquarian images of non-European peoples, although the majority are well beyond my price range: a good early photograph by a named photographer of non-European people, especially Japanese and Koreans, or Native Americans, can easily cost £500 and beyond. A set of such images in an elegant album can cost over £10,000. A sociologist, an economist, or an art historian could all construct a research project enquiring into cultural value and market forces in venues ranging from humble village halls to the salerooms of London and New York auction houses.

All of the issues touched upon above, and many more besides, are examined in more detail in the course of this book, following the lines of enquiry produced by 'found' images such as the postcard above, as well as images created by the social researcher. In broad terms social research with pictures involves three sets of questions: (i) what is the image of, what is its content? (ii) who took it or made it, when and why? and (iii) how do other people come to have it, how do they read it, what do they do with it? Some of these questions are instantly answerable by the social researcher. If she takes her own photographs of children playing in a schoolyard, for example, in order to study the proxemics of gender interaction, then she already has answers to many of the second two sets of questions. The questions may be worth asking nonetheless: why did I take that particular picture of the boy smiling triumphantly when he had pushed the girl away from the slide? Does it act as visual proof of something I had already hypothesized? How much non-visual context is required to demonstrate its broader validity? And so on. Sometimes – perhaps quite frequently – our initial understandings or readings of visual images are pre-scripted, written in advance, and it is useful to attempt to stand back from them, interrogate them, to acquire a broader perspective.

1.3 Unnatural vision

Seeing is not natural, however much we might think it to be. Like all sensory experience the interpretation of sight is culturally and historically specific (Classen 1993). Equally unnatural are the representations derived from vision – drawings, paintings, films, photographs. While the images that form on the retina and are interpreted by the brain come in a continual flow, the second-order representations that humans make when they paint on canvas or animal skin, or when they click the shutter on a camera, are discrete – the products of specific intentionality. Each has significance by virtue of its singularity, the actual manifestation of one in an infinitude of possible manifestations. Yet in Euro-American society we treat these images casually, as unexceptional presences in the world of material goods and human social relations.

This is partly because for centuries vision – sight – has been a privileged sense in the European repertoire, a point well-established by philosophers, social theorists and other cultural critics. Native speakers of English are quite accustomed to the use of visual metaphor in the language: 'Look here . . .' says one beginning a discussion, or argument; 'I see what you mean . . .' says their interlocutor conceding defeat. The

point is sometimes over-emphasized. Classen points out that the historical importance of other sensory experiences in Europe tends to be
ignored by those anxious to establish the historical dominance of visual-
ity (1993: 6–7 and passim), while other societies have established ocular
significance quite independently. In Hindu India, for example, the core
aspect of much religious devotion before temple idols or pictures of
deities is direct eye-to-eye contact between deity and devotee. Diana Eck
(1985), Lawrence Babb (1981) and others have shown how *darshan*
('seeing [the divine]', or the mutual exchange of looks) structures much
Hindu ritual. Moreover, in Hindu philosophy vision can carry the same
implications of understanding as we recognize in contemporary English
usage; early Indian society also used the term *darshan* to refer to schools
of thought, 'points of view', distinguished by differences in practice or
politics (Eck 1985: 11). What distinguishes the Hindu approach to *darshan*
from mere 'seeing' in English is that it is an active gaze: Babb cites an
example from the famous Bombay Hindi film *Jai Santoshi-ma* in which
the (female) deity's gaze when angered is like fire, desiccating the
unworthy (1981: 393).

Among the Jains – the Indian religious group with which I have
worked – a newly-made idol of a *tirthankara* (one of the religion's revered
founder figures) is considered to come to life, or be animated, only after
a ritual is performed in secret and at night during which bright staring
glass eyes are fixed to the carved eye sockets. Eck notes that Hindu
images are imbued with life by opening the eyes with a golden needle, or
by the final stroke of a paintbrush; the deity's first glance is so powerful
that it can kill a man and so the image is first shown a pleasing thing,
such as sweets, fruit or flowers, or even its own reflection in a mirror
(1985: 7). In some Jain and Hindu temples, especially those on busy city
streets, screens are placed just inside the threshold to prevent inadvertent
darshan on the part of those who are temporarily or permanently impure
who may be passing by – menstruating women, for example, or those
classed as untouchable. Also in India, and elsewhere in the world,
fragments of mirror glass are incorporated into embroidered textiles to
divert or reflect back the gaze of the evil eye. Women, especially childless
women, may refrain from looking too long at another woman's child for
fear of witchcraft accusations. The anthropologist in India and other such
societies needs to spend as much time considering how and at what
people look, as listening to how and what they say.

While vision may be a privileged sense in some Euro-American
contexts, these societies are also strongly in the thrall of language – both
oral and written. In many cases the use of vision and appreciation of the
visual is compartmentalized or constrained, as appropriate for some

contexts but not others. This containment is largely effected by language, by placing the visual and visible aspects of culture within a language-based discourse that has primacy. Such containment of social and cultural activity – of breaking up the business of living and hence the organiza-tion of society into named and categorized chunks – is perhaps a distinctive feature of Euro-American society. While the appreciation of fine art (a social skill and a class-bounding diacritic as Bourdieu et al. have pointed out [1991]), going to the cinema or taking family snapshots are all straightforward cultural practices predicated upon a visual sense, these and many other activities must be enmeshed in language to become meaningful or valuable. Moreover, while cultural activities that centre on vision and the visual are valued in some contexts, they are clearly not in others. Education provides a good example. Preliterate children, and even pre-linguistic infants, are encouraged to engage with picture books, not in order to develop their visual sense but in order to familiarize them with books of words they must learn to value and rely on in later life. As Alice noted before she disappeared down the rabbit hole, the absence of pictures denotes the intended adult readership of a book. While some higher education disciplines such as art history clearly must engage with the visual manifestations of culture, others that are expressly concerned with the organization and flow of social life, such as sociology, place a far greater reliance on language both to investigate and then report on human social relations.

It is almost as though the disembedding of visual culture, and its containment in a discourse of 'art', has caused a suspicion of images in other contexts, and a consequent need to constrain and limit the work that they do. This is apparent, for example, in the contrast between the bland disregard for language that some artists and fine art photogra-phers employ by captioning their works 'Untitled', and the apparently exegetical or descriptive captioning employed by academics (and others, such as newspaper editors) for images that are inserted into primarily written texts (see Chapter 2.2).

1.4 Reading narratives

The study of images alone, as objects whose meaning is intrinsic to them, is a mistaken method if you are interested in the ways in which people assign meaning to pictures. (Ruby 1995a: 5)

The idea of 'reading' a photograph or other visual image merely extends the range of a term normally applied to the written word and is used commonly by commentators on a whole variety of visual forms, from fine art landscapes to television soap operas. There are, however, some important differences which are not always made explicit, or which are perhaps not even recognized by some who use the term. First, although I use the term fairly casually throughout this book, I do not wish to suggest that there is a 'language' of images or image components that follows some kind of quasi-grammatical rules, either universally or in more socially specific contexts. Within any particular sociocultural environment, we may learn to associate certain visual images with certain meanings, but these are normally highly context dependent and often transient. In popular Indian cinema a sharp camera zoom in onto the face of a character (together with a musical climax) is commonly read as an indication of intense emotion on the part of the character, perhaps associated with the revelation of a hidden fact. On British television by contrast, the same camera movement would be read today as a melodramatic cliché, perhaps prompting associations with amateurish 1960s or 1970s soap opera. Sequences of images, however, or individual pictorial elements, have no inherent para-syntactic or structural association, other than that which an interpretative community – the audience – is educated to expect by convention.

Secondly, 'reading' to some extent implies that the 'message' being read lies within the visual image, that it is speaking to us and that all we need to do is listen. On the contrary, it is human beings who speak to one another, literally and metaphorically through their social relations. But, as anthropologists are well aware, human beings frequently displace those conversations onto inanimate objects, giving them the semblance of life or agency. When we read a photograph, a film or an art-work, we are tuning in to conversations between people, including but not limited to the creator of the visual image and his or her audience. Those other participants include gallery curators, television producers, aid agencies, and a whole variety of other persons who present images to a viewing/reading public.

In *The Photography Handbook* Terence Wright describes three approaches to reading photographs: looking through, looking at, and looking behind. These approaches he associates with realist, formalist and expressive strategies of authorial intention (Wright 1999: 38 ff.). The labels in themselves do not matter here; what Wright is saying about photographs, which would hold true for any visual representation, is that a reader can consider both their content and their context. For some photographs, or in the eyes of some readers, the content is primarily a matter of information, as though one were looking through a window at some object beyond: this is my partner, this is the house where I stayed on fieldwork. In the eyes of others the way that content is presented is deemed important – the arrangement of elements, the angle of light, and so on: this tiny baby in the crook of that heavily-muscled arm, lit to produce deep shadows 'says' something about strength and fragility, experience and innocence. With other images, or in the eyes of still other readers, it is the context within which the image was produced that assumes prominence: this image of a naked Aboriginal woman, standing in profile against a measuring rule, was taken in accordance with a now-discredited nineteenth century theory of human biological variation.

The properties of the images, and the interpretation of readers, are not fixed. The nineteenth century anthropometric photograph (reproduced in Spencer 1992: 101) was intended to be read for its informational content, but would now be read as an insight into the social, intellectual and perhaps even sexual background and interests of its unknown photographer and those like him. In what follows I focus in particular on the first and third of Wright's approaches – looking through and looking behind – but I employ a slightly different terminology, one that stresses the element of readership or audience, and one that is concerned with the social rather than the individual construction of meaning.[3] The content of an image I refer to as its internal narrative – the story, if you will, that the image communicates. This is not necessarily the same as the narrative the image-maker wished to communicate, indeed it can often be markedly different. This is linked to, but analytically separable from, what I call the external narrative. By this I mean the social context that produced the image, and the social relations within which the image is embedded at any moment of viewing.

Although I often use these terms in opposition, in practice they are of course intertwined, and elements of external narrative – information about the nature of the world beyond the photograph – are always involved in readings of the internal narrative. If you show me a photograph of a woman in a white dress and veil, a man standing beside her in a morning coat, then it is probably a wedding photograph, though I cannot know that the women is your sister unless I know her too or you tell me so. If you show me the same photograph in the pages of a magazine, with certain textual elements attached, then I am more likely to assume the two are actors, dressed up for an advertising shoot to sell wedding attire. Either way, I draw upon internal and external narratives in my reading: in the one case to tell myself a story of romantic love within a familial context; in the other to tell myself a story about consumption and the commodification of romantic love within a possibly global context.

Good visual research rests upon a judicious reading of both internal and external narratives. At root all visual objects represent nothing but themselves; their very existence in the world as material objects is proof of nothing but their autonomy. Consequently, their materiality, their similarity to all other objects in their class and their uniqueness as particular manifestations of that class all need to be assessed by an initial reading of the internal narrative. Simultaneously, all films, photographs and artworks are the product of human action and are entangled to varying degrees in human social relations; they therefore require a wider frame of analysis in their understanding, a reading of the external narrative that goes beyond the visual text itself.

Notes

1 On the history of the visual in anthropology, see MacDougall 1998b, Morphy and Banks 1997, Pinney 1992a; for sociology, see Harper 1998, Stasz 1979.

2 In fact, the image, but not the postcard, travelled back to India again. After I purchased it I photographed it front and back, digitized the slides, and took printouts to India with me on a research trip in 1999, during which I wrote this passage.

3 While the affective power of an image is often strongly related to formal properties of composition and so forth, this is an aspect I only touch on in passing. One reason for this is that formalist analytical approaches, which tend to stress the skill or even genius of individual producers, have dominated approaches to the history of art and of photography and have obscured the more sociological approaches I am concerned with here.

2

Encountering the visual

Figure 2.1   Samuel Finlak using an old sheet film camera, adapted to make several exposures on one sheet. Atta village, Adamaoua Province, Cameroon, 1984. Photographer: John Fox

2.1 On television

This chapter raises some of the basic but sometimes unquestioned assumptions surrounding the visual image in Euro-American society in order to make the point that social researchers need to be aware of their own influences and orientations before they attempt research on the visual and visible aspects of culture and social life. This is especially true when conducting visual research outside one's own society or with sections of society that may stand in a very different relation to public or private visual culture. For example, take television viewing in Britain. In the 1970s, a television manufacturer ran a print advertising campaign featuring a photograph of an elegant woman seated in a cool, modernist interior, the room dominated by an equally elegant white television set. The copy ran along the lines of: 'Sophisticated people don't watch television. This is what they don't watch it on.'

The advert played upon the fact that the British middle classes – who were, of course, the initial purchasers of television sets in the period of post-war economic and consumer growth – soon began to distance themselves from television viewership as the increasingly prosperous working classes began to buy in, a transition marked by the arrival of commercial television in 1955. Middle class people increasingly claimed only to watch television for the news, or for 'quality' drama serials, particularly literary adaptations. A social practice of viewership quickly developed: for example, middle class children in the 1950s and 1960s frequently had their viewing 'rationed' by their parents to an hour or so of putatively educational programmes in the early evening, and it was considered the height of middle class bad form to have the television on when visitors arrived. When I began anthropological fieldwork with South Asian migrants in the British Midlands in the early 1980s, as a product of a good middle class upbringing I was disconcerted to find myself conducting interviews in people's homes over the blare of the television. I had difficulty in maintaining a clear frame of reference as I tried to listen to what was being said by my informants, while involuntarily picking up on what was being said or shown on the television. What I failed to do at that time was to see the television not as an irrelevant and irritating intrusion, but as a social interlocutor. More recently, during fieldwork in India in a town where terrestrial television reception has only been possible for the past few years (and very recently augmented by the arrival of satellite for the wealthier), I have conducted three-way informal interviews, with the staff from the CNN Asia News desk mediating conversations between myself and my informants concerning recent economic change in the town.[1]

2.2 Visual forms produced I: representations of society

As mentioned in the previous chapter, social anthropology and sociology have had a rather troubled relationship with the visual image, and its use in the representation of social knowledge and of society itself. Nonetheless, the value of making and then displaying filmic or photographic representations of the subjects of research has never been entirely denied. Many academic social scientists may show a series of slides or a short piece of video tape to introduce a research population when teaching in the classroom, for example. This is commonly the case when the objective of the lecture is to highlight the relationship between people and their environment (forlorn scenes of urban decay, for example, as a backdrop to a lecture on juvenile criminality, or shots of precipitous mountain passes to illustrate the arduous nature of pastoral nomadism). These illustrations may then be followed by illustrations of the research subjects in close-up and long shot to place them within such environments. In such cases, students are visually introduced to people and places of which they may have no direct experience.

A similar trope can be identified in the use of photographs to illustrate academic monographs and – especially – classroom textbooks, which are often far more heavily illustrated than a monograph intended for a professional readership. For such page-turning and load-lightening illustrations, one photograph is essentially as good as any other. The intentionality and directedness of the image is frequently sociologically diffuse, concerned more with the author–teacher and reader–student relationship, than the social relations between those depicted. For example, in the course of a discussion on family and kinship in North America, one introductory anthropology textbook uses a photograph of a woman sitting at a table outdoors with a young boy and girl, apparently discussing a drawing one of them has done. The caption reads: 'In contemporary North America, single-parent families are increasing at a rapid rate. In 1960, 88 percent of American children lived with both parents, versus about 70 percent today. What do you see as the main differences between nuclear families and single-parent families?' (Kottack 2000: 197). While there is no reason to suppose that the woman is not the mother of the two children and that she has no partner, there is no evidence from the image itself to confirm this either. On the other hand, neither the caption nor the main body of text say anything about this particular image: why are they outdoors, for example? The photograph is intended to be read at only the most superficial level and the student reader is intended to respond to the caption text, not the image.

In cases such as these the multivocality of the photographic image – its ability to communicate multiple narratives – is not so much suppressed or constrained by the caption and context, as irrelevant. The work that the photograph does in such contexts is relatively light: it breaks up the text on the page, it hastens the end of the chapter, it illustrates a broad issue in which specific details are not especially relevant. The social contexts of both image production (why was this photograph taken? by whom? when? under what circumstances?) and of whatever social relations are depicted (who are these people? what are they doing? why are they doing it?) are rendered relatively unimportant. In such introductory texts, and equivalent classroom uses, the aim of image use is frequently no more than to familiarize the reader or listener-viewer with a group of people previously unknown, or to act as a relatively arbitrary visual hook on which to hang a more abstract argument.

The same is equally true in more public contexts, such as the use of photographs in newspapers. These are sometimes used to illustrate a story concerning a person or a topic considered unfamiliar to the reader. In early February 2000, for example, British newspapers were full of images of Jörg Haider, leader of the right-wing Freedom Party that had just joined the Austrian coalition government and prompted Europe-wide fears about the return of fascism. Unknown in Britain until this point, Haider's images told the readers very little about him but served as a visual clue to allow readers to follow the story over the days as it unfolded. Far more redundant are the photographs used to illustrate stories on the business and finance pages of most newspapers. Abstract and complex issues concerning mergers and takeovers, market rises and falls, are difficult to illustrate photographically. A need seems to be felt by editors that the pages should nevertheless be broken up with photo-graphic images, in addition to any more meaningful charts and graphs used. A typical strategy is to employ an arresting image, one that attracts attention through composition or lighting, but which performs no objective informational function. A story about the growing strength of small companies in the pension fund sector is illustrated with a photo-graph of a seascape. Shot on a long lens, the image is cropped into portrait mode (taller than it is wide) so that the waves fill most of the frame, a thin strip of foreshortened shingle at the very bottom. Two indistinct figures are visible emerging from the shingle, the heads and shoulders of an appar-ently elderly couple. The caption reads: 'All at sea . . . The pensions industry is set for its biggest shake-up yet' (The *Guardian* 27.1.00, photo-graph: Thomas McGourty). Apart from the apparent elderliness of the couple – presumably both in receipt of a pension – there is nothing to link the image to the story except the clichéd caption. Yet how else might one photographically represent changes in the pension fund industry?

Much of what I have said concerning illustrative and introductory uses of still photographs in academic texts and more public print media is equally true of moving images – film and video – in such contexts. The ability to see a newsreader on television, as opposed to merely hearing them on the radio, would seem to add little to one's understanding of the news, and the popularity of television news broadcasts is probably best assessed through a consideration of television viewing practice more generally. Nonetheless, television executives clearly consider that a static shot of a woman or man reading an autocue is insufficient to hold viewer attention, and hence almost world-wide such shots make up only a small percentage of the visual content, the rest being dominated by animated graphics, filmed location reports and the like. Of these a large percentage of shots are essentially 'wallpaper' shots – images that are largely or even completely redundant, either because they merely illustrate what is being said by the reporter or journalist, or because they are simply pleasant but bland images of location providing low-key visual interest as a background to a verbal presentation that is either abstract in nature or temporally remote.

Of course, even such bland wallpaper shots are open to multiple readings, and to forms of frame analysis that could attempt to find a broader cultural logic linking verbal and visual elements. But from the standpoint of the overt intentionality of the images – providing pictures to accompany sound under intense time pressure – the very ephemerality of the production as a whole may undercut most if not all attempts to seek deeper meaning. These images are highly contingent upon the circumstances of their production, and are often beamed live or almost live to the viewer, with very little time to consider image content or subsequent editing. Consequently, readings of the internal narrative – that is readings of the text of the image alone, uninformed by any ethnographic investigation into the social relations of such production – are largely unverifiable.

Within the realm of less time-constrained factual and educational documentary production, where more care can be taken to select and edit images such that images and sound perform complementary work, image use may nonetheless not go far beyond the mere illustrative. This was certainly true of what Nichols and others have called the 'voice of God' approach, characteristic of documentary film in its pre-Second World War Griersonian heyday, but still routinely encountered today (Nichols 1988: 48). In this mode, a relentless and authoritative narration drives the film forward, telling the viewers what they are seeing on the screen and interpreting its significance. However, many uses of film, videotape and photography in social research attempt to go beyond the merely introductory or illustrative, and seek to say something about society or social life. I will concentrate more on the production and content of documentary and ethnographic films, and on corpuses of ethnographic photographs, in Chapters 5 and 6. For the moment I simply want to consider these as forms of visual representation considered to be of use by some social researchers.

There is an immediate problem, one that lies at the heart of all social research – visual and non-visual. While it is relatively straightforward to create or select a visual image that illustrates a material object, it is much more difficult to create or select a visual image that illustrates an abstraction such as 'society' or 'kinship' or 'unemployment'. Or rather, there is a dissonance between an individual's very real experience of – say – unemployment, and a photograph of the unemployed individual. Metaphor is commonly employed to overcome this problem of abstraction: an unemployed man can be photographed in a bleak urban waste-land, the empty building plots and boarded up windows standing as metaphors for the emptiness of his life and the closure of opportunity. Metonymy is also employed: a photograph of a single African child, stomach bulging due to malnutrition, stands for all starving people in that society. But divorced from a wider context, or lacking an explanatory caption, such photographs are, ultimately, no more than a man standing on a street or a child with a large stomach.

2.2.1 *Interpreting* Forest of Bliss

If there is difficulty in visually representing conditions of human existence in an unambiguous way, these difficulties are magnified when broad abstractions – prototypically 'society' and 'culture' – are attempted. To illustrate the problems, I wish to examine one example in depth: Robert Gardner's film, *Forest of Bliss* (1985).

The film was shot in and around the sacred Hindu city of Benares (Varanasi, also known as Kashi and described as *anandavan* – 'forest of bliss' – in some Sanskrit texts). It is difficult to say in a few lines exactly what it is 'about' – a problem that forms the subject of numerous articles in the journal *SVA Newsletter* in the late 1980s. However, most of the scenes in the film depict aspects of the death business for which Benares is famous – activity at the cremation grounds on the bank of the river Ganges, collecting and transporting firewood, plucking flowers and making garlands that are placed on bodies and also on images of deities. All this activity takes place almost wordlessly; very little is said by the subjects of the film, and what is said is not translated. The film has no voice-over commentary, no subtitles, only a single opening inter-title, a quotation from W.B. Yeats's translation of a Hindu sacred text, one of the Upanishads: 'Everything in this world is eater or eaten, the seed is food and the fire is eater'.

This then is a film which intends to rely upon image and (non-language) sound to convey whatever it is seeking to convey. The soundtrack is equally as rich and dense as the visuals, if not more so – certain sounds, such as the creaking of oars on a boat, acting as a kind of aural punctuation. Watching and listening to the film is undoubtedly a great sensual pleasure for many, and perhaps moving for the individual – a visual and aural poem on the round of life and death, on things changing while they stay the same; in short, a filmic attempt to bypass language and offer a universally comprehensible account of great but highly abstract themes. But what, if anything, is the anthropological or socio-logical relevance of the film? Certainly, many visual anthropologists assumed there was intended to be some, not least because Gardner had made several earlier films normally labelled as ethnographic. That is, documentary films of non-European peoples shot in an observational style, and normally relying on the long-term fieldwork of an anthro-pologist to provide sociological insight. I will consider three different responses to *Forest of Bliss*, all by social anthropologists.

First, Alexander Moore (1988) takes up the challenge to provide a reading of the film reliant on internal evidence alone: 'I made some guesses about what was happening, educated guesses drawing on my non-expert's knowledge of Hindu culture . . . The film starts with an old man. . . .' he begins confidently. As the review continues, his tone begins to falter: 'We see. . . ., It is possible . . ., We see . . ., One assumes . . ., We see . . ., I assume . . .' and so on. At each stage Moore attempts to extra-polate from what he is seeing a wider sociological pattern or cultural significance but is frustrated that he can never be sure of the validity of his assumptions. In the end, while praising the film's visual and emotional qualities, Moore is ultimately damning: 'an irresponsible, self-indulgent film'. He is also concerned that the film's particular subject matter – the disposal of corpses – may seem repugnant to some (Western) viewers without any other information to help them contextualize what they are seeing. The implication would seem to be that a visual 'experi-ment' in cross-cultural communication such as this would perhaps have been better with a less emotive subject, but that as it stands the film may risk alienating rather than attracting viewers.

Moore is used to dealing with visual imagery and its sociological uses (see for example Moore 1990). By contrast, Jonathan Parry is a social anthropologist who would be unlikely to claim any expertise in the field of visual anthropology. He does, however, have extensive field research experience of Banaras, and is the author of a monograph on the rituals of death in the city (Parry 1994). Indeed, some of his field informants are featured in Gardner's film. His reading of the film is consequently very different from that of Moore (1988). Parry points out that although he has an unusually intimate knowledge of things and persons seen in the film it provides no clue for him of Gardner's intentions in depicting them, except that he finds Gardner's vision 'bleak' and has an 'uneasy suspicion' that Western viewers will conclude that India is 'an ineffable world apart', in effect enforcing a kind of cultural apartheid. What he does do, however, is mention in passing that the content of the film allowed him to 're-live something of what I experienced during my first few weeks of fieldwork . . . above all the film evokes the intense frustration of initial incomprehension'. Parry then goes on to provide additional information that either presents a broader context for some of the objects, persons and actions seen in the film, or that undermines or radically recasts what a viewer might assume (including Moore). But the implication of Parry's statement about 'initial incomprehension' is clear – the film reflects the superficial understanding of and emotional response towards the business of death in Banaras that one would expect on a brief exposure. Further and more detailed fieldwork should have served to correct this impression, but this Gardner appears not to have done. Parry concludes that images of action, without explanation of possible meanings, are unintelligible and go against the grain of any social research methodology.

A third viewpoint on the film is provided by Ákos Östör, the film's co-producer. Östör worked with Gardner on a series of films, including *Forest of Bliss*, and like Parry has a long-standing ethnographic engagement with India, well beyond Banaras. Östör is at pains to demonstrate that *Forest of Bliss* is not about death in Banaras (or anywhere else); rather, it is a witness to 'the great truth of Banaras: the non-finality and transcendence of death' (1989: 6). He justifies and demonstrates this not by reference to an external narrative such as the context beyond the frame of the film (his knowledge of the Banaras ethnography or his knowledge of the circumstances of the film's production) but by reading the film as a film, and not as a written monograph with most of the words missing. The film is 'an invention, not a copy of reality' (1989: 6) and it tells its story largely through aural and visual metaphor. He points out that the audience should be alerted to the importance of metaphor by the opening Yeats/Upanishad quotation (in which an abstract statement is amplified by reference to metaphor) and gains its significance from being the only piece of text/language in the film that is comprehensible to most viewers outside India.

Indeed, some of the film's metaphors are so transparent that even the most casual viewer can be fairly confident in their reading of them. For example, the idea of flying high above the noise and confusion of the world is a fairly stock metaphor for freedom and liberation in both India and the West, and *Forest of Bliss* is peppered with shots of children flying kites and birds wheeling overhead. Gardner also exploits the metaphorical potential in shots of steps, stairways and ladders to convey the idea of movement from one state to another (Robert Gardner, personal communication; see Figure 2.2). Östör concludes his article by citing a number of other reviews of the film, all of which note the strength and

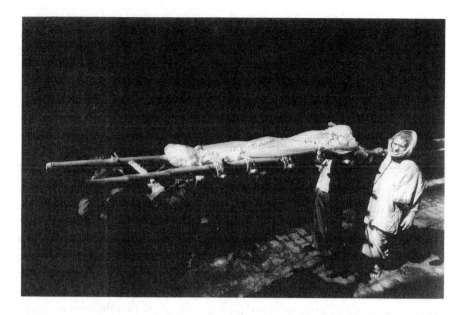

Figure 2.2   Image from Robert Gardner's film *Forest of Bliss*; corpse being carried to the cremation grounds on a bier constructed like a ladder. Benares, India, 1985. Photographer: Jane Tuckerman

value of metaphor and which demonstrate how the reviewers' under-standing of the film's intent arises from the film itself: from the relation-ship between picture and sound; and from the linkages between and within scenes. Östör's barely disguised criticism of Moore and Parry is that they almost wilfully failed to see (in both the vision and comprehen-sion senses of the word) what was right in front of them.

These three initial responses to the film were followed by several others, and although the arguments became more vehement and impas-sioned, interested readers can follow the story in subsequent issues of the *SVA Newsletter*. The three nonetheless serve to highlight some relevant points. First, the readings draw upon a variety of perspectives external to the film. Moore, for example, provides the most 'closed' reading, casting himself in the role of interested layman, unable to draw upon any other contextualizing information or understanding (except, I would suspect, a previous familiarity with Gardner's work). Parry brings an expert knowledge of both the local ethnography and the broader anthropo-logical paradigm with which the film appears in dialogue. Östör refrains from invoking knowledge of his and Gardner's initial intentions (which would not be accessible to Moore, Parry or most other viewers) to prove his point about the 'correct' reading of the film, though his exposition of other critics' positive views serves to achieve this end, and instead provides a reading from the internal evidence of the film alone. While he shares this approach with Moore, the difference lies in the fact that Östör claims the correct way to read the film is visually rather than to search in vain for an absent linguistic translation and exposition: 'Moore and Parry expect a voice to whisper in their ear an extended commentary on what is already in front of their eyes' (1989: 5).[2]

2.2.2 Still and moving images

Östör's claim that Moore and Parry have viewed *Forest of Bliss* as a series of absent and present ethnographic points highlights one of the most significant yet frequently overlooked differences between film (and video) and still photography: a film is not a sequence of still images, or even scenes, to be read individually. In a well-edited film (or even a badly edited one) the sum is greater than its parts, just as a well-written ethography cannot be treated merely as a series of free-standing observations. It is the cumulative effect of the individual shots following one after another to make up scenes, and scene following scene, that creates the message of the film. A film cannot merely be reduced to its constituent parts.

Extreme disruptions or manipulations of time and space continuity are a distinctive aspect of commercial feature films (for example, the looping of time in Quentin Tarantino's *Pulp Fiction* [1994], in which the closing scene takes the viewer right back to the time and place of the opening scene, though from a different standpoint); I can think of only one commercial film which unfolds in real time (Alfred Hitchcock's claustrophobic *Rope* [1948]) and only one which maintains a strict integrity of space (Robert Montgomery's largely unwatchable *Lady in the Lake* [1947], where the camera is enslaved to the viewpoint of the main character, a detective). Even the most observational of observational documentaries will still contain edited jumps of both time and space, while adhering to a strictly chronological sequencing. Yet, while 'off duty', as viewers of commercial feature films, social scientists seem aware of editing conventions and apparently enjoy the creative playing off of one scene against another to gradually build up the plot or develop characters, they often seem unable to bring the same visual literacy to their viewing of documentary films made by or for other social scientists. In my own experience of watching films with other social scientists I have noticed a pronounced desire to read the film as a sequence of animated photographs, each accompanied by explanatory narration. When this desire cannot be fulfilled, as in *Forest of Bliss*, the tendency seems to be a retreat into incomprehension, or to claim that the film is superficial, unable to communicate with the depth of a written monographic account.

Academic social scientists are not alone in this approach to the documentary moving image, of course. Amateur videographers, especially infrequent users on holiday, may actually produce material to be read in this way by treating their video camera as a stills camera, to take 'shots' of the scenes and places they visit, which are then presumably viewed much as a slide show would be viewed.[3] There is nothing inherent in the technology of video recording that determines such an approach, though a prior technical familiarity with still cameras is probably a contributory factor. So too is a prior familiarity with viewing slide shows or, more commonly, photographic albums where single images become the repositories for sequential but self-contained verbal narratives. Thus in some cases we may be correct in trying to read a length of film or video footage as a series of still images, but it would be a mistake to assume this is the correct way to read all documentary footage encountered (see also Banks 1989b).

2.3 Visual forms produced II: representations of knowledge

> Self-consciousness about modes of representation (not to speak of experiments with them) has been very lacking in anthropology. (Geertz 1975: 19, n. 3)

So far I have mentioned only what might be termed the public face of visual studies in anthropology and sociology – the films that have been produced, the photographs that have been published – and I shall discuss these issues in more detail in later chapters. First, however, I wish to discuss some of the less-obvious uses of visual images by social scientists and others, particularly tables and diagrams. These are techniques used to present information, both concrete and abstract, where spatial arrangement and non-linear order are necessitated and where the inevitable linear sequencing of words is insufficient. Non-indexical and often non-figurative visual representations such as these (that is, images that are not mechanical representations of reality, such as photographs) are common in social science texts and form a sub-category of the overall design issues surrounding the production of academic texts. (In many cases authors do not draw their own maps and diagrams, or lay out the final form of any tables used, but rely instead on the publisher to employ professional graphic designers.)

The distinction between text and image, as found in illustrated academic textbooks, is not absolute. The syntax of languages such as English
is sufficiently strong that the visual or design elements of the printed
word in academic contexts is normally limited to mere style, contributing
little or nothing to meaning (though see Tufte 1983, 1990, and 1997 for
impassioned arguments to the contrary).[4] But there are occasions on
which the strict linearity of language is insufficient to convey the
information required, where the spatial – and hence visual – arrangements of the language elements need to be considered. The most basic,
and ancient, examples of what Jack Goody refers to as non-syntactical
language are lists, inventories and tables (Goody 1986: 54–5). Tables are a
particularly good example of a basic form of hypertext (see Chapter 6.5),
allowing multiple links to be made between units of information
(linguistic or otherwise). These links are essentially visual – it is the eye,
looking over the layout of the table on the page, that presents the brain
with a pattern of intended associations between information units:
scanning the columns of a railway timetable I can see when the next train
home is, looking along the rows I can decide which is the fastest route.
Tables and other lists are an intermediate form, midway between the
linear flow of language and the open-endedness of a photograph or
picture, demanding a combination of linguistic and visual reading skills.
Nearer to the 'pure' image lie various forms of the diagram, where
textual elements act as labels and where the frame that holds the
elements together, such as the cells of a table, is more fluid or less
predictable: Alfred Gell has written to great effect about the analytical
power of diagrammatic representation in anthropology and its ability to
organize complex ideas (see Gell 1999: Introduction and Chapter 1).

2.3.1   Diagrams of Nuer lineages

A good example of the use of diagrams to present social knowledge
and social understandings can be found in Evans-Pritchard's classic
ethnography of the Nuer, a cattle-herding group in the southern Sudan
(Evans-Pritchard 1940). Evans-Pritchard, like many anthropologists of
the time, sought to describe the social structure of the Nuer – the pattern
of economic, political and kinship ties between people that regulated
their social relations. One of the distinctive features of Nuer society was
that there were no obvious leaders or persons of political authority. Nor
was Nuer society contained within any kind of formal administrative
framework, beyond the overall British colonial authority of the day. The
question thus arose of how the Nuer were able to maintain social order,

and deal with conflicts and disputes. The answer lay in what is sometimes called a segmentary lineage system. A Nuer clan – the largest
grouping of Nuer who can trace common descent from a single ancestor
through male descent lines – is divided into lineages, segments of the
clan which trace descent to specific ancestors within the clan (Evans-
Pritchard 1940: 192).[5] Of particular interest to Evans-Pritchard was the
relationship between these segmentary lineages and he spends a considerable part of his ethnography making this clear, employing numerous
diagrams as he does so.

At one point, for example, he draws on the familiar Euro-American
analogy of the 'family tree' and presents several tree-like diagrams (such
as Figure 2.3a) illustrating the segmentary relations between lineages of

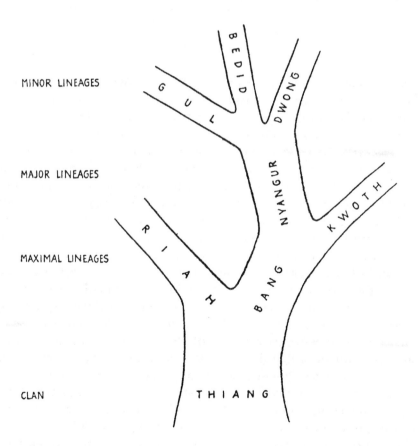

Figure 2.3a Lineages of the Nuer Thiang clan. Reproduced from Evans-
Pritchard, *The Nuer: A Description of the Modes of Livelihood and Political
Institutions of a Nilotic People*, 1940: 198. By permission of Oxford University
Press

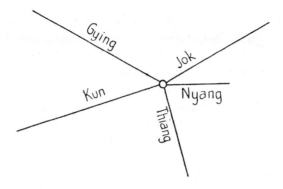

Figure 2.3b   Lineages of the Nuer Gaatgankiir and other clans. Reproduced from Evans-Pritchard, *The Nuer: A Description of the Modes of Livelihood and Political Institutions of a Nilotic People*, 1940: 202. By permission of Oxford University Press

particular clans. Evans-Pritchard notes that the Nuer themselves could speak of a lineage as a *kar* or 'branch', although they also used other terms such as 'hearth' (*thok mac*) and 'entrance to the hut' (*thok dwiel*) (Evans-Pritchard 1940: 195). Later in his text Evans-Pritchard notes that the Nuer did not represent their lineages to themselves in the form of a tree, however, but as a number of lines radiating out from a single point (as in Figure 2.3b, drawn originally with a stick on the ground, pre- sumably without the lineage name labels). Broadly speaking, the length of the lines and the proximity of one line to another indicated the relationship between the lineages. In Figure 2.3b, however, not all the lines/lineage names actually belonged to the Gaatgankiir clan; Evans- Pritchard's Nuer informant was also trying to indicate something of the nature of territorial relationships at the time: the Gying lineage was not part of the Gaatgankiir clan at all, for example, but was territorially associated with a group of which the Kun lineage formed part. While confusing, and not logically consistent, the Nuer representation is seek- ing to perform work that the Evans-Pritchard 'tree' diagram ignores. In seeking to understand the segmentation of Nuer lineages and their inter- relationships Evans-Pritchard could abstract 'pure' genealogical relation- ships, while his Nuer informants 'evaluate[d] clans and lineages in terms of their [present] local relations' (Evans-Pritchard 1940: 203).

Evans-Pritchard is well aware of this. Earlier in his text, when he is seeking to explain political affiliations among the Nuer he employs a very different type of diagram – an abstract, ideal-type representation (see Figure 2.4). This diagram rests on the fundamental understanding

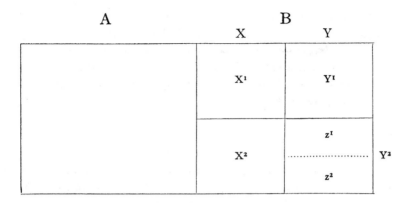

Figure 2.4 Segmentation and opposition among the Nuer. Reproduced from Evans-Pritchard, *The Nuer: A Description of the Modes of Livelihood and Political Institutions of a Nilotic People*, 1940: 144. By permission of Oxford University Press

that the Nuer lineage system was relative, not absolute. The lineage – maximal, major, minor or whatever – that a man assigned himself to when questioned depended upon the context of the enquiry. In the context of disputes, for example, a man or a village could choose to ignore a higher level genealogical linkage in favour of a lower level linkage that would unite them in conflict against a local enemy. Conversely, disputes that opposed lower-level groups could be set aside as groups united against a common enemy. Figure 2.4 represents well this contextual pattern of fission and fusion as Evans-Pritchard called it (1940: 148): 'In the diagram . . . when Z^1 fights Z^2 no other section is involved. When Y^1 fights X^1, Y^1 and Y^2 unite, and so do X^1 and X^2 . . .' and so on (1940: 143–4). The cleavages between the segments were not permanently in force but only articulated according to political or military expediency. Indeed, when the Nuer – a politically dominant group in the region – mounted cattle-raids or military expeditions against the neighbouring Dinka population (a sedentary group lacking the segmentary lineage structure of the Nuer), the entire Nuer population was theoretically or conceptually unified – in this case the diagram in Figure 2.4 would contain no lines of cleavage at all.

Although Evans-Pritchard's conceptual diagram is extremely simple, his use of it and the accompanying textual explanation later proved extremely influential for a generation of anthropologists seeking to move away from functional explanations (the so-and-so people do this thing because of that practical advantage) towards structural explanations (the underlying structure of this society is such that that action makes sense).

Here the fractal or metonymic aspects of the diagram – parts mirroring the structure of the whole – play a part. This is well seen in a famous analysis of the Indian caste system, which uses a written description of the Evans-Pritchard diagram (without, oddly, reproducing it or any variant) to overcome the limitations of other visual and non-syntactical textual representations.

2.3.2   Diagrams of Indian caste

From their first encounters with Indian society, European observers were made aware of a form of social division that had no complete parallel with class or any other form of stratification common in European society. The term 'caste' (from the Spanish and Portuguese *casta*, some-thing not mixed) was employed from the sixteenth century by scholars and others to describe what were perceived to be the four main blocs of Indian society (more specifically, Hindu society): Brahman – the caste associated with priesthood; Kshatriya – associated with rulership and military action; Vaishya – associated with trade and commerce; and Shudra – associated with artisanship and service.[6] Initially, these 'castes' were also sometimes described as 'races' (a common and rather vague term in the seventeenth and eighteenth centuries, lacking the specific and grossly inaccurate biological associations of the late nineteenth and twentieth centuries). Early attempts to describe and map the differences between these 'races'/castes were often visual: drawings, and later photographs, of 'types' in which it was hoped that visual attributes of physiognomy and dress would reveal inner sociological truths. Photo-graphy was often employed in academic endeavours to judge human social difference; Christopher Pinney cites William Johnson's *The oriental races and tribes . . .* (two volumes, 1863 and 1866) as having specifically scientific anthropological intent (by the understandings of the day) in its use of photographs that could aid the reader in distinguishing between different types of Indians (Pinney 1997: 28–9; see also Pinney 1992b). By the twentieth century, the 'races and types' genre of photography was well established for popular consumption, as many postcard reproduc-tions of the time make clear. Figures 2.5a and 2.5b – from India and Tunisia respectively – are typical of the genre, the Indian image probably produced for the woman herself, or her family, but then reused; the Tunisian image probably not taken with the interests of the subject in mind, but according to the pseudo-scientific agenda of anthropometry (see also Edwards 1996 and Spencer 1992 respectively).

Yet such visual representations alone merely produced an array of equivalences, an endless series of 'types' with little or no visual evidence

Figure 2.5a Undated hand-coloured studio portrait of a young Indian woman, apparently re-used as a postcard, printed in Germany for sale in India, captioned 'A Bunya girl'. Photographer unknown

to indicate the relationships between them – as though one had the names of many Nuer lineages but no idea of how to order or arrange them. In the Indian context some ordering principle was necessary, the stimulus being both intellectual and administrative. The imperative for an ordering was heightened by later observers discerning another order of 'castes', initially thought to be subdivisions of the basic four, which

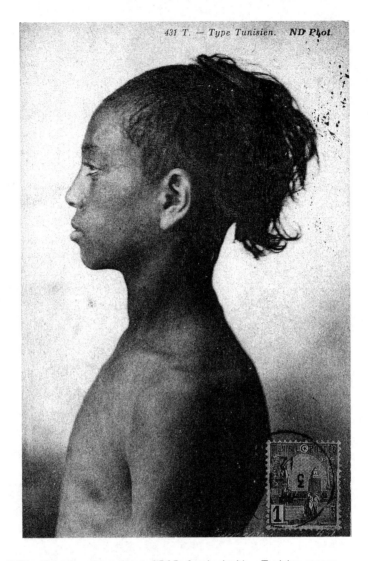

431 T. — Type Tunisien. **ND Phot.**

Figure 2.5b French postcard, ca. 1912, franked with a Tunisian stamp, captioned '431 T. – Type Tunisien.' Photographer unknown

generated many more 'types' – known commonly in the literature by the Hindi term *jati* (meaning, type or kind or species). The answer, from 1871, was to typologize information known about the various castes and *jati*s in decennial censuses, attempting to subsume the many *jati*s (which were often associated with particular occupations or territories) into one of the four main caste categories. From the census and the associated descriptive literature produced by British colonial administrators, together with amateur and professional ethnographers, emerged the idea that castes and *jatis* were somehow ranked in a hierarchical fashion – a hierarchy that could be represented in tabular form and where visually an entry at the top of a table was considered to be in some way superior or of higher social status than an entry towards the bottom of the table. This non-syntactical textual representation gave rise to a view of caste that dominated for decades – the 'football league table' view as Declan Quigley has dubbed it (1994: 27). Although many attempts were made over the nineteenth and early twentieth centuries to understand quite what principle of hierarchical ordering underlay this league table view, most subscribed to a greater or lesser extent to a unilinear ranking (see Figure 2.6).

A partial change of direction came with the work of the French anthropologist, Louis Dumont, who set aside a variety of single-case functional and descriptive explanations (the Y caste is higher than the Z caste because Ys do not accept boiled food from the Zs, but in turn lower

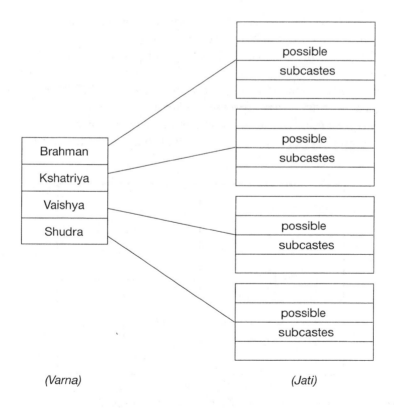

(Varna)   *(Jati)*

Figure 2.6   The 'football league table' view of caste

than the X caste which does not accept boiled food from the Ys) in favour of an overarching structural explanation which saw the castes as parts in relation to a whole ('Hindu society'), ranked not in terms of their relations with one another but with reference to the whole – a shared view of the nature of society (Dumont 1980). Instead of a league table of the four main castes – by now known as *varna*, an ideological set of divisions, as opposed to the on-the-ground divisions of *jati* – Dumont envisaged a single *varna* structure, containing a number of structurally opposed segments. He drew directly on Evans-Pritchard, and in particular on Figure 2.4 above:

> a careful reading [of *The Nuer*] shows . . . the structural principle of the 'distinctive opposition' – which is conceptual – even if [Evans-Pritchard] expresses it for the most part in the language of oppositions of fact, of conflict . . . In a certain situation group A and group B are opposed, each united against the other. In another situation, we see group A_1 and A_2 face to face, segments of A which but a moment ago were not differentiated, and so on. (Dumont 1980: 41–2)

Where Evans-Pritchard only saw the principle of segmentation at work on the ground among the Nuer (at least according to Dumont), Dumont realized that for India the fractal diagram of parts related to the whole could perform a purely conceptual work of representation, demonstrating how the four main 'castes', the four *varna*s of Indian society, were ideologically rather than empirically related.

Redrawing Figure 2.4 above for Dumont's vision of the Indian caste system would produce something like Figure 2.7. With the fundamental

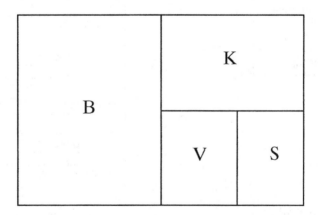

Figure 2.7   The four main 'castes' of Hindu society, conceptualized in terms of their relative structural opposition (after Dumont 1980)

principle of (religious) purity acting as the point of differentiation, the Brahmans (B) are opposed to the rest of society by virtue of their spiritual values, their closeness to divinity sustained by an active avoidance of (spiritual) pollution; but the Brahmans and Kshatriyas (K) are united in their structural opposition to the rest of society by virtue of their joint command of power – spiritual in the case of the Brahmans, temporal in the case of the Kshatriyas. In turn, the Brahmans, Kshatriyas and Vaishyas (V) are structurally opposed to the Shudras (S) by virtue of a ritual they all pass through, that the Shudras do not. Dumont does not envisage these as physically manifest oppositions – there are no feuds between Brahmans and Kshatriyas that are set aside when Brahmans and Kshatriyas in turn feud with Vaishyas. Rather, the internal logic of Hindu society views each as standing in relation to the whole, their relative position governed by their relative purity. The relationships between the *jatis*, which are not in fact merely subsections of the four main castes but an on-the-ground working out of the same principles, are articulated according to the same fractal logic.

There have been many challenges to Dumont's view of the structural ordering of Indian/Hindu society, not least from Quigley who uses a completely different set of diagrams based on a core–periphery model, or orientation towards and away from the centre (one central element, labelled with a caste or occupational name, joined by arrowed lines to a cluster of other such elements around it) to propose an alternative view based on the model of a king and his court. There is also a fractal logic to Quigley's view, each caste or occupational group viewing themselves at the centre of a universe of action and exchange, yet in turn seen by others as an element in their constellation (Quigley 1993: Chapter 7). Although the parallelism is structurally superficial, Quigley's model has an affinity with Evans-Pritchard's diagrammatic representation of the Nuer view of lineages (Figure 2.3b above). Yet Evans-Pritchard, Dumont, and Quigley are all united in their understanding that a mechanical listing of the parts of society – lineages, castes, whatever – is as unable to provide a satisfactory sociological account of society as a portfolio of photographs of the society's members. Diagrammatic abstraction, when carefully considered and clearly laid out, can exercise great efficiency.[7]

2.4 Visual forms encountered

The Euro-American society that produced the academic disciplines of anthropology, sociology and other bases for social research is, of course, not the only society that produces visual representations of itself and others. From the earliest Neolithic cave paintings to today's video diaries humans have manifested a capacity for visual self-representation. Visual image production and consumption in the social sciences is – or should be – distinguished only by being grounded in particular discourses of sociological knowledge, just as image production and consumption in – say – astronomy is distinguished by being grounded in particular scientific discourses (see Lynch and Edgerton 1988 for a particularly good exploration of the latter).

But if it is – or should be – relatively straightforward to identify the overt knowledge basis of some image forms encountered (such as the Nuer lineage diagrams above), discerning a more generalized and less formally academic interest in human social relations can be more prob-lematic. We cannot discount modernist abstract art, or astronomical photographs of distant galaxies, as having no social representational properties, simply because human beings are not their overt subject matter. While the internal narrative of the image may concern some non-social issue, the external narrative concerning the image's very existence is quite clearly the product of human social relations. But equally, the presence of human subjects as part of an image's internal narrative does not automatically communicate an overt and sociologically grounded concern with their social relations. Nor does it mean that the social researcher who encounters such images can ignore the external narrative. This is particularly the case when familiar visual forms are encountered in what might be considered to be unfamiliar contexts.

2.4.1   Encountering indigenous media

Although Euro-America (including, of course, Japan) has been the location of most mechanical visual media innovation and production, the rest of the world has not been slow to embrace these media and to devise socially appropriate contexts for their use and consumption. Indian-run photographic studios were in operation as early as the 1850s, less than twenty years after the development of the daguerreotype (Pinney 1997: 72, citing Gutman 1982), and in 1912 D.G. Phalke, the 'father of Indian cinema', travelled to England to buy his first movie camera and stock (Chabria 1994: 8). David and Judith MacDougall's 1991 film *Photo Wallahs*, explicitly subtitled 'an encounter with photography in Mussoorie...' gives a powerful sense of the deep embedding of still photography in India today.

Away from investigations into mechanical visual media in the metro-politan centres of the non-Euro-American world, there is by now a large anthropological and sociological literature on indigenous uses of mechanical audio-visual media, as well as a much longer tradition of investigating other non-Euro-American visual media – the so-called anthropology of art literature.[8] A comprehensive overview of the anthropology of art literature lies beyond the scope of this book, and I shall deal more fully with indigenous media collaborations in Chapter 5, sections 4 and 5. Here I will briefly discuss only one example: the anthropologist Terence Turner's encounter with Kayapo video production. The first stage of the encounter, of course, was the Kayapo meeting with video. Turner, who has been working as anthropologist with the Kayapo, a Brazilian indigenous group since the 1960s, had on various occasions facilitated access for British television crews wishing to make ethnographic films on Kayapo life (see Beckham 1987 and 1989, for example). The Kayapo, a large and powerful group in the region and well used to dealing with the outside world, appreciated the potential of video representation as a result of this exposure (Turner 1990: 9) and acquired their first video camera in 1985, followed by editing facilities in 1990 (Turner 1992: 7). Especially after they had the ability to edit, copy and safely store their video footage, Kayapo video production became fully localized.

Turner itemizes at least five different aspects of their video use. First, and superficially the most obvious, was its use to document rituals and ceremonies, in the recording of which Turner sees – as part of the internal narrative – a distinct Kayapo aesthetic or cultural sensibility (1992: 8–10). But he also discerns a number of distinct external narratives surrounding video use – narratives which might not be evident, let alone readable, to anyone unfamiliar with Kayapo society. One is an aspect of documentary use, videotaping an event; the example Turner gives is of a young political leader who took a group of followers from his village to establish a new village of which he would become the leader, and who videotaped the founding of the village and aspects of their life there. The tape was not a mere historical document, however, to conjure up fond memories in years to come. As Turner says: 'The Kayapo do not regard video documentation merely as a passive recording or reflection of already existing facts, but rather as helping to establish the facts it records' (1992: 10). Indeed, the leader in question re-staged the event of arrival in the new village some time after, specifically for the video camera, as no camera operators or equipment had been available the first time around. Another politicized documentary aspect has been the use Kayapo have made of video recording their encounters with the Brazilian state, most notably in 1989 during a series of protests against a proposed dam project on the Xingu river which would have flooded Kayapo land. In these encounters the manifest content of the videotape, its internal narrative, can be seen as largely irrelevant. The Kayapo knew that national and international media would be present at the protests; they were also well aware that the sight of a 'primitive' Indian, bedecked in paint and feathers yet wielding a highly sophisticated example of late twentieth century technology, would create an arresting image (Turner 1992: 7). Such images duly appeared in the international media (see Figure 2.8). A final aspect of Kayapo video use, which Turner remarks must be present in other cases of indigenous media use but which is rarely commented upon, is the social and political importance of becoming a camera operator or a video editor in Kayapo society. As Eric Michaels has noted for Aboriginal Australian television (cited by Turner 1992; see also Burum 1991), questions concerning the ownership of and

Figure 2.8 Kayapo camera-operator filming at an Alta Mira dam protest, Brazil, 1989. Photographer: Christine Hugh-Jones

access to visual media technology are questions about power relationships within society. For the Kayapo, the contact with outside society that becoming a camera operator or video editor entails, creates a form of cultural capital, enabling the individual to act as a mediator and cultural broker between Kayapo society and the outside world. This mediatory role is an essential prerequisite for political leadership within Kayapo society and Turner states that several of the current younger chiefs rose to power in this way (1992: 7).

Of course, the ownership and use of visual media in Euro-America is surrounded by a multitude of external narratives that require sociological investigation. The point is that simply because the Kayapo can be observed using video cameras and producing films, does not mean that the observer can assume she knows what they are doing with them. Turner makes no mention, for example, of any special significance accorded to those who appear in Kayapo video production simply by virtue of their mere appearance; a category of 'celebrity' does not seem especially relevant, although some Kayapo have briefly become 'celebrities' in Euro-American society by virtue of their association with Euro-American 'celebrities'.

2.4.2 The image as evidence

For the Kayapo, as for many other image producers, their videotapes constitute evidence of something – a village settled, a political grievance aired – no matter what other readings of the external narrative a social researcher may bring to the images. In Chapter 5.2 I consider the ways in which a social researcher herself may create images for the purposes of documentation. Many, perhaps all, societies create images for this purpose although the notion of 'documentation' itself is a socially constructed notion. For example, the Plains Indians of North America used animal hides as a canvas on which to paint maps of space and time, recording the successful hunts and harsh winters of previous years, or the personal war records of warriors (see Figure 2.9; see also Brownstone 1993; King 1999). This 'map' does not conform to the topographical conventions of European mapping, but it does document a 'where' and a 'when' of past events of practical significance that could be read by its makers.

Once a convention has been established, it can then be used to document things that lie beyond experience. Figure 2.10 shows a famous pilgrimage site for the Indian Jains, the sacred mountain of Girnar-ji near the town of Junagadh in Gujarat State. The image is fixed to the wall of a Jain temple in the city of Jamnagar where I have conducted fieldwork;

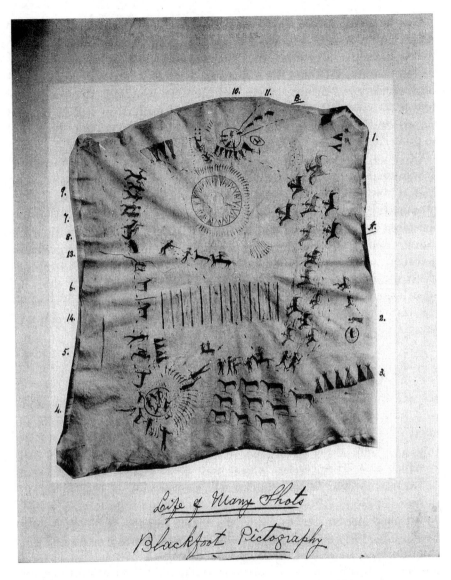

Life of Many Shots

Blackfoot Pictography

Figure 2.9   The Life of Many Shots, painted by himself on a cowhide as a personal war record. Image painted before 1895

it is carved in low relief on a marble slab, then painted and glazed for protection. While the mountain of Girnar-ji, and the temples that crown it, are perfectly real and can be visited easily from Jamnagar, the visitor's eye – or a camera – would not see it in the way the painting represents it. For one thing, the path that winds around the mountain is brought to the

Figure 2.10   Detail of a low-relief painted and glazed image of the Jain temple complex on Mount Girnar-ji, Gujarat, India from a Jain temple in Jamnagar, India. Painting created late twentieth century

forefront of the image, so that every step of it is visible. While the wall painting is one of many in Jain temples that 'document' the existence of the pilgrimage site, its topography and important features such as the temples, it also acts as an aid to devotion, enabling worshippers in a distant temple to walk the path to the summit in their mind's eye. The iconography of the painting, while unfamiliar and even kitsch to a Euro-American viewer, is entirely conventional to the Gujarati Jains – a view of things as they really are, at least within a devotional framework. So much so, that other, unseen, places can be depicted in the same way using the same conventions. Figure 2.11 depicts a view of the entire earthly realm according to Jain cosmology; it shows the sacred Mount

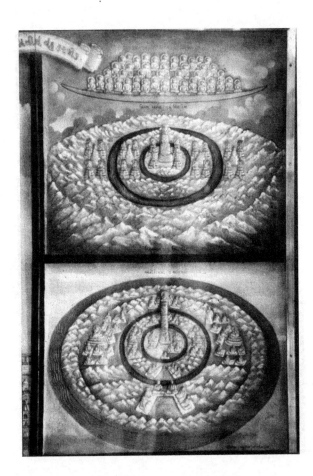

Figure 2.11   Detail of a low-relief painted and glazed image of the 'middle world' of Jain cosmology, consisting of concentric rings of land-mass and water, with the sacred Mount Meru at the centre, from a Jain temple in Jamnagar, India. Painting created late twentieth century

Meru at the centre of the world, surrounded by circular seas and continents (the known world for the early Jain cosmographers – modern India essentially – is but one part of the central continent). The style is much the same as that of the painting of Mount Girnar-ji and, like the wall painting of the pilgrimage site, the wall painting of the earthly realm is at once documentary – this is how the world is – and devotional.

Paint on canvas or stone is, of course, an infinitely malleable medium, a technology that is not limited to mimicking what the eye can see. But even still photography, an apparently objective mechanical recording medium, can be ambiguous in its capacity to 'document'. Figure 2.12 is a

Figure 2.12 Studio portrait of young woman. Utelle, France, 1913.
Photographer unknown

reproduction of a photograph taken around 1913 in a village in southern
France. It seems a typical studio portrait of the period – a young woman
in a simple but elegant dress looks up from her book, her head resting on
her hand, a dreamy suggestion of clouds behind her. Yannick Geffroy, the

French ethnographer who collected this image in the early 1970s, points out that the image is more likely to document her aspirations rather than her lived reality. Her pose suggests education and leisure – both of which cost money, and both of which were unlikely to have been within the grasp of a possibly illiterate peasant woman from a once-prosperous but later backwater of rural France. In one sense, the camera does not lie: this woman posed before the lens, her elbow on that table, that book open in front of her. But the image alone tells us less of the life she knew and more the life she dreamed of, the life she wanted to be hers and for herself and others to see (Geffroy 1990: 383).

But away from turn of the century peasant backwaters, 'documentation' has come to have a specific set of meanings in metropolitan Euro-America, one not necessarily shared by other societies in their use of figurative visual media, photographic or otherwise. Through the late nineteenth and twentieth centuries visual documentation – primarily still photography, but also latterly videotape and other mechanically-recorded traces – assumed the status of 'evidence'. A great deal has already been written about this issue, from the anthropometric photography of Victorian anthropology as evidence of human 'racial' types (Spencer 1992) to the security video of the James Bulger abduction as evidence of a crime (Mirzoeff 1999: 1–2). In fact, in neither case is the visual actually evidence of what it claims: the Victorians were simply wrong in their assumptions that human cultural and social variation were visible upon the skin and in the physiognomy of their subjects, and the security video simply shows the boys leading the toddler James Bulger away from the shopping centre, not the subsequent acts of violence for which they were convicted. The point is that Euro-American society has constructed photography – and, in due course, videotape – as a transparent medium, one that unequivocally renders a visual truth; that this is a social construction, and not an inevitable technological consequence, is well demonstrated by John Tagg among others (Tagg 1987). When confronted with claims of visual evidence a social researcher should first of all enquire about the basis of truth claims in general within that society or section of society, before going on to consider the ways in which images are adduced in support of truth (see also Scherer 1992).

2.5 'Us' and 'them'?

In the passage above, as elsewhere in this and the previous chapter I have implied a distinction between visual forms produced by and largely for Euro-American society, and forms produced within other societies or by subordinate or minority groups within Euro-American society (the category of Euro-American society I am using here is broad and fuzzy, and could quite easily be labelled 'the West' or something similar). Anthropologists and other social scientists are familiar with what is sometimes called 'the great divide' that separates 'us' from 'them', though the diacritic feature or features vary with the context of academic production. These features may be qualitatively or quantitatively assessed – 'primitive' rationality versus scientific rationality for instance, or pre- and post-demographic transition, or relative level of GNP. The distinction I have so far maintained rests rather self-reflexively on an historical contrast between those societies which produced and institutionalized the academic and applied disciplines of social research, and those that did not. That is, in the nineteenth and twentieth centuries Europe and America created forms of knowledge, or refined earlier forms, explicitly concerned with understanding the nature of society. These knowledge regimes were then applied within these societies and extended beyond them, and were intimately linked with the consolidation of the political and economic hegemony of global powers.

Today, the academic and applied use of social research is not geographically specific – every nation state in the world has some kind of government department devoted to the collection of demographic and census data, for example, and most nation states will maintain universities with departments of sociology, anthropology, economics and the like. But there is still a distinction to be made between those who conduct social research and those who are the subjects of that research, and this applies as much to visual research as to any other kind. Consequently, there is still some value in maintaining a distinction between those who create and utilize visual forms in the service of self-conscious social research and those who create and use them for other ends, but the distinction is contingent, suitable for some arguments only, and the differences highlighted by the distinction are probably outweighed by the similarities. There are two principle similarities. First, the use of any visual form, by anyone, will depend in varying degree upon a level of skill and familiarity with that visual form. I do not here particularly mean technical skill, though this is clearly a requirement to make best use of some visual forms, but rather a skill of social comprehension and social appropriateness. For example, until recently and maybe still today, strip cartoons and various types of animated film, were not considered appropriate media for 'high' literature or academic monographs in Euro-American society.[9]

Comprehension of the socially appropriate uses and subsequent readings of particular visual forms lies normally within the realm of tacit or implicit knowledge, though some fine art practices became increasingly self-conscious and self-referential in the course of the twentieth century. Thus, within all societies visual practice is an embedded social practice but it is likely to be embedded in a variety of different ways. Terence Turner's research on video use by the Kayapo of Brazil, discussed above, demonstrates both that the embedding may be rapid and that socially appropriate uses may be diverse. To both use and read visual forms in social contexts, therefore, normally requires no skill beyond the range of social skills to which all members of society have access. But to use, read or redeploy visual forms within explicitly sociological contexts requires not just a familiarity with the specialized knowledges of the social and human sciences, but also a foregrounding and analytical disembedding of the tacit social knowledge that enmeshes visual forms. 'I could have done that' says a member of the public in response to a Damien Hirst dead sheep in formaldehyde, runs the anecdote (substitute any abstract, installation or performance artist of choice). 'Yes, but you didn't', replies Hirst.

The second area of similarity between 'us' and 'them' is really just an extension of the first. Just as all visual forms are embedded in social practice, so too do all visual forms created or researched within the social sciences require an open, broad context reading and a recognition that analytical reading frames are context-specific, limited-use tools. A visual sociologist may uncritically accept the transparency of a photograph in her morning newspaper, but then apply a full range of critical skills when faced with a similar image encountered in the field. Take the newspaper photographs of Jörg Haider mentioned above (Section 2.2). I passed over these in my own newspaper reading easily enough, skimming the stories as they appeared day after day. But if I were engaged in a field-based research project into the social construction of 'whiteness' in the formation of English ethnic identity, I would be extremely alert if presented with one of these images – Haider triumphally clasping his arms above his head, for example – by one of my informants. So too, the Indian Jains, who casually accept the representational conventions of pilgrimage paintings encountered in the temple (see Figure 2.10), had no difficulty reading a black and white photograph of Mount Girnar-ji that I took on my own visit to the pilgrimage site, but wanted me to narrativize it: had I found the climb up the mountain difficult? which of the many temples had I visited? and so on. Consciously and unconsciously, critically and uncritically, we all – observers and observed – slip easily between reading internal and external narratives of images. Visual social researchers may feel a disciplinary duty to elucidate the external narratives within which images are enmeshed, but that does not mean that others are incapable of doing so.

Discussing similarities and differences between 'our' and 'their' visual use – 'we' do visual things to 'them' or conduct research on 'their' visual forms – is only a meaningful proposition within positivistic research paradigms, that is those which understand the task of social science to be to collect objectifiable data from research subjects who need have little concern for or comprehension of the project. Indeed, some forms of psychological research and covert sociological observation crucially depend upon the subjects of research remaining ignorant of the research process completely. Non-positivistic paradigms do not work in this way. Where social knowledge is seen as contingent and context-dependent, something that is constantly fashioned by actors, not a set of rules embedded within the individual or collective consciousness, then the collaboration of the research subjects is not merely required but is a recognition that they are active creators and shapers of the research process.

While willed and active collaboration may form the basic premise of some visual research projects (see Chapter 5.3) it is inadvertently present in all.[10] During the course of my own early fieldwork in India I found myself taking many of my photographs at public events organized by the Jains, such as feasts and temple ceremonies. On one occasion I took a number of photographs at a feast held in an open courtyard, organized to celebrate the conclusion of a period of fasting. A reading and under-standing of the internal narrative, of the images' content, was undoubtedly important to my later analysis: the overall context of the building and courtyard in which the feast took place, the segregation of men and women, the seated feasters and the standing feast givers, and a variety of other spatial features (see Figure 2.13).

However, after I had taken a few such photographs, I began to take closer portrait shots of various friends, including those who had brought me to the feast. This they tolerated for a while, and then gently began to suggest other people I should photograph. They were particularly insistent that I took a posed photograph of the woman who had paid for the feast, as she ladled a dollop of a rich yoghurt-based dessert into the bowl of one of the feasters (Figure 2.14). Looking at this image now alongside the wide-angle and contextualizing images, I can see how the 'directed' photograph is a collaborative image. It was composed and framed according to my own (largely unconscious) visual aesthetic and is part of my own corpus of documentary images of that feast. But it is also a legitimization and concretization of social facts as my friends saw

Figure 2.13   Group of Jains feasting at the conclusion of a nine-day period of dietary austerity. Jamnagar, India, 1983

Figure 2.14   Feast donor serving those who have completed the dietary austerity. Jamnagar, India, 1983

them: the fact that the feast had a social origin in the agency of one person (the feast donor) as well as being to some extent inevitable, precipitated by the period of communal fasting that had preceded it; the fact that the donor was (unusually) a woman and that in the photograph she is giving to men; the fact that this was a good feast during which we ate the expensive and highly-valued yoghurt dessert. Analytically, I 'knew' these social facts, because I had been told them on this or other occasions, but by being directed to capture them on film I was made aware not only of their strength and value but of the power of photography to legitimize them.

Notes

1 A recent British situation comedy, *The Royle Family* (1998, 1999) written by actress Caroline Aherne, trades heavily on class-based stereotypes of television viewing practice. It portrays the life of a white working class British family smoking, eating, drinking and talking in front of a permanently-on television set. Their conversations – a series of non sequiturs about themselves, their friends and relations – are often guided and shaped by apparently randomly selected snippets from the stream of sound and pictures.

2 My own opinion is that Östör found himself somewhat backed into a corner by Moore's incomprehension and Parry's hostility and hence provided an extremely 'closed' account of the internal narrative, relying on the film text alone. Of course, the film does not exist out of time or any other context any more than the men and women depicted in it. Part of the developing external narrative surrounding the film are the debates that have subsequently accreted around it. Taking this context into account, one could equally well say that the film is 'about' the contested trajectory of ethnographic film at the end of the twentieth century: see Ruby 2000, especially Chapter 3.

3 This, at least, is my observation on the streets of the historic and much-visited city of Oxford.

4 This discussion relates solely to conventional academic work in the social sciences. Obviously in other contexts, such as the concrete poetry movement of the 1960s, or the fashion/style magazines of the 1980s, typeface, layout, design and the overall look of the printed word on the page in combination with images and other design elements have all been as important as the syntax of the language elements. Even within academic contexts, the importance of considering textual information visually was only brought home to me when I volunteered as a 'blind reader', reading academic works onto audio-tape for visually-impaired academics and students. The most demanding task was the reading of tables, discussed in the text below. This necessitated specifying the number of columns, and then reading the rows cell by cell,

repeating the column head for each cell, to allow the hearer some chance to reconstruct the vertical and horizontal dimensions in their mind.

5 While not especially relevant to what follows, it is important to realize that here, as in most other anthropological discussions of kinship and genealogical relatedness, the links discussed are descriptions of *social* relatedness in the present, not descriptions of a history of biological descent. Statements about them are, therefore, statements about who is socially recognized to be related to whom, not who is biologically the descendant of whom.

6 The history of caste in India, and European attempts to grasp indigenous principles of social organization, is complex, contested, and well beyond the scope of this book. See Dumont 1980 for one highly influential overview, Quigley 1993 for an alternative explanation, or Sharma 1999 for a basic account.

7 As I noted above, Dumont actually fails to present his view of structural opposition in diagrammatic form, although he describes the essence of Evans-Pritchard's diagram; moreover, his (non) diagrammatic advance relates only to the representation of the ideological *varna* scheme, not to the on-the-ground *jatis*, the functional units of marriage, occupation, residence, etc., where he appears to revert to a league table view (Dumont 1980: 89–91; Quigley 1993: 31–5). A small number of diagrams are employed elsewhere in *Homo hierarchicus*, some to good effect such as his diagrammatic representation of hierarchical encompassment (Dumont 1980: 242, Figs. 1 and 2), and some to poor effect – such as his comparison between societies oriented towards holism, such as India, and societies oriented towards the individual, such as Euro-America, which I find cluttered and spatially confusing (Dumont 1980: 233, Fig. 5).

8 'Indigenous' is used here in a loose sense, to indicate third and fourth world peoples who form a minority population within their nation states of residence and who have limited if any control of the dominant media of the state, such as national television and newspapers. Key readings on indigenous media use include Dowmunt 1993, Ginsburg 1991 and 1994, Michaels 1986 (see also Ruby 2000, Chapter 9, on Michaels's work), and Turner 1990, 1991 and 1992. Recent comprehensive texts within the anthropology of art include Coote and Shelton 1992, and Gell 1998.

9 The exceptions are usually highly particularistic, such as animated computer modelling to show sequences of some kinds of scientific or statistical data, or self-consciously boundary-challenging, such as the . . . *for Beginners* strip cartoon series originally published by the Writers and Readers Publishing Collective (*Marx for Beginners*, Rius 1976; *Freud for Beginners*, Appignanesi and Zarate 1979; etc.), or cartoonist Martin Rowson's strip cartoon versions of T.S. Elliot's *The Waste Land* (1990) and Laurence Sterne's *Tristram Shandy* (1996).

10 The following two paragraphs and referenced photographs are a partial reworking of a section of Banks 1995.

3

Material vision

Figure 3.1 P.C. Parekh, an Indian businessman, showing a photograph attached to the minutes of a business meeting, part of his own personal archive. Jamnagar, India, 1998

3.1 Object and representation

All I want is a photo in my wallet
A small remembrance of something more solid
All I want is a picture of you.

'Picture This' (Chris Stein/Deborah Harry, 1978)

Debbie Harry's desires are both ubiquitous and unique: many of us carry photos in our wallets, yet each of us carries photographs that are uniquely meaningful to ourselves. The photo in my wallet is not the photo in your wallet. But is that creased and ragged-cornered photo-booth photograph in your wallet any less 'solid' than the person or persons it represents? Most photographs, films, videotapes and certain types of art objects represent or stand for the thing depicted, at least in some contexts. With photography, as with most mechanical forms of reproduction, the thing depicted is a concrete thing, manifest in the world at a particular point in space-time – my lover, your dog, their garden. The object and its representation are linked indexically in a photograph; light reflected from the object causes chemical changes on the surface of the film, subsequent manipulation in the dark room notwithstanding. One material object is substantively linked to another material object. Practically speaking, the linkage lasts only for the fraction of a second it takes to expose the film. The death of a person does not cause all the photographic representations of them to fade; the destruction of a photograph does not cause the person depicted to die.[1]

In fact, in Euro-American society the idea of an enduring link between a person (or thing) and their representation, especially a photographic representation, is quite commonplace. Take the following familiar examples: pinning a picture of the autocratic boss to a dartboard and throwing darts at it; shredding a photograph of a lover who abandoned you; airbrushing a Party colleague who has fallen from favour from an official photograph of the Party faithful; tying a photograph of Princess Diana to the railings of Kensington Palace and laying flowers before it. In these and many similar examples, the initial link between the person and their photographic representation is not merely indexical but symbolic – and it is the symbolic linkage that endures. The photograph is not just a representation of a person, but a representation of a representation – the qualities or actions or knowledge associated with the person represented. It is a change or shift in the social relations between persons that causes action to be done to the photographic representation: he thinks he's so powerful, but I'll get him right between the eyes; she left me and destroyed our relationship, so I will shred her photograph; he was in the way on my rise to power so I had him removed; she brought beauty and pleasure into our lives but then died and left us, so we will adorn her photograph with beautiful but soon-fading flowers.

The symbolic linkage can be more banal, and less obviously a product of social relations. If I show my friends a photograph of my new Aston Martin, improbably purchased with the royalties I have received from this book, I am claiming something about the wealth and status I have, or aspire to. But as with all symbolic linkages, there has to be a common cultural field that we share in order to interpret the symbolism correctly, and we establish our co-presence in that cultural field through sociality, through the sharing of social relations. Social researchers need to be alert to this intertwining of the material, the symbolic, the social and the cultural; they also need to be alert to the contexts in which one element appears to be privileged, and the social mechanisms which permit that privileging.

3.2 The materiality of visual forms

Similar to the need to distinguish between external and internal narratives in the reading of images, it is important for the social researcher to distinguish between the *form* of a visual image and the *content* of a visual image. While linked, form and content are at least analytically separable and it is often helpful to consider the extent to which form dictates or mediates content. In all cases of mechanical image production and reproduction, such as video and still or moving photography, as well as in many non-mechanical cases, the material characteristics of the form serve to shape or even constrain the possible content. Conversely, through paint or other non-mechanical media it is possible to represent both those things that can be seen with the naked eye and those that cannot (but see Latour 1988 on the rise of scientific rationalism and the consequent difficulty of representing 'heaven' in religious painting).

By the time of the development of still photography in the mid-nineteenth century, the possibility of photographing that which could not be seen had been both ideologically and mechanically circumscribed, and indeed special attention was and continues to be paid to photo-graphic images which appear to breach this, such as Elsie Wright and Frances Griffiths's images of fairies (the 'Cottingly Fairies') which so captivated Sir Arthur Conan Doyle, or the attempts of psychics and others to photograph ghosts, ectoplasm and the like (see Figure 3.2).[2]

Consequently, with marked exceptions which are generally recognized as such, film, video and photography serve to depict only a limited and finite range of all possible content, partly as a result of convention (for example, Jay Ruby's exploration of a genre of photography, post-mortem images, that was thought no longer to exist for reasons of taste rather than practicality [Ruby 1995a: 3]) and partly as a result of material con-straint. Thus the social researcher should consider in advance of research both what kind of images she might possibly encounter, as well as the various media that may be encountered.

In considering the relationship between form and content, attention should also be paid to the extent – if any – to which one is privileged over the other in any particular social context. Attention paid to the materiality of the visual image, and the materiality of its context, can serve to illuminate the distinctive texture of social relations in which it is performing its work. In a survey of Catholic homes in southern Europe a

Figure 3.2   One of the 'Cottingly Fairy' photographs: a fairy offers harebells to
Elsie Wright. Photographer: Frances Griffiths

researcher might expect to encounter images of the Madonna. But in one
home she might find a framed chromolithograph of Mary and her angels

hung on the wall over the bed, in another she might find a photograph of a particular statue of the Virgin to which the householders accord special respect tucked into the corner of the frame of another picture, and in yet another she might be shown a damp patch on the wall of the kitchen that forms the rough outline of a woman praying and which the house-holders and their neighbours sincerely believe to be a divine apparition. The social relations surrounding and enmeshing the images will be very different in each case. In the first, the medium is commonplace and its material form probably of little concern to the householders: for them, the content is what matters. In the second, the householders have formed a particular relationship with a material object – a specific statue of the Virgin at a certain pilgrimage shrine – and they represent that relation-ship through another material object, the photograph. In the third, the unusual material form is what animates what is otherwise commonplace content, and this physical form will bring about a whole train of social relationships involving the Church hierarchy, the press, visiting pilgrims and the like.

While this example is both hypothetical and (in the last case) unusual, some researchers have used the form versus content distinction to problematize the 'meaning' ascribed to a visual image. For example, in 1996 the National Gallery in London organized an exhibition focused on a single painting: John Constable's 'The Cornfield' (1826). Prior to the exhibition, the organizer and staff of the Gallery used notices in a local newspaper and next to the painting itself in the Gallery to find members of the public who had reproductions of the painting in their homes. Some of these reproductions then became part of the exhibition, together with a videotape in which people described what the painting (or their reproduction thereof) meant to them (Chaplin 1998: 303–4). The selected reproductions were in a variety of media but were typically utilitarian objects decorated with a reproduction of a part or the whole of the painting: tea towels, plates, firescreens, thimbles, clocks, wallpaper.[3]

One, perhaps not terribly surprising, finding from this exercise was that some of the 45 people who answered the newspaper advertisement 'were unaware of the existence of the original painting and had never heard of John Constable' (Chaplin 1998: 303). The domestic objects, even if not used for their functional purpose but displayed ornamentally (as doubtless the decorated plates and thimbles were), were part of an assemblage of material items within the home that conveyed meaning in conversation with one another, and with their owners and their visitors. Vague yet comforting associations of a golden rural past, of leisure and days out in the country, of childhood innocence, triggered by the reproduced content of the known or unidentified original painting are combined with the class and status imperatives to maintain a nice, well-ordered and well-decorated home triggered by the material form, existence and display of the decorated objects. It is the consumption of material goods and their decorative content that would appear to give meaning to these visual artefacts, not merely their association with what Alfred Gell has called 'the art cult' (Gell 1992: 42; see also Gell 1998: 62–4, 97).

3.2.1 Displaying family photographs

In the example above, the material forms of the Constable reproduction place their owners in a particular relation to the art world that gives the painting meaning, even if this place is rather peripheral prior to the 1996 exhibition. Chaplin, however, does not discuss how these visual images stand in relation to other visual images in their homes, nor how they mediate or represent relationships between their owners and others in their more immediate social environment.

David Morley cites a number of studies to show that domestic television sets frequently act as a dual medium for the display of visual images, as there is a common tendency to place a variety of physical objects on top of the set, especially photographs – the viewer thus receiving two images for the price of one, as it were (Morley 1995: 182 ff.). In Euro-America the photographs displayed on the top of television sets are commonly family photographs, very often studio portraits or at least posed pictures representing important life cycle events, as opposed to holiday snapshots which tend to be hidden away for more intimate consumption in albums. From my own observations, British middle class householders rarely make a distinction in their displays between photographs of the living and photographs of the dead, a marked contrast to photographic displays I have observed in India. My mother, for example, now elderly and living in the suburbs of a northern town, has on her television set a photograph of her deceased husband with her still living sister, taken on the occasion of my graduation, several photographs of her only grandchild as a child (though the 'child' is now a teenager), and a graduation photograph of her daughter who later died, together with a photograph of the still-living spouse. My brother and I – both childless – are not represented at all, though she told me this was simply because we had not given her photographs of ourselves. For all of these images, as far as I can establish, the frames around the photographs are cheap high street items, selected only for their ability to fit the photograph and be self-standing on the top of the set but otherwise unmarked, socio-logically speaking. Content is all, and form or medium entirely sub-sidiary. To some extent the television set top acts as a kind of shrine for the display of a family's significant images and other objects such as china ornaments and holiday souvenirs, the bounded and pier-like surface acting as a more suitable space than a run of shelves or another item of furniture that is already designed to hold objects, such as a table or sideboard. Mantelpieces, in homes that have them, may serve a similar shrine-like function.

In Indian homes by contrast I have never seen family photographs displayed on a television set, though I don't doubt that some are as television sets themselves become more prevalent. More particularly, photographs of the living are also rarely on show in any context, but are generally confined to albums (the ubiquitous wedding album) or tucked away in their envelopes in drawers or boxes (day trip snapshots, photographs sent by relatives overseas). Photographs of the dead, how-ever, are frequently displayed,[4] as are photographs or other visual representations of sacred places – shrines, temples, mosques – together with chromolithographs of divinities and other sacred persons where appropriate. In most of these cases the materiality of the image is marked, sometimes quite literally. In relatively wealthier urban homes I have visited in western India, where access to studio portrait photo-graphy was possible during the past few decades, a standard practice is to enlarge a studio photograph of the deceased person in the prime of life, sometimes to have it hand coloured, and then to frame and hang it on the wall in a prominent position. In Hindu homes it is common to hang a garland of fresh or artificial flowers around the frame of the image on the anniversary of the death of the person. Incense may be burned in front of such photographs, and the foreheads of those rep-resented may be dotted with vermilion or sandalwood paste.[5] Photo-graphic images of the dead, intermingled with photographic and artistic representations of sacred places and persons, can also be found away from the domestic context – in the meeting halls of religious groups and caste communities, for example (where the dead will be revered religious or community leaders). In cases such as these the content of the images is obviously important, but so too is the material form around and upon which social acts are performed. In the domestic context there is little or no cultural space for a 'mere' photograph of a living family member.

In his work on the social production and consumption of photography in central India the anthropologist Christopher Pinney provides a num-ber of related examples from a village community, one with less access to wealth and the material trappings of urban domestic life than my own informants. He found no correlation between the wealth or status (i.e. caste status) of the villagers and the number of photographs they might have displayed, nor in the arrangement of such photographs. He did, however, find a number of framed groups of images hung on the walls of some homes (Pinney 1997: 154–64). These can be seen as biographical narratives of an individual or family and therefore do include photographs of the still living. They are not, however, family photographs in the Euro-American sense. Typically, for example, the assemblies of images will also include photographs or chromolithographs of deities or shrines, or of family members visiting such shrines or performing other auspicious acts. All in all, the physical association between the variety of images in a single frame is the point of the display rather than it being an attempt to provide a catalogue of relatives.

Clearly a great deal more can be said about family photographs, their use, their circulation and so forth, but I believe the discussion above should be sufficient to alert the social researcher to a consideration of their materiality; or, as has recently come to be the case, their apparent immateriality. In the late 1990s computer manufacturers began a series of aggressive campaigns to market relatively cheap multimedia computers to domestic consumers for recreational use (rather than the office-like management of home finances, for example). A persistent theme in many advertising campaigns, particularly around Christmas time, was the ability offered by the technology to send digitized photographs and video clips to distant family members. With a multimedia computer, a digital camera and access to the Internet (the latter two also aggressively marketed at this time) the possibility was offered of an archive of family photographs, freely exchanged between family members and others, that had no apparent physical form whatsoever. In Section 3.5 below I will address some of the problems that computer-based and other digital media pose for those attempting to incorporate a material perspective into their study of visual images. First, however, I wish to consider another aspect of the materiality of visual objects: their commodification and exchange.

3.3 Exchanged goods

One further social attribute of family photographs, beyond their capacity to memorialize the dead and to display to the living, is their role in social exchange, generally intra-familial exchange. On the whole, photographs do not serve as the opening tokens in exchange relationships, but they most certainly serve to maintain relationships.[6] They distinctively do this by maintaining relationships between persons who are and remain geographically separated. Of course, many other things are exchanged between such persons – letters, telephone calls, birthday cards and gifts – but in these contexts photographs are perhaps uniquely inscribed with qualities of permanence (materiality), display potential, memory and personhood (both representing the person and being gifted by the person). The materiality of photographs so exchanged is by no means their dominant property, nor possibly their most important, but it is certainly not a property that should be overlooked by social researchers: their visible presence, for example, contrasted with the perhaps acutely experienced absence of their subject, should be of interest to psychologists, while their role as counters of exchange in the materially imbalanced relationship between parents and children (or grandparents and grandchildren) should be of interest to social economists and economic anthropologists.

Photographs like these are, however, generally reproductions struck from a negative, allowing both parties involved to own a copy. Coming from and largely remaining within a private, familial sphere of exchange, they also rarely have any market or other value to those outside the sphere. (Indeed, the morality of kinship and friendship relations in Euro-America is predicated upon keeping these relations distinct from the sphere of capitalist economic value.) Some photographs do, however, cross over into the world of market relations and here their materiality plays a very important part.[7]

3.3.1 Market exchange

The commercial market in photographs has developed only in the last few decades, and still only accounts for a very small part of the fine art market with which it is usually allied – around five per cent of the turnover of one large auction house, I was told. While one or two of the big auction houses do have photographic departments and hold regular photographic sales, the rest tend to sell photographs either in memorabilia sales (signed photographs of the Beatles at pop memorabilia sales, for example) or in fine art or book sales (Victorian photographs in Victorian painting sales, for example). There are also few specialist photographic dealers, and the most significant retail outlet for old photographs in Britain are rare book and print dealers. Nevertheless some photographs or collections of photographs can sell for considerable sums, and both the market itself and the prices paid are increasing year by year. For example, a set of the 'Cottingly Fairies' photographs mentioned above (and including an original print of Figure 3.2), was sold at Sotheby's in

London in July 1998 for almost £22,000. However, the collection included a first edition of Conan Doyle's credulous book about the photographs and their makers (*The Coming of the Fairies*, 1922) and so in this case the price raised is probably more indicative of the value placed upon Conan Doyle memorabilia than the value placed upon the photographs themselves. To understand more about which photographs sell in their own right it is necessary to learn a little more about the market and the collectors.[8]

A number of factors determine the market value of a photograph at auction. Understandably perhaps, the internal narrative or manifest content of a photographic image is said to be most important, but surprisingly the material condition and properties are said to be of relatively little importance. Also influencing value are the status of the photographer (named and known better than unknown), the age and type-scarcity of an image (that is one, or only one of a few from a type or class defined by age, provenance, content, etc.), mounting, format, and technical process employed. The high value accorded to content parallels that of the fine art market, although in this market the value accorded to particular painters is so strong (albeit fluctuating) that there is heavy reliance on the Romantic aesthetic imperative (see note 3) which links the imputed universal and objective beauty – and hence value – of the artwork to the 'genius' of individual painters. In the world of marketable photography the linkage is less strong until we come to the celebrity photographers of the second half of the twentieth century (such as Robert Mapplethorpe, Helmut Newton, Irving Penn).[9] Prior to this, and especially in sales of nineteenth and early twentieth century photography, content appears to dominate.

A good example is seen in the sales of what might be loosely termed 'ethnographic' photographs. In general, photographs of people fetch more than photographs of landscapes or buildings, portraits – especially in colourful native clothing – fetch more than scenes, and photographs of women fetch more than photographs of men. But where the subjects come from is also important. It is generally acknowledged that photographs of Japan and Japanese subjects are always popular; in Britain these tend to be bought by local dealers and then sold on to Japanese customers. Korean subjects became increasingly sought after in the 1990s, however, reflecting the boom in the Korean economy and the development of a self-conscious and commoditized nostalgia for the nation's past. In 1998 one auction house valued an album of around one hundred Korean photographs pre-sale at £600–900 on the basis of their poor physical condition but sold them for over ten times as much. Early

Figure 3.3 Studio portrait of Korean men, possibly traders; this image has never been put up for sale, but is typical of those that command a high price at auction. Hong Kong, 1870s or 1880s. Photographer unknown

photographs from Korea are far scarcer than those from Japan (as a result of the differing historical relationships between these countries and the metropolitan centres of the West from which the photographers came) which also contributes to their increased market valuation (Figure 3.3).

The salesroom market has increasingly turned towards younger buyers and to individual buyers. In the early days of photographic sales, buyers were largely dealers, who preferred albums that could be split up and the images sold to particularly targeted clients. Increasingly the market for 'ethnographic' photographs is less the museum-based ethnographic photographic collections (which have effectively been priced out of the market) and more wealthy individual buyers, often from the countries represented by the subjects. While all the evidence above would seem to indicate that content, therefore, dominates material form in the sale of photographs, the shift from dealer purchases to individual purchases represents an underlying emphasis on the unique materiality of the photographs.

I was told that one of the reasons that a market in old photographs was so slow to develop were fears concerning the uniqueness or rarity of the object bought. Buyers accustomed to purchasing unique and provenanced paintings, or prints or books of finite and known print runs, initially looked with suspicion upon investing in photographic prints where the status of the negative 'original' was unclear.[10] How could they be sure that this was a unique print, or that no more would be discovered or – worse – made? One solution adopted by the auction houses was education, helping potential collectors to appreciate the unique value of individual prints, as well as educating them in basic photographic history. One auction house even ran a once-a-week evening course, taught by a photographic historian, which concluded just as the auction house held a major photographic sale, allowing – encouraging – the course members to put their new-found appreciation into practice. By such avenues collectors are brought to an awareness of the beauty or scarcity of certain photographic categories: all pre-1870 photographs are rare, salt prints and platinum prints are more beautiful than albumen prints; some individual prints can be (claimed to be) closer to the photographer's original intentions than others. These largely material or artefactual properties, together with factors of content discussed above, can all contribute to the value of a print purchased at auction.

I have concentrated in this section largely on the auction house sale of historical photographs, though clearly there is more research to be done and many parallels to be explored between the commoditization of photographic images and the commoditization of fine art images.[11] A related area of access to a world in which social exchange and market commoditization are intertwined in the materiality of images is the theft of photographs. Many anthropologists have pointed out that theft, fraud and cheating are various forms of 'negative' exchange (but see Davis 1992: 24–5) and that items once stolen or illegally removed from one sphere of exchange often then circulate in another sphere of exchange (from art thief to collectors of illicit art, for example). One curator of a small historical photographic collection told me that fear of theft was not a terribly pressing concern, partly because the images in the collection were largely not by 'named' photographers (as defined by the market – the makers of most of the images were in fact known), and partly because the majority of the prints were in small formats – quarter plate or half plate – and not the full plate and large formats that the market values. An unsavoury instance of theft which does, or did, occur from historical photographic collections is mentioned in Paul Harris's film about photographic collections and exhibitions, *Scenes from a Museum* (1994). In the film, Alison Devine Nordström, the Director of the South-east Museum of Photography, claims that a number of images have disappeared from certain collections over the past century. In one case, the missing images are all nudes, in another, images of naked boys in particular (the loss of the images is detectable by comparing early records of the collection with the images actually in the files). In Sections 3.5.2 and 3.5.3 below I will deal more directly with the circulation and exchange of photographs deemed pornographic. However, the ease with which any images can be stolen from collections is, as noted above, partly related to their size.

3.4 Size matters

One of the most obvious aspects of image materiality is size, especially with regard to photography in the period before the ubiquity of the 'En-print' when a wide variety of image sizes and formats were used. In a review of a book on American memorial photography (Stanley Burns's *Sleeping Beauty*, 1990) Jay Ruby complains that Burns has enlarged some of the images, and cropped others: 'presumably in an effort to adhere to some design principle, thus "enhancing" the photographs' value as objects of artistic contemplation' (Ruby 1991: 84). Why should this matter, apart from the fact that unless one has access to the original one will never know what has been lost in cropping? Ruby's answer is that in losing or distorting an aspect of the photograph's materiality an ability to comprehend or uncover its place in human social relations is also lost or distorted. Ruby provides an excellent example of this in his own later book on American memorial photography. In the caption that accompanies a tintype postmortem photograph of a child, dated 1879–1890s, he notes: 'The size of this tintype [8 $\frac{3}{8}$ × 6 $\frac{7}{16}$ inches] would indicate that it was produced to be framed and hung on the wall. It is too large for an album' (Ruby 1995b: 73, Figure 28). Ruby links this with a particular type of post-mortem photograph at the end of the nineteenth century, designed not merely to convey the sentiment of 'the last sleep' but to cheat death by portraying the subject as alive. In the case of the particular tintype to which he refers, open eyes have been painted onto the surface of the image, perhaps to render it more suitable for open display. Equally, the particular size of *cartes-de-visite* images (albumen prints, mounted on 4.5 x 2.5 inch cards, and popular in the second half of the nineteenth century) is closely associated with one of their social functions – to be left or sent as a visiting card on social occasions.

Today, photographic negative size is largely standardized for the amateur photographer, with the 35mm format, although of course prints from negative film can be supplied in a variety of sizes and on a variety of media such as table mats, porcelain plates and even mouse mats. Nonetheless, the dimensions of other photographic forms have some social resonance, especially those without negatives.[12] Instant Polaroid photographs are often associated with the recording of images that either have to perform their work immediately, or must not advertise their existence too widely. Such photographs are instantly recognizable by type for many viewers with their black back and asymmetrical white border (deeper at the bottom than at the top). Consequently, they can be used to indicate a certain type of photograph in other media – typically feature films and television programmes – where the putative content of such photographs could not be shown for reasons of taste or decency: dismembered corpses or illicit sexual activity in crime thrillers, for example. Again, the dimensions of the passport photo booth strip of four images are also instantly recognizable to many Euro-American viewers, and a snatched glimpse of a sequence of four images in a teenager's pocket or bag can communicate a narrative about a Saturday afternoon messing around with mates at a shopping centre, or bashful pride in a new girl- or boyfriend.

Similarly for cine-film and videotape, differences between formats – including the dimensions of the actual film or tape – are more than merely technical matters.[13] The huge variety of 35mm and 70mm commercial projection systems patented over the years for commercial feature films have succeeded or failed not so much because of technical superiority or novelty, or even audience appreciation, but due to the willingness or reluctance of cinema chains to invest in the necessary projection equipment. Meanwhile, until the advent of domestic video systems, 8mm and later Super-8 film was very much the province of the amateur cinematographer, though used occasionally by professional filmmakers partly for reasons of cost and partly to convey certain aesthetic sentiments through the graininess of the stock. A knowledge of the originating medium of documentary films encountered can suggest a great deal concerning the social relations involved in their production (for a more technical discussion of film and video formats see Barbash and Taylor 1997: Chapter 5; for an historical discussion, see Salt 1992).

3.5 Transformations: digitization and computer-based media

Some of the more evangelistic proponents of new digital technologies like to proclaim a future world of bits, not atoms; a world in which materiality, the tying of objects to time-bound trajectories through space, is transcended by virtuality, the liberation of knowledge from its material containers.[14] There is certainly some truth in this: many cash transactions now take place by electronic transfer rather than the exchange of gold bars; some of us who haven't written a letter in years send dozens of emails a day; electronic copies of important literary and historical texts are freely available on the Web, as are digital copies of the contents of many photo and film libraries.

There are, however, some downsides to this, particularly with regard to materiality. During the course of my research for this book I interviewed a number of curators and archivists working with photographic and film collections. For the most part, they were agreed on the potential benefits offered by digitizing their collections. This was particularly so in the case of film archivists who were acutely aware of the access difficulties posed by film, especially fragile old film. One photographic curator, however, pointed out that while digitization was of great value in providing access to certain collections or parts of collections, the policies behind digitization projects often reflected a primarily content-based approach to images, a privileging of the internal narrative. In some cases this could be helpful to users, who may initially require knowledge at this level before going further. But an overwhelming focus on 'pictures of . . .' could also lead to only certain parts of collections being digitized for reasons of cost: typically a 'cherry-picking' approach that selects arresting images, signature images, or images by 'names'. A collection of these images, available on the Web or on CD-ROM, would therefore fail to present the originating collections in their entirety, and the knowledge that could be derived from the relationship between images in a collection would be overlooked. The danger, she felt, lay in seeing digitization programmes as a cure-all for problems of access to collections (a highly politicized topic in British museums in the late 1990s) and consequently diverting cash and time resources away from more fundamental but less glamorous research into the photographs themselves, research which inevitably involves dealing with the materiality of the photographic objects. Less-experienced scholars, encountering only digital copies of images documented on the basis of content alone, might – uncritically or even unwittingly – come to accept this bias. Insight and evidence gained from the originals, such as inscriptions and stickers on the reverse of the image, changes in emulsion tone and texture through age, and so on would be ignored.

Of course, materiality is not sidestepped altogether – all digital images require a material storage medium[15] – and the social relations engendered or created by the exchange and circulation of images persist, albeit in new forms. So too, in the case of digitized copies of photographs and film, do concepts of authenticity and originality remain.

3.5.1   Digital manipulation

Nowhere is this more apparent than in the case of digitally altered photographs. Photographic prints – and negatives – have been physically altered since the beginnings of photography. At times this has been for aesthetic effect, at times for political or social reasons. While some early photographic manipulation had the aim of enhancing the seeming verisimilitude of the image (Wright 1999: 162–3), other examples appear purely decorative. The Victoria and Albert Museum in London contains some early albumin prints by its founder, Henry Cole, of scenes in Bologna. On the surface of the prints, Cole has added drawing ink and sometimes pigment, giving the photographs the appearance of ink and watercolour sketches. Similarly, in India, the hand-colouring of black and white prints may have diminished but has not entirely ceased since the introduction of cheap colour print film (Pinney 1997: 138–40).

For years, photographers have retouched both negatives and prints in the darkroom, removing speckles and dust or hiding blemishes on the faces of subjects. Many of us are also familiar with the tendency of dictatorial political regimes to airbrush political rivals out of earlier official photographs. In the world of digital photography all this and more is now within the reach of anyone with access to a scanner, a domestic computer and basic image manipulation software. While the unacknowledged manipulation of photographs has always been a cause of concern for some, these worries appear to have increased dramatically with the advent of digital techniques. Frequently, these worries centre on issues of truth and 'reality'. For example:

> [a] century and a half ago photographs relieved paintings of the burden of recording reality; now, in turn, computers have weakened photography's claim on depicting the 'real' world. For all of computers' extraordinary precision, their impact in news photography has been to obscure the boundaries of fact and fiction. In other words, to blur. (Leslie 1995: 113).

Setting aside the fact that it is doubtful whether pre-photographic representational Western painting traditions were ever wholly or even in part concerned with 'recording reality', it is clear that this author (a journalist) considers this to be the work of pre-digital photography. For most visual anthropologists, photographic historians and such, this is a highly dubious claim. What is true is that photography is frequently called upon to authenticate the experience of reality after time has passed. Photographs are treated as active witnesses, not passive or even accidental objects of evidence. We tend to conflate their object nature with their objectivity, their self-authenticity (this is a photograph) with the authenticity of their representation (this is a dog – cf. Sekula 1982: 86). Digital photographic manipulation worries because it lays bare the gap between material object and objective representation.

Nonetheless, digital images – while composed of perfectly fungible bits rather than stubbornly unique atoms – can be digitally granted digital uniqueness. There are two main ways to achieve this, which should be employed by anyone concerned about copyright and unauthorized reproduction on the Web (see also Chapter 6.6). The first is manually to alter the image with image processing software after it has been digitized in such a way that the overall readability is generally preserved but interrupted. Figure 3.4 shows a digital image on the Web treated in this

Figure 3.4   Frame still taken from A.C. Haddon's 1898 Torres Strait Island footage, digitized and overprinted with the word 'COPYRIGHT' as a watermark (detail). Torres Strait, Australia, 1898, digitally manipulated 1996. Photographer: A.C. Haddon

way. In this case, the overprinting of the word 'copyright' is relatively regular, and it should be possible for a skilled mathematician or programmer to write an algorithm that inserted new data bits almost seamlessly to complete the image. It is unlikely, however, that anyone would go to the trouble, certainly for a single image. This is a form of watermarking on the 'surface' of the image, which does not prevent its digital reproduction but which clearly signals that any subsequent reproduction has a source, an origin point.

The other method involves inserting a digital watermark invisibly into the code of the image file, in the form of a unique reference number. In one commercial system the code, once inserted, cannot be removed even after the image has been extensively manipulated – a form of electronic tagging. This is also a passive system, however, and relies on a concerned viewer using software to check a suspect image. If a watermark is revealed then the software can use the Web to identify the image owner (see Figure 3.5). In neither case can unauthorized reproduction be prevented or even noticed, but in both cases the digital image carries meta-content, information external to the image, which can make explicit

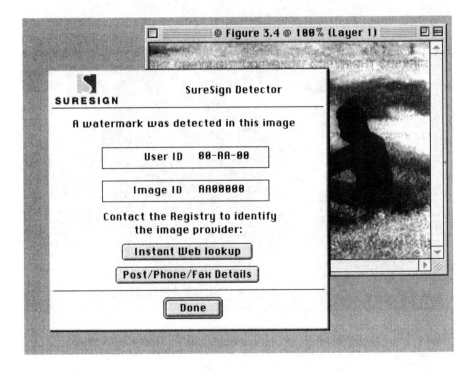

Figure 3.5   Screen shot showing digital watermarking software in action

a claimed linkage between image and owner, whereby the owner's unique identity is virtually conferred on the image.

3.5.2 Digital pornography: constraining the virtual

One category of photographic images to which both physical and digital manipulation has been extensively applied is pornography, ranging from the airbrushing out of pubic hair in early 'health' magazines, to the digital grafting of a famous person's head onto the body of a nubile or beefy naked porn model. Until the late 1990s 'sex' was often cited as the most frequent term entered into Internet search engines (it was overtaken by 'MP3' in 1999 in response to the rise of digital audio files on the Web). Certainly, the Web is awash with pornographic images, 'soft' and 'hard', and their early appearance quickly gave rise to a moral panic which shows little signs of abating. While the relevance of Internet pornography is not immediately apparent to a discussion of the materiality of visual forms, the fears prompted by the ease of access to such images – a property of their very immateriality – crystallize a number of more widespread social concerns which link moral boundaries with physical boundaries.

The Internet provides a medium of exchange and circulation for images (of all kinds), principally through newsgroups and the Web, that is subject to minimal internal regulation and which transcends regional and national boundaries. Unlike the market in physical goods – which can be controlled with more or less success by governmental and parastatal agencies, thus hindering for example the flow of printed and videotaped pornography from mainland Europe into the British Isles – the 'trade' in bits over telephone and data wires is hard to see, let alone block. As still photographs and video frame grabs can be digitized and stored for little cost, they make ideal commodities on the Web: some given away freely, some for purchase in a variety of ways. In response, a number of initiatives have grown up to limit or prevent access to certain kinds of Internet content. It is relatively easy for states and agencies such as Internet service providers (ISPs) to block newsgroup content, as the groups are organized into a relatively clear and stable hierarchy and because newsgroup content must be downloaded from particular distribution nodes. An ISP may choose not to carry any of the alt.sex.xxx groups for example, and technically this is a relatively simple procedure to automate.

The Web, however, is a fluid, rapidly changing network, where content is drawn directly from the millions of Web servers around the world. Most ISPs pass this content through a cache, where it is stored for any later users, cutting down the costs of data transmission for the ISP. While an ISP may choose to filter the material that passes through the cache automatically, this can rarely be very effective and consequently most material on the Web is freely accessible. One commercial solution to this is to place the filtering burden on the consumer. Software can be purchased which, when configured and password protected (usually by parents or teachers in respect of the children in their care), automatically blocks access to nominated Web sites. The irony is that this must be done manually, not digitally. Typically, a software filter company employs teams of researchers who scour the Web for offensive content (of all kinds, not merely pornography) to compile lists that the filtering software draws upon. Purchase of the software normally provides a subscription to periodic or constant updates of these lists. We thus have a situation in which, taking the case of pornography, the digital and non-material images become hedged around with materiality, virtual objects which must be manually constrained.[16]

3.5.3   Digital pornography: exchange and circulation

In late 1993 and throughout 1994, a number of British newspapers carried stories claiming that 'computer porn' had been seen by one in ten children at British secondary schools, and was circulating freely on floppy disks in playgrounds and in the streets (see, for example, *The Sunday Times* 5.12.93; The *Guardian* 16.6.94; *The Times* 16.6.94). Teachers cited claimed not only to have seen this material, but to have identified their own school's children in some images which, it was claimed, would lead these children into a 'culture of abuse'. Later reports shifted the figures higher, to a third of all boys' schools and noted that 'computer porn' was common at 'upmarket boarding schools' (The *Guardian* 7.10.94). In short, the reports had all the hallmarks of a moral panic, linking unfamiliar new technologies with children, pornography, abuse and lack of control. The addition of 'upmarket boarding schools' added a further element of class, as though even the twin bastions of wealth and privilege could not hold back the tide. In fact, as one commentator points out, hard factual evidence for these or any other claims regarding the spread and dissemination of digitized pornographic images is extremely scarce (Calcutt 1995). In Britain at least, the newspaper scare stories above, and others like them at this period, relied on two documents: a 1994 report prepared for the UK government's select committee on computer pornography, and an unpublished survey by a researcher at a British university – the latter providing the findings for the news stories above.

The author of the report, Vicki Merchant, had sent 28,000 question-naires out to British schools, and received more than 7,500 replies (not a terribly poor response rate for an unsolicited postal survey). Nonethe-less, however carefully the questionnaire may have been prepared and the responses analysed, it was grossly misinterpreted by the press. While the *Guardian* article quoted above claimed that most material was passed in disk form between children in the playground or streets, and that some had brought material into classrooms and loaded it onto school computers, in fact the respondents to the questionnaire were not the children but their teachers and headteachers. The 'evidence' for the claims amounted to little more than 'hearsay and staffroom gossip' and vague assertions such as 'many respondents say that children with home computers are aware of computer porn and "know someone who has a disk"' (Calcutt 1995: 753–4). While asking some respondents for their opinions concerning the actions or opinions of others can be a valuable research technique in some contexts, this seems unlikely to have been one of them, but rather to have contributed to the climate of half-truths and stereotypes that are a hallmark of moral panics.

In the early to mid-1990s domestic Internet access was rare in Britain, with the major period of growth not occurring until the end of the decade. So any 'computer porn' in the possession of school children at this time was more likely to have been scanned locally than downloaded from the Internet. That being the case, 'computer porn' is a misleading epithet, as the nature of the medium does not *cause* the local circulation and consumption of pornographic images, it merely extends it from the conventional printed medium to a digital one. Calcutt cites another news story from the time of the 'computer porn' panic that fails to understand this, and indeed borders on the hypocritical. In 1993, the British Sunday paper, *The Observer*, claimed that children had been selling one another scanned images from Madonna's book *Sex* (*The Observer* 28.2.93). While the story pointed out that the images, though explicit, were not in fact illegal under British law, it failed to mention that the same newspaper had been the first to publish images from the book, back in November 1992, in its colour supplement. The children – assuming the claim to have any truth in it at all – could just as easily, and far more cheaply, have scanned from the newspaper as from the (expensive) book (Calcutt 1995: 754).

Whether deemed to be pornographic or not, the bits of digital images can be exchanged and circulated as freely as the atoms of printed images, and in doing so engender or alter relations between persons. While apparently immaterial, a researcher's understanding of the use and consumption of the digital can benefit greatly from a consideration of the materiality of parallel media.

Notes

1 Social anthropologists are familiar with more permanent linkages, a phenomenon that was once called contagious magic. In many ethnographic as well as fictional accounts of witchcraft for instance, manipulation of an object that was once substantively linked to a person, such as a lock of hair, is believed to effect a change in the person as though the substantive link still remained.

2 In these cases, and in other more recent ones such as the many photographs of UFOs that have circulated among aficionados and in the media in the last couple of decades, the emphasis is very much on the photograph as documentary proof or evidence; more particularly, the mechanical reliability and material existence of such photographs attests to the material existence of the object represented. The photograph is as much *about* materiality as it is a material object in its own right.

3 Chaplin's own analysis of the 'meaning' of the painting does not pay any particular attention to these diverse media, or indeed to the unique physicality of the painting and its relationship to these reproductions. Instead she adopts Howard Becker's idea of art worlds to argue that a large number of people perform a number of ideological and practical tasks to create and valorize a work of art. Together they form an art world that gives and sustains the painting's meaning; as the social relationships between these persons change, so do the meaning and value attributed to the image. This contradicts the Romantic aesthetic imperative which claims that meaning and value emanate from the art work itself, normally as a result of the genius of its creator (Becker 1982). While the owners of the 'Cornfield' objects are clearly participants in the same art world that gives meaning to the original – not least because all the items listed appear to have been purchased as market commodities which links them to the market exchange of fine art paintings themselves – nonetheless they would appear to be on its periphery. The owners and the objects are more directly associated with other arenas of value creation and social meaning in which 'art' is not a significant ideological feature.

4 Normally, these are photographs taken in life, sometimes explicitly taken in middle or old age with the aim of being used subsequently as memorial images. Chris Pinney cites examples of existing wedding or other photographs being reworked for memorial representation where no other image exists; he also cites cases of post-mortem photographs being taken by family or studio professionals and used as the basis of a retouched memorial image (Pinney 1997: 139, 205).

5 Pinney describes an unusually elaborate set of actions performed by a man toward the photograph of his deceased father (Pinney 1997: 145).

6 There are important exceptions. In India, photographs of prospective brides and grooms used to be – and still are to some extent – exchanged between families seeking marriage alliances for their sons and daughters. In cyber-space, Internet dating sites are full of lonely heart adverts accompanied by photographs, which state that respondents should send a digitized photo-graph in exchange.

7 At another level, family photography is, of course, deeply enmeshed within capitalist market relations as its practice is not possible without equipment, film stock and processing purchased from the market. The sociologist Don Slater is one of the few commentators on popular or mass photography to take this material (and materialist) aspect into account (Slater 1983).

8 Most of this section is based on interviews I conducted with staff at British auction houses in 1998 and 1999. Though my interviewees were unfailingly helpful and generally forthcoming, a slight aura of secrecy and vagueness characterized some of the responses I received, in order to protect the privacy of their regular customers.

9 One interviewee told me that a 'name' alone was not sufficient – the named photographer must also be judged to have contributed significantly to the history of photography. This claim must I think be taken with a pinch of salt: within this art world it is generally a fine art aesthetic that determines and writes the history of photography as a history of 'names'; hence the argument is effectively circular – collectable 'names' are those that the market has deemed important. A photographic historian I interviewed was particularly disparaging on the subject of 'names', claiming that undistinguished back-street studio photographers could be talked-up in sales catalogue blurbs to the status of unappreciated-in-their-own-lifetime geniuses with little historical justification other than to raise the market value.

10 As Walter Benjamin notes: 'the whole sphere of authenticity is outside technical . . . reproducibility', and yet it is authenticity that the collector seeks (Benjamin 1992: 214).

11 I also attempted to discover if there was a parallel market in old film material. While several auction houses, and associated dealers, trade in film memorabilia – film stills and posters, autographed photographs of film stars and other ephemera – none dealt directly with film stock. I was given two reasons for this: first, old film stock – nitrate especially, but also 'safe' acetate – degrades so easily that there is very little material to collect or sell; secondly, as one approaches the present there are so many prints in circulation of many films that they have no rarity value. That is not to say that there are not collectors of old films, particularly silent Hollywood classics. Paolo Cherchi Usai indicates that there may in fact be many private collectors, many of whom are exceptionally secretive and unwilling to let others know what they have or how they acquired it (Usai 1994: 24).

12 Even within the otherwise bland format of 35mm there are variations. One such is 'Lomography', a photographic movement of artists and students devoted to the use of an obscure and basic Russian camera with an

idiosyncratic lens. In a reversal of the normal trend to valorize expensive 35mm cameras for the clarity and precision of their images, devotees of the Lomo claim that its technical limitations allow them to explore new angles and compositions in their work, creating new kinds of images.

13 Failure to pay attention to the physical specifications of film formats can have quite practical – and unpleasant – consequences. If a researcher thinks she may have uncovered some (highly flammable) nitrate stock, she should leave well alone and call her nearest film archive; see Usai 1994: 19–20.

14 'Unlike atoms, bits aren't consumed by consumers. They can regenerate – infinitely' (Negroponte 1997: 112). The mysteries of quantum physics apart, the atoms of materiality are unique in their occupation of a distinctive point in space-time, constituting similarly unique physical objects – books, photographs, people. In contrast the 1s and 0s of binary code can constitute virtual objects anywhere, anytime. I have a photograph and, for a friend to see it on the other side of the world, I must either post it to her, in which case she has all the atoms that compose it and I do not; alternatively I make a photographic copy and post that, but then she has her set of atoms and I have mine and they are not the same. If on the other hand I digitize the photograph and email it to her, I am not sending her the digitized version, merely the instructions for her computer to recreate it. My friend's computer and my computer both devote some of their bits to temporarily recreating the same thing. But materiality cannot be denied: the atoms of my monitor's glass configure unique scratches, providing a home to unique dust particles and a film of cigarette tar. The carefully dusted monitor in my friend's no-smoking office shows her a subtly different image.

15 These media are proving to be far more problematic than their analogue counterparts of paper, ink and chemicals. More for commercial than technical reasons, the physical formats of digital media appear to have an extremely short lifespan. The magneto-optical disks on which I originally stored backups of the HADDON Catalogue (see Chapter 6.4.2) are now essentially unplayable as my current computers will not recognize the external disk drive and the manufacturer has stopped updating the software drivers. Doubtless the CD-ROMs on which I currently store digital copies of my fieldwork photographs will go the same way in a few years.

16 A number of commercial filtering software products exist and links to these are provided on the Web site associated with this book. See also Chapter 6.4.1 on computerized visual recognition systems which could, in theory, perform the filtering task automatically.

4

Research strategies

Figure 4.1   János Tari taking still images in a Jewish cemetery to use as visual aids in planning a film on the Hungarian Jewish diaspora. Makó, Hungary, 1989

4.1   Silk thread to plastic bags

In the previous three chapters I introduced a wide range of examples and issues fundamental to visual research in the social sciences. In this chapter and the next I deal with what for many readers is the most important issue of all – visual social research in practice. As in the previous chapters I draw on a wide range of examples, some drawn from the work of others, some drawn from my own research, and again there is a bias towards anthropological research from outside Euro-America, with a particular focus on India. The justification for this bias is partly that this is the material I know best, but more importantly the issues encountered in 'exotic' research locations often serve to highlight the taken-for-granted aspect of research with culturally and socially familiar subjects. I therefore begin the chapter with an example drawn from my own research in India to demonstrate the sometimes unanticipated course that visual social research may take. I then move on to consider a range of research practices involving pre-existing images: watching television with subjects; interviewing subjects with both archival and contemporary films and photographs; and conducting research in film and photographic archives and libraries. In Chapter 5 I then turn to the. creation of images by the social researcher, followed in Chapter 6 by a discussion of the presentation of visual research results. That these three chapters have a more practical focus than those that have gone before does not mean that there is no necessity to continue *thinking* about images: theory (or critical analysis as I would prefer to call it here) and practice are intertwined in the social sciences – one cannot proceed without the other.

Like all social research, visual research can sometimes lead in un-expected directions. The analytical shift in the social sciences away from positivism and its static view of social facts, towards a more processual and contingent view of social knowledge makes following the unexpected and unanticipated a methodological necessity. For example, like all visitors to India, on my first research trip in the early 1980s I was intrigued and delighted by the embroidered and mirror-work textiles that are – or were – a distinctive feature of rural crafts in Gujarat and Rajasthan (see Figure 4.2). Unfortunately, I could see no direct connection between these artefacts, which were largely fashioned by rural women, and the middle-class urban businessmen and traders who were the subjects of my research at the time. Nonetheless, I asked friends in the small city where I worked if they had any at home, or whether their wives or mothers or sisters had ever made any of their own. Some brought out a few examples or directed me to towards those on sale in the local *khadi bhavan* (a chain of state-funded shops that sell local handicrafts) but these were crude by comparison with those that I had seen in museums, or framed and hanging on the walls of upper middle class homes in Bombay and Delhi. Eventually, I contented myself instead with making a small private collection of the textiles, acquired largely from professional dealers in the nearby big city of Ahmedabad, at the end of my field trip. In the ensuing years I learned more about the textiles, noticing for example the distinction between square panels used for decorative or functional purposes (such as wrapping a bride's trousseau or decorating a bullock), doorway-framing *torans* that have a decorative function but also a greater symbolic and performative aspect (adding or confirming auspiciousness on those that pass beneath them), and the five-sided *ganesh sthapanas* that use the same materials and

Figure 4.2 *Ganesh sthapana* from Gujarat or Rajasthan, India, collected in Ahmedabad, India, in 1983. Date and maker unknown

techniques to create a portable or home-made shrine to Lord Ganesh, the elephant-headed Hindu deity (see Hitkari 1981).

Later I realized that there was in fact a connection, though not a direct one, between the textiles and the more sociological research I was conducting at the time with Gujarati migrants in Britain. Many of the textiles, like most rural women's handicrafts, were originally never fashioned to enter the market but rather were dowry objects, created by women to take to their marriage homes and eventually passed on to their daughters.[1] Such trousseau objects routinely form part of a dowry but are often overlooked in the academic literature on dowry which focuses instead on market purchased commodities, such as pots and pans and gold jewellery, that fathers must buy for their daughters. One reason that such textiles had first entered the market in Gujarat, enabling me to purchase some in Ahmedabad, was a severe drought at the end of the nineteenth century, which had forced many rural families to realize whatever assets they had in order to survive. The same drought also acted as a precipitating factor for the first major wave of migration from western Gujarat of the trading families I was studying. Unable to maintain significant trade from the sale of agricultural produce, some men moved on to the British colonies and protectorates of East Africa, from which their descendants again moved on to Britain in the 1960s and 1970s. Thus the same precipitating event had caused a change in the circulation of artefacts on the one hand and a change in the circulation of persons on the other.

Further consideration of the textiles led me to realize that my own aesthetic perceptions needed to be questioned. The embroidered mirror-work textiles of Gujarat and Rajasthan are a staple of the lower end of the ethnic arts market, routinely encountered in the West. My own first encounter with these textiles came when I was a student in Britain in the 1970s, when ethnic fashions were all the rage (and all we could afford as students). Then, the primary aesthetic emphasis was on authenticity – aged, time-worn items that had obviously seen some use or, alternatively, new items fashioned in that image. In the case of mirrorwork textiles this would be evidenced by a few broken stitches, and the occasional broken or missing mirror fragment. Colour range was also important: bright acid colours from aniline dyes were acceptable, but only so long as they were used sparingly and tempered with rich dark tones.[2] The 1990s saw a rise in artificially aged and reconstructed textiles available in the ethnic artefact shops of the West (and also in India, for sale to tourists): fragments of old or new textiles were machine sewn together in a random patchwork, and then overdyed with brown, shifting the tonal range to deep purples, browns and blacks. With these Western aesthetic criteria in place, it is no surprise that I found the few modern embroideries of my Gujarati Jain friends, or those available in the *khadi bhavan* to be disappointing, with their clear colours, skimpy threads and a marked preference for chain stitch over satin stitch. Clearly local aesthetic preference differed markedly from that which attracted tourists in India and purchasers in London.

It was methodologically important to get past my own preconceptions of what constituted authentic mirrorwork textiles and to deal instead with what was actually being produced by my urban informants, which was embroidery but not mirrorwork. As part of a more recent investigation into the visual culture of the Jains – the religious group with which I work – it was also important to include an appreciation of the aesthetic that is manifest in domestic and private contexts, as well as the public contexts of temple decoration and painting. Many urban teenaged girls, in the months or years between schooling and marriage, spend some of the time when they are not cooking, cleaning or preparing food, engaged with handicrafts such as embroidery and beadwork. Such craft activities are widespread and by no means confined to Jain women. Nevertheless, while ubiquitous, they are also relatively undervalued, at least by men. They form a private, domestic aspect of Jain visual culture in contrast to the public visual imagery of, for example, temple paintings. I began to formulate a hypothesis that the visual transmission of Jain culture was in fact in the hands of women, as they taught their daughters to sew and fashion beadwork. The products of their labours, which adorn most Jain homes I know, might constitute a low level, background visual presence of colours and symbols which could serve to ground more abstract notions of the nature of the soul or other doctrinal points.

I was, therefore, slightly surprised when I talked to some unmarried girls as well as married women to find that they did not draw any strong association between their craft activities and their religion. The designs they were using for both beadwork and embroidery tended to be pan-Indian signs of auspiciousness – swastikas, lotus flowers and coconuts on water pots – and although these can be construed as having Jain significance, the women I spoke to did not seem particularly concerned about this. Finally, Pannaben, in response to my insistent questions concerning specifically Jain designs and motifs, decided that the iconographic representation of Trisala-mata's fourteen auspicious dreams might constitute the kind of Jain images I was seeking. (Trisala was the mother – *mata* – of the last in the series of 'great heroes' that the Jains revere as the founders and propagators of their religion; while she was pregnant, Trisala dreamed of fourteen auspicious things which alerted her to the fact that her son would be a great hero.) Not that Pannaben had ever used these designs herself, preferring stylized floral motifs instead. But to be sure that I knew what the fourteen signs actually were, she disappeared for a moment and returned with a plastic carrier bag. This carrier bag was both an advertisement for and a product of her brother-in-law's printing press, and on it the fourteen dream symbols were used to frame the company's name and address (see Figure 4.3).

As we looked at the symbols on the bag, she told me of her young sister-in-law's recent marriage which had taken her to another city to live, and we continued to talk of the movement of girls from one place to another – often several hours away – as they leave their natal home to join their husband's family. Despite the fact that Chayaben, Pannaben's sister-in-law, had had to move from the town where she had grown up (which Pannaben had not, having been married locally), leaving behind

Figure 4.3   Printed design on a plastic carrier bag, showing the fourteen dreams of Trisala-mata as an arch of symbols. Rajkot, India, 1999

her parents, her friends and her familiar surroundings, Pannaben insisted that she had been lucky. Her husband had a good business – evidenced by the bag – and was a good man, a good religious man, as evidenced by the designs the bag carried.

So from an initial and casual interest in old and seemingly exotic textiles, which I approached through Western aesthetic categories and nostalgic yearnings for the richness of pristine rural Indian cultural forms, I had been led past insights into migration and the circulation of labour in colonial India and the British Empire more widely, through to a point where I came to see even the designs on a cheap plastic bag as constituents of a local discourse concerning marriage and gendered social relations in modern urban India. In the following sections of this chapter I shall outline some of the visual research strategies that social researchers have employed as part of their investigations into more broadly-based social phenomena, including instances where the use of such strategies was accidental or unintended.

4.2 Researching image use and production in social contexts

In the previous chapters I have provided instances of things people do with pictures; of how films, photographs, and other visual forms are stitched into the fabric of people's lives, reflecting and representing social persons and social relationships like the tiny mirror fragments stitched into Indian textiles. All visual forms are socially embedded, and many visual forms that sociologists and anthropologists deal with are multiply embedded. Using archival photographs to prompt memories or comments from informants in the course of an interview, for example, involves an appreciation of at least three social embeddings or frames.

First, there is the context of original production. Perhaps a photographer visited a small rural community in the early years of this century and took a number of images. She or he could have been a middle-class metropolitan traveller on holiday using their new camera to record picturesque views and images of quaint rustics, or a government official documenting the village and its surroundings for possible future military strategy and planning purposes, or an itinerant professional photographer with a mobile studio hoping to take and then sell back some portraits of the locals. Then there is the context of the photographs' subsequent histories. Perhaps they or the negatives remained together in a trunk in an attic, or in a cupboard in a shop – with or without identifying labels – to be eventually sold at auction, donated to a picture library or archive, split up among family members, until at some point they or their copies came into the possession of the social researcher. Both these frames serve to edit the corpus of photographs. First, the original photographs represent a finite part of the infinity of all possible photographs that could have been taken on that occasion and even that finite part is probably only a subset of all the photographs taken – minus those that did not come out or were damaged in processing and discarded. Second, in its subsequent history a photographic collection may have been split up for sale, or an archive accepted only that part which was considered relevant to its collection policy, or all photographs of a notorious black sheep were subsequently destroyed by a family. Thus when the third frame is considered – the context in which the social researcher deploys the photographs in the course of an interview – the images' previous embeddings influence what happens next; the shadowy hand of all previous social embeddings hovers over the current one. The next section – on watching television – concerns visual material with a generally limited number of previous embeddings, though previous broadcasts of the same material, feature films recycled on television, and soap operas produced and originally broadcast in one market but subsequently replayed elsewhere should all be noted. The visual material dealt with in subsequent sections is more obviously multiply embedded.

4.3 Watching television

Television and film are the products of and reliant upon technological processes to which most ordinary people have limited or no access, whether they live in the heart of the Amazon rainforest or the depths of an urban housing estate. These technologies of production are themselves socially embedded, and again the social relations of image production are often beyond the social experience of those that anthropologists and sociologists normally work among. While the hirings and firings of television executives reach the news pages of British broadsheet newspapers, and the infidelities and broken hearts of soap-opera stars and chatshow hosts frequently fill the pages of the tabloids, most television viewers have little knowledge of how television programmes are produced. Consequently, much social research on television has concentrated on consumption, occasionally treating viewers as passive vessels filled with more or less wholesome messages, but more recently seeing viewers as active subjects engaged in the construction of meaning (but see Morley 1992: 26–39 for some caveats).

As with almost all other discussions in this chapter, this section is primarily concerned with research into television and cinema as an aspect of a broader social research project, rather than as an end in itself. In contrast to, say, still photography, television and film are objects of social research in their own right – who watches? when? how? – quite apart from whole research fields devoted to analysing the content of television programmes and films, which is an area closer to literary criticism or cultural studies than empirical sociology. While interesting and revealing, such approaches lie beyond the scope of this book.

Some basic points need to be borne in mind, however, and many issues concerning research on television viewing as social practice are well summarized by James Lull in his book *Inside Family Viewing* (1990), especially in the final chapter on methods. Lull's advocated approach is 'ethnographic', by which he means researchers should spend between three and five days living with a family in their home and taking notes on television programme choice, discussions over television programmes, the degree to which the television is actually watched as opposed to providing background noise for other activities, and so forth.[3]

In one project, Lull sent trained undergraduate students into 85 homes in a Southern Californian town for two days to conduct this kind of 'ethnographic' observation, followed by a structured interview session on the third day (1990: 52–3). Lull advocates this kind of approach for a number of reasons, not least the fact that the two days of observation facilitated a far higher degree of trust and co-operation from the research subjects than would be the case if the researchers had 'cold-called' with a questionnaire. Lull notes, as have many other social researchers, that gaining access to the heart of a Euro-American family for a prolonged period is no simple matter, whatever the nature of the research, and the refusal rate is high. For this reason, constructing a viable random or stratified sample from a voter's list, electoral role or telephone book is unlikely to be successful. Like others, Lull advocates approaching neighbourhood organizations, establishing trust with them (which may involve clearing and possibly modifying the research) and then contacting their members with the approval and support of the organization: 'Groups such as girls' clubs, boys' clubs, Parent Teacher Associations, and community nursery schools have been especially co-operative' (1990: 175).

Lull also briefly discusses what one might call remote surveillance techniques of research: installing cameras and microphones into homes (with the knowledge and consent of the families involved) to record every last detail of viewing practice (1990: 164, 177). Sociological and psychological studies such as this have revealed what most of us already know from our own experience: that most Euro-Americans spend a great deal of time not watching television when it is on. Peter Collett, a psychologist who employed set-top cameras for observation, in fact demonstrated that those who spend most time physically in front of the set, spent least time actually looking at the screen (cited in Lull 1990: 164; see also Root 1986: 25–6). Following on from this David Morley, whose work on television mentioned in the last chapter (Section 3.2.1) stressed the importance of the television set as a material object, has indicated that television should be considered primarily as an audio medium with pictures. This is particularly so in the home, at the point of consumption, but also in the studio, at the point of production. Morley cites his own work as well as that of others to confirm that an apparently simple question from a researcher – what do you like to watch on television? – has no simple answer. 'Do you mean sitting down watching?', responded one woman from Morley's own sample. 'Sitting down watching' for this woman and – one assumes – for many other women was a rare occurrence. More typically, she would be *listening* to the television from the kitchen, only coming in to the room where the television was for an occasional glance at the screen (Morley 1995: 174).

While listening to the television is an observed aspect of domestic 'viewing' practice, Morley suggests that television producers appear to be aware of this, providing audio cues that indicate when attention should be directed towards the screen. When first introduced for mass consumption in America in the 1950s, television was perceived as a form of domestic cinema, demanding the viewers' full visual attention. Unfortunately, it was also realized that women, while the primary domestic consumers, would simply not have the time during the housework-filled day to watch in a concentrated fashion and would therefore switch off, missing the crucial advertising breaks.

> The solution which gradually emerged to this problem . . . was the redesign of television programming, not on the model of 'private cinema' requiring close visual attention, but on the model of radio: television as 'radio-with pictures', where the narrative is mainly carried by the soundtrack and the visuals play a subordinate, 'illustrative' role. (Morley 1995: 177)

Busy housewives could now keep the television on constantly while they worked, dropping in and out of the pictures while following the soundtrack. A rise in volume when the advertising break started would catch their attention and bring them back into the room.

Television producers, of course, are greatly interested in what people watch, when and how. In Britain, audience viewing figures are gathered and published by organizations such as BARB (Broadcasters' Audience Research Board), while other surveys and focus group work are commissioned by television companies to provide finer-grained feedback. Clearly the imperative to satisfy advertisers and programme sponsors plays a large part in directing this research, but in Britain at least there is also a broader concern with ensuring audience satisfaction, partly as a result of a public service ethos that still pertains, and partly because commercial television franchises awarded by the government are granted on the basis of 'quality' as well as profitability. Social research on television consumption and domestic viewing practice, therefore, cannot wholly ignore the social relations of television production, though in fact remarkably few studies seem to consider this with any seriousness. In an article on ethnographic film broadcast on British television, André Singer points out that ethnographic films do not fall out of the sky ready made, nor do they appear on television screens free of human agency –

although many reviewers of such films appear to treat them in this way or at least appear to have little understanding of how a film is made (Singer 1992; see also Loizos 1980). Singer does note, however, that through the 1980s and 1990s there was a shift in balance with fewer documentary projects than before beginning life as a result of individuals' ideas and decisions within television companies and a greater emphasis on the power of market forces (1992: 271).[4]

In one of the most exhaustive investigations into how television is made, the media sociologist Roger Silverstone spent the best part of two years with a BBC production team, following the course of a science programme, from the initial production meetings through to the eventual screening. Silverstone published his account as an extended diary, though one that while full of detail gives little indication of his research methodology. 'The research period produced a mountain of notes', he states, 'I was collecting data: observations, transcripts, perceptions, interpretations, details, photographs, judgements' (Silverstone 1985: 201–2). The implication is that the study of television production required few if any special skills (though Silverstone had himself once been employed as a BBC researcher and to some extent already knew the ropes). This is probably entirely correct: there is nothing mysterious about television production and observing the process should pose no more problems than observing social processes of the actors in any organization. Silverstone makes no claims to providing a visual analysis, and there is no obviously visual emphasis in his account. What he does do, however, is to ground production issues sociologically and empirically, such as in his description of how decisions were taken by the producer and editor to use subtitles as opposed to voiceover commentary to translate foreign-language dialogue.

4.3.1 *Soap opera in India and Egypt*

All this points to the necessity of researching television viewing practice from a number of different perspectives, including a consideration of the broad political and social context within which programmes are created and screened. Veena Das and Lila Abu-Lughod, for example, have both investigated television soap opera in developing countries as a site for negotiating local social practice and the global demands of modernity. Both come to the conclusion that the messages of television are neither all-pervasive, nor are they the distillation of producers' intentions. According to Das, the Indian soap opera *Hum Log* ('we people') was devised explicitly as an educational, pro-development vehicle. Broadcast in 154 half-hour episodes by the Indian government-owned television channel Doordarshan in the mid-1980s, the serial depicted life in an urban middle-class household and 'created a space from which the norms of family and society could be interrogated' (Das 1995: 180). Das relies on two main empirical research strategies and one analytical insight in her investigation of this space. Empirically, she relies on an analysis of readers' letters sent to the television station to gauge the nature of audience response (no social researcher apparently having carried out any fieldwork at the time the serial was broadcast) (1995: 177 ff.); she also relies on an earlier investigation by other researchers into the bureaucratic decision-making steps that brought *Hum Log* to the Indian viewers' screens (1995: 173). Her analytical insight concerns the gap between responses rooted in rhetoric and those rooted in experience (1995: 180). Das contends that the pro-development messages of *Hum Log* – maintaining strong familial relations and personal morality, while granting greater personal freedoms to women and encouraging their participation in the labour market, for example – are stock components of Indian bureaucratic and political discourse, and as such tended to provoke stock rhetorical responses from viewers in their letters. She thus cautions against taking these spontaneous responses to the serial as talismans of authenticity, as insights into the hearts and minds of the viewers (1995: 171). At least some of the letters received revealed not what viewers might 'really' be thinking, but merely their familiarity with this discourse and their ability to respond in kind.

Lila Abu-Lughod goes even further in her conclusions, after examining the highly popular Egyptian television soap opera *Hilmiyya Nights* in its broader social and political context. Like *Hum Log*, the intention of *Hilmiyya Nights* was explicitly didactic, although it was not in any sense a government-sponsored or even necessarily government-approved project. The serial, broadcast over a five year period from 1988, charts the relationships between two wealthy men and their families from the Cairo neighbourhood of Hilmiyya over the course of half a century but, as Abu-Lughod notes, did not concentrate solely on the psycho-dynamics of the characters' relationships, their tears and laughter, ups and downs, marriages and divorces in a way that has come to been seen as typical of American and British soap operas such as *Dallas* or *Eastenders*. Instead, the writer and producers explicitly tied these domestic events to a wider reading of post-war Egyptian political history: 'Above all, *Hilmiyya Nights* promoted the theme of national unity' (1995: 196). Abu-Lughod's investigative strategy was to interview key figures in the Egyptian television industry, as well as to interview two disparate groups of Egyptian viewers – female domestic servants in Cairo, and the inhabitants of a village near Luxor in Upper Egypt, several hundred kilometres beyond Cairo's metropolitan orbit.[5]

Her chief conclusion is that the social and political importance of the serial was more a construction of its producers than a perception of the viewers. As she says, 'a socially and politically conscious group of culture-industry professionals . . . constructed as their object "a public" in need of enlightenment', and, having 'faith that mass media have powerful effects', they duly created a product to meet this need (1995: 199–200). The domestic servants that Abu-Lughod interviewed nonetheless read against this 'need', albeit inadvertently. For example, some particularly admired the serial's glamorous leading lady, a *femme fatale* who, while manipulating the men around her, meets an unglamorous and inglorious end, in accordance with the serial's moral tone. This end was unremarked upon; what was admired was her strong character and flouting of moral norms. Equally, both the domestic servants and the Upper Egyptian peasants seemed untouched by the serial's political and social messages of self-reliance, political autonomy and anti-consumerism, receiving them as they did within a stream of other messages from American soaps, local chat shows and advertisements for running shoes (1995: 206–7). Abu-Lughod asserts that their experience of television was compartmentalized, lacking any necessity of connection to their experience of life, and that *Hilmiyya Nights* was just one item in that compartment, however much enjoyed. Even the serial's self-professed aim, to introduce the urban working classes and the rural peasantry to a form of high-minded modernity, by returning to them knowledge of their own national history, was too little and came too late. As Abu-Lughod wryly comments, the viewers were already well-acquainted with modernity: 'the more common form of modernity in the post-colonial world: the modernity of poverty, consumer desires, underemployment, ill health and religious nationalism' (1995: 207).

The main lesson to be taken from Abu-Lughod's study by the social researcher considering an investigation into television is a surprisingly refreshing one: that perhaps television is not quite as socially important as its producers would have us believe. Television – perhaps the most self-absorbed and self-regarding of the mass media – constantly constructs its own viewers, and exercises its agency within a hall of mirrors, shifting its production to meet the needs of these constructed viewers, then commissioning further research to evaluate the success of these shifts upon the constructed objects. Social researchers perhaps need to exercise especial care when entering this charmed circle, to be certain that they have set their own research parameters rather than having uncritically accepted those set up before them. One way out is to take the suggestions of the previous chapter and to pay attention to the materiality of visual culture, in this case the material and social placing of the television set and its output. One consequence of this is to shift analysis away from earlier communication models of television viewership. While the 'reader response' or audience-focused school of analysis that developed in the 1970s and 1980s de-centred the notion of the media producer acting as the only agent (see Morley 1996 for a good and recent overview; see also Banks 1996a: 118–24), with viewers merely as passive subjects of the producer's action, nonetheless even according viewers agency in interpreting media messages in accordance with their class, gender or ethnic background still rested on a premise of messages being sent, received and interpreted.

4.3.2   Television as a social presence

In Chapter 2.1 I mentioned briefly how the CNN news readers had acted as a third interlocutor in conversations between myself and Indian informants. This was effected by the material fact and presence of the television in the room as I conducted interviews. In contrast to a study which focused on messages, in which I might observe my informants watching CNN, take notes of what they said during transmission, and then quiz them about what they thought afterwards, a focus on the materiality of television – the placement of the set and satellite dish, on how people are sitting, and an engagement of the observer with both the material objects and the human actors – brings about an alternative research approach to viewing practice. By considering the television as a literal presence in the room and as a literal voice in the conversation – like an elderly relative sitting in the corner, mumbling away to themselves and occasionally saying something interesting, as I once heard it described – it becomes an embodied agent.

Its very presence during my interviews was partly a consequence of nationwide changes in the Indian broadcasting industry, partly a consequence of local economic development. Until the mid-1980s, the small city where I conduct fieldwork had not even had terrestrial television reception, so even those who could afford to buy a set would have had no use for it. The arrival of satellite broadcasting in the 1990s, which bypassed the slow and inefficient spread of terrestrial services, coincided with a major economic change in the city which meant that some – including many of my informants – could afford to purchase sets and satellite subscriptions. Once purchased, a place had to be found for it in the home – often difficult in the cramped spaces of traditional old city houses. Traditionally, Indian homes have few spaces allotted to specific functions apart from cooking and bathing. Most space is multi-functional, used for eating, sleeping, talking, doing homework – often at the same time – in contrast to the 'one room, one use' norm in Euro-America (Prasad 1998: 185). Consequently, it is largely impossible for a television set to become the dominant agent in the construction of a room's use, and it is forced to become another component in the fluid construction of social space. Certainly, the television set sends out a series of messages – both through its broadcast images and sound and through its very presence – but these enter into rather than dominate a set of social relations between persons. How it inserts its messages is dependent upon where people sit, stand or lie, on whether visitors are present or not, on what other activities people are conducting at any one moment. I have noticed on occasions that speakers will seat themselves on the floor beside or even in front of the (still on) television, not particularly to drown it out, but simply because at that moment it is not considered to be playing a particularly important part in the social conversation.

4.4 Doing things with photographs and films

In general, televised material is simply encountered, both by the social researcher and those who consume it, though there are some exceptions. Researchers with a specific interest in television consumption will also wish to note which member of the household has the dominant voice in programme selection, for example, which will determine in part what the other members see, or pay attention to the strategies – if any – by which a household plans its viewing in advance. Alternatively, one group of anthropologists working on a long-term project to study the social role and cultural presence of television in Bali, asked informants to record certain programmes and types of programmes in between field visits, which were then watched with informants during field visits (Hughes-Freeland 1997). With still photography and some uses of film and video a researcher can be more proactive, selecting both the visual material to be viewed and the circumstances of its viewing. Some thought should thus be given to how this is done – the examples discussed below range from the arbitrary or accidental, to the highly structured and planned.

4.4.1 Photo-elicitation with archival images

On the surface, photo-elicitation is a straightforward method to understand and to utilize. It involves using photographs to invoke comments, memory and discussion in the course of a semi-structured interview.

Specific examples of social relations or cultural form depicted in the photographs can become the basis for a discussion of broader abstractions and generalities; conversely, vague memories can be given sharpness and focus, unleashing a flood of detail. According to John and Malcolm Collier (1986: 105–7) an additional benefit is that the awkwardness that an interviewee may feel from being put on the spot and grilled by the interviewer can be lessened by the presence of photographs to discuss; direct eye contact need not be maintained, but instead interviewee and interviewer can both turn to the photographs as a kind of neutral third party. Awkward silences can be covered as both look at the photographs and in situations where the status difference between interviewer and interviewee is great (such as between an adult and a child) or where the interviewee feels they are involved in some kind of test, the photographic content always provides something to talk about. But although the basic principles of photo-elicitation rest upon a fairly transparent reading of the internal narrative of photographic content, issues of photographic multivocality and the complexity of the entanglement of photographic objects in human social relations means that photo-elicitation (and the more rarely used film-elicitation) is not always so straightforward in practice.

For clarity, we can examine variation in the practice of photo-elicitation by considering the sources and types of photographs used. In some cases, sociologists and anthropologists have taken their own photographs with the specific aim of conducting photo-elicitation interviews, though probably more commonly they use photographs they took earlier for other reasons. In other cases, interviewers have used photographs taken by others, possibly decades ago, which are either owned by the subjects of research or very strongly connected to them in some way, such as photographs of their ancestors lodged in a museum or archive. In both these instances, the reasons for the subjects to want to see the photographs and their understanding of intentions of the interviewer in showing them are relatively straightforward, at least on the surface. More problematic are cases where neither subject nor interviewer has any particularly obvious link to the images, and where the intentions of the researcher may be unclear to the subjects. The most extreme cases of this would perhaps be in certain kinds of lab-based psychology experiments, where subjects are shown a sequence of images – photographs of faces, ink blots, Chinese ideograms – and asked to make simple preference choices without being told what the purpose of the experiment is, or even being deliberately misled, in order to minimize the risk of subjects double-guessing the researcher's preferred outcome.

The use of photo-elicitation in such controlled circumstances is relatively rare in qualitative sociological and anthropological investigations. Indeed, the French anthropologist and psychologist Yannick Geffroy (whose work has already been mentioned in Chapter 2.4.2) and the Italian anthropologist Paolo Chiozzi, both describe accidentally stumbling across the technique in the course of fieldwork (Geffroy 1990; Chiozzi 1989). In the early 1970s Geffroy and a fellow student at the University of Nice were conducting research on popular traditions surrounding a saint's day festival in a village in the hinterland behind the famous Côte d'Azur in the south of France. This involved interviewing elderly members of the village, not only about how the festival had been celebrated decades earlier but also about more general aspects of village life at the time. While fruitful in some ways, both Geffroy and his informants would sometimes find these enquiries about the past frustrating: 'Some descriptions of events could be difficult to express. Often during interviews, we heard these words: "You should have seen how . . ."'. Geffroy describes how the turning point came one day when an elderly woman decided that in fact they could see, and see now: 'During her interview . . . she stood up suddenly saying "But . . . wait a minute" . . . She went and opened the doors of an old wall cupboard from which she brought out a large cardboard box, full of photographs, old photographs. . . . These family photographs, by helping her memory to recall events and their contexts, allowed us to glean more data and facts from the emotions she was reliving' (Geffroy 1990: 374).

In a similar vein, Paolo Chiozzi describes himself as being 'overwhelmed with information' when he first began to use photographs in the course of his interviews (1989: 45). In the mid-1980s Chiozzi was conducting research in the Tuscan town of Prato, which had grown fourfold in the previous three decades as a result of migration from elsewhere in Italy. From his account, older inhabitants of the town seemed to be experiencing a sense of 'cultural disintegration' as they sought to come to terms with the recent social and economic changes, but he found specific information and coherent accounts of change hard to come by; not, he thought, as a result of any mistrust on the part of his informants, but simply because of a lack of engagement with him and his project. One day during the course of his research an elderly man told him that his family home in the town's market place had been bombed in the Second World War. By chance, Chiozzi had with him the catalogue of a photographic exhibition that had been held in the town and which depicted the town and the area at the turn of the twentieth century. Looking through the catalogue they quickly identified the house from some general views of the market square. But the elderly informant was not simply seeing his childhood home, a place of personal nostalgic significance, he was seeing a territory – a specific part of the large square that was home to a specific neighbourhood community – and he described the kinship relations between those who lived there, the histories and life courses of particular families in the period leading up to the war in great detail. Choizzi notes that although he continued his accounts into the post-war period, his recollections became more vague as the town grew and the neighbourhood began to break up: 'It seemed that [he] only then realized how great a transformation had occurred in Prato during his lifetime' (Chiozzi 1989: 45–6).

In another piece of research, this time with rural communities in the hills of northern Tuscany, Chiozzi used photographs from the beginning. While his informants again reacted positively to being shown old photographs of the region, they also insisted that Chiozzi re-photograph the same sites in an attempt to make manifest what they saw as the loss of their cultural identity (Chiozzi 1989: 46). Although Chiozzi does not dwell on this aspect, it would seem that although in one sense the changes in the landscape and habitat patterns of the valley were per- fectly visible to the original inhabitants' eyes, their insistence that a photographic record be made was a way of concretizing this, of external- izing in material form something that until then had been tacit, internal, subjective.

4.4.2 Photo-elicitation with contemporary images

Both Choizzi and Geffroy were largely concerned with social memory in their use of photo-elicitation, and consequently deployed photographs from the periods in which they were interested. But photo-elicitation is equally relevant as a technique with which to investigate contemporary issues. Two recent photo-elicitation studies concerned with ethnic boundaries and ethnic interaction make this point well. In the course of research with Vietnamese refugees in California, Stephen Gold encoun- tered a range of stereotypes related to an 'internal' ethnic boundary between ethnic Vietnamese and Chinese-Vietnamese, the latter having been an economically powerful but disliked minority in Vietnam (Gold 1991). Gold cites some previous sociological findings which indicate that self-help strategies resulting in economic co-operation and development within American ethnic groups were a key determinant in the successful adaptation of relatively recently arrived migrants and was consequently concerned to discover whether the Vietnamese/Chinese-Vietnamese divide was hindering this process among the broader community of refugees from Vietnam (1991: 9).

He made a small selection of his own photographs of both Vietnamese and Chinese-Vietnamese families and individuals in California to conduct photo-elicitation, initially with four key individuals. Each individual – two from each ethnicity, one older and one younger – was shown the photographs in the same order but not confined to a strict interview schedule. All were aware of Gold's broader research frame, and all knew him well. While Gold states that he carefully selected the sample photographs according to certain criteria (variety of social settings, apparent clarity or ambiguity of ethnic markers such as the language of shop signs, and so forth) it does not seem that the photographs were originally taken with the intention of conducting a photo-elicitation exercise.

Gold's first enquiry was in the form of a straight test: could his interviewees correctly identify the ethnicity of the individuals represented merely from a reading of the photographs' manifest content? Setting aside the issue of whether ethnic identification is ever straightforward, no matter how much information is available, Gold notes that while the two older informants guessed 'correctly' with a greater frequency, none of the four were 'correct' in all cases. The exercise nonetheless indicated the variable criteria by which people might make such guesses. While some sought to make judgements based on physiognomy – the shape and size of a photographic subject's nose, for example – others looked to more subtle as well as contextual factors. Images of women in particular were felt to be likely carriers of ethnic clues: for example, the barely noticeable high heels worn by two women in one photograph were said to be clear indicators of Vietnamese ethnicity on the stereotypical grounds that the Vietnamese were more closely associated with the French colonial rulers than the Chinese-Vietnamese, the French generally are fashion conscious, ergo the women are French-influenced Vietnamese (Gold 1991: 13–14). Gold also reports a few findings from his second line of enquiry – to use the photographs to prompt people to discuss the stereotypes each holds of the other and to elaborate upon these. Both sides commented on the greater family orientation of the Chinese-Vietnamese, their willingness to work long and hard and to utilize kin ties in developing and consolidating business ventures, though one suspects that this kind of information would have been forthcoming anyway, regardless of the use of photographs. Nonetheless, as Gold says and others have confirmed 'The photos gave respondents an object on which they could focus their discussion of their culture and experiences' (1991: 21).

By contrast, Patricia van der Does and four other graduate students at the University of Amsterdam, elicited information concerning what they call 'ethnic integration' (rather than 'adaptation') despite their apparent inability to photograph it in their study of a Dutch neighbourhood (van der Does et al. 1992).[6] Van der Does and her colleagues set out to employ photo-elicitation as the major research methodology of their project, rather than as a supplement to a broader-based investigation. The overall aim, influenced by the Chicago School of urban sociology, was to investigate the relation between social interaction and the physical environment in the Schilderswijk neighbourhood of The Hague. This particular neighbourhood was chosen because it is associated with crime, poverty and urban deprivation: 'hard drinking, slang-speaking women with screaming, dirty kids and car-tinkering unemployed husbands, living in run-down "cockroach-slums" ' (1992: 6). It is also an area of high ethnic diversity: white Dutch, Surinamese and Antillians, Turks and Moroccans.

The students worked on the project for a period of nine months, the photographing sessions and interviews taking place over a two-month period. As photo-elicitation had been selected as the major research strategy from the outset, they elected to create the photographs with their informants. Each student was taken by an informant on a tour of the neighbourhood, with the informants rather than the students select-ing the images to be taken, to the point of looking through the camera's viewfinder to be sure that the shot was what they wanted. The five key informants then looked through the photographs individually, and made suggestions for further photographs that should be taken. This became an iterative process: interview – more photographs – follow-up interview – still more photographs, and so on. Each informant was also asked to make a ranked selection of six to ten images that were 'most important to their view of the neighborhood' (1992: 10). These selections were then shown to the other interviewees, providing a cross-check of views and opinions. While the subject matter of the photographs lay very much in the hands of the informants, the students seem to have been anxious to avoid directing the subsequent interviews with leading questions; to some extent they were working collaboratively with their subjects (see Chapter 5.3) while still seeking to adhere to more objective or quasi-scientific research paradigms.

Perhaps the most interesting aspect of the research, and surely the one most commonly encountered, is that while the students and their inform-ants had no difficulty in selecting and visualizing the places they wished to photograph and discuss – streets, squares, playgrounds, houses – they all had great difficulty in constructing images of social relationships to discuss. 'We found . . . that our informants have a general idea of their social contacts, but that no single image was able to capture this impression. We found, indeed, that our informants found it difficult to verbalize what such photos should look like' (1992: 63).

This is well demonstrated in the students' attempts to document and explore issues of ethnic 'integration': 'It is striking that none of the informants had a photo taken to illustrate the existence of a large amount of immigrants in the quarter, although they often spoke about the presence of immigrants' (1992: 55). Nonetheless, a number of the photographs inadvertently, as it were, showed white and non-white neighbourhood residents together, and yet could be differently interpreted (see Figure 4.4): an image selected by a Surinamese man, which peripherally showed a number of white Dutch women sitting with their children on a bench in a playground, and a number of Moroccan and Turkish women with their children on an adjacent bench, was claimed by the informant to indicate a lack of integration (presumably because of the bench segregation), while another informant (a younger Moroccan man) claimed the opposite on being shown the photo for cross-referencing purposes (1992: 56). Indeed, it seems clear for all the informants – white Dutch and non-white immigrant – that race and ethnicity, and the integration or not of recent migrants, were important topics; yet at the same time these

Figure 4.4 Photograph that may or may not show 'ethnic integration' – Moroccan and Turkish women on the right, white Dutch women on the left. The Hague, Netherlands, 1991. Photographer: Patricia van der Does

were topics that, perhaps as a result of government policy, could only be alluded to rather than explored directly.

4.4.3 *Learning from photo-elicitation*

These four cases – Geffroy, Chiozzi, Gold and van der Does et al. – present a variety of overall contrasts and lessons, from the limited objective and near-experimental aspect of part of Gold's study (and, to some extent, that of van der Does and her colleagues) to the far more open-ended and phenomenological aspects of Geffroy and Chiozzi's studies. The difference is not, I think, unconnected to the fact Chiozzi and Geffroy were using old photographs, about which they initially knew little, although there was clearly a strong link between the photographs and the interviewees. As I said above, photo-elicitation exercises employing images that are not produced by the researcher, nor have any particular link to the subjects in terms of their production or manifest content, seem relatively rare – and probably for good reason. If one of the aims of photo-elicitation is to increase the degree of intimacy between researcher and subject, then arbitrary images, removed from one context and deployed in another, would seem unlikely to promote this. Furthermore, other aspects of the images such as their perceived embedding within another social context may come to dominate the course of the interview, possibly working against the intended research aim. For example, most years I set my visual anthropology students a photo-elicitation exercise, in preparation for which they read much of the material described above. No particular topic or set of images is assigned, however, and the students are free to construct their own exercises. Most commonly they select one or more informants, usually fellow students from other cultural backgrounds, and conduct an interview based on the informants' holiday photographs or snapshots they have brought from home. Occasionally, however, student researchers have used their *own* family or holiday photographs with informants, a possibly interesting exercise, but one which inevitably involves the informant having to make guesses about the researcher's background and which therefore focuses the interview on the researcher rather than the informant. While there can be a kind of bounce-back effect – 'Oh, I see you do it this way; in my country, we do it that way' – it hardly seems the most efficient way to solicit information about other people's cultural norms and social practices. Moreover, the peripheral content of other people's family photographs may prove more interesting to many research subjects: why is it out of focus? how much did that car in the background cost? – or even: what kind of camera do you have? what lens did you use?[7]

However, there have been occasional good examples. In one case, a North American student researcher interviewed a British friend who had recently become engaged, with the aim of exploring attitudes towards marriage. Rather than ask to see pictures of her fiancé, or other family members, he purchased a bridal magazine from the newsagent and used this as the basis of the interview. While initial questions and responses focused on which dress she might choose from the variety pictured in the pages of the magazine, and on other pragmatic and personal issues, the context of the images led eventually to a discussion about the magazine itself; for example, the blatant collusion between advertisers and publishers, such that editorial-copy fashion shoots were largely indistinguishable from paid advertising-copy. This in turn led to a discussion on the tension felt between economic and commercial pressures on the one hand, and the ideology of 'pure' emotion that was supposed to lie at the core of marriage in Euro-American society on the other.

In this last case, the fact that the images used had only a generalized relevance to the interview subject meant that a certain distance from personal circumstances could be maintained, allowing the interview to explore broader sociological topics: a displacement from the personal to the social.[8] A similar strategy can be seen in Gold's work with Vietnamese and Chinese-Vietnamese refugees in California. None of the interviewees appeared to have had any control over the initial taking of the photographs used, nor the sample selected for photo-elicitation, nor – with one exception – did any of them appear to know or recognize any of the photographic subjects (which would have negated the 'test' of their ability to discern an ethnic difference). As a result, ethnic chauvinism – an issue of personal relevance and about which the older generation at least would have strong feelings – could be discussed with some degree of detachment and yet rooted in detail, such as the fondness of Vietnamese women for high heeled shoes.

Additionally, there are strong indications in some of the cases described above that the work of extrapolating from personal memories or experiences prompted by photographs is not solely the task of the researcher alone. Research subjects are not treated (or refuse to act) merely as containers of information that is extracted by the research investigator and then analysed and assembled elsewhere. Rather, the introduction of photographs to interviews and conversations sets off a kind of chain reaction: the photographs effectively exercise agency, causing people to do and think things they had forgotten, or to see things they had always known in a new way, as in the case of Chiozzi's elderly informant who came to a new understanding about the break-up of his neighbourhood community. They serve to bring about a research collaboration between the investigator and subject, an issue that I discuss at greater length in Chapter 5.3.

4.4.4   Film-elicitation

For a variety of reasons, film (and video) are less often used in interview contexts than photographs. One significant aspect of the difference, briefly returning to the subject of the previous chapter, is the materiality of the respective media. Most obviously, an envelope or album of photographs can be viewed anywhere, in almost any circumstances, while even a video cassette of a film will require a player and a power source. In the same vein, photographs can be passed around, picked up and discarded, carried out to the light or examined with a magnifying glass to get a better or a closer view. The time-based properties of film and video, by contrast, impose their own constraints upon viewing practice and researchers need to be aware of these. For example, if specific information is sought relating to the manifest visible content of archival film footage, where the structure within and between scenes is arbitrary or merely chronological, then a researcher might do better to digitize and print off specific frame stills to use in interview contexts.

Nonetheless, there can be value in showing whole films or sequences of film to informants, and this is well exemplified in Stephanie Krebs's work on the Thai dance-drama known as Khon (1975). Her research took place in the early 1970s, well before videotape was available to the amateur, yet the nature of the enquiry demanded moving rather than still images. Krebs had hypothesized that gestures used in the dance communicated meaning, and represented key or core Thai cultural values that were distilled within the dance-drama. She systematically shot sequences of the dance, first using Super-8 film and later using 16mm film and cameras, to provide material for a set of interlinked elicitation exercises. The Super-8 material was shown, unsatisfactorily, to informants using a modified projector, and the 16mm material was shown on a small or baby Steenbeck editing table. It must be said that Krebs's view of film is unabashedly realist, at least for herself if not her informants: '[film is a] "slice of reality" . . . the informant MUST accept at least part of the screened event as reality' (1975: 283–4, emphasis in original). This positivist and realist approach allowed her to set up and control experimental parameters – for example, showing the same sequence of film to a number of informants and asking them the same questions, as free of prompts and cues as possible, or screening a section without sound to determine whether dance gestures communicated unambiguously or only in the context of the accompanying song.[9]

While she largely shot and edited her own film material, Krebs was essentially working with raw footage and asking her informants to concentrate entirely upon manifest content (or at least assuming that is what they were doing). She assumes that in most societies a realist reading is normative and unproblematic, and that even in societies unfamiliar with moving pictures it would be relatively straightforward to 'introduce' the members to this form of representation and then begin elicitation.

A more sociologically-focussed approach, and less positivist in orientation than that of Krebs, was taken by the anthropological filmmaking team of Tim Asch, Patsy Asch and Linda Connor in their exploration of the life and work of Jero Tapakan, a Balinese masseuse and spirit medium. The first film in the series, *A Balinese Trance Seance* (1980a), shows Jero at work as a medium, meeting clients on the veranda of her village home and going into trance to allow the deities and other spirits to speak through her to the clients. Unlike Krebs's material, *A Balinese Trance Seance* is a fully-edited film, complete with titles, voice-over commentary and subtitled speech.[10]

After the film was completed, the team returned to Bali and screened it (on video, in a house in a nearby town) for Jero, taking note of her reactions and filming the proceedings. The resulting film, *Jero on Jero: a Balinese Trance Seance Observed* (1980b), is relatively brief (around 17 minutes) and not especially captivating visually. It is shot entirely within the rather bare room where Jero watches the earlier film (clips from the earlier film are inserted at points) and consists mostly of a three-way conversation between Jero, Linda Connor and the player-monitor kit screening the films: Jero talks to her screen representation and talks to Linda; Linda talks to Jero and talks about (rather than to) the screen representation/player-monitor; and the player-monitor talks to both of them.

In an article describing this performance of the film, Patsy Asch and Linda Connor note a curious reversal of what one might expect (Asch and Connor 1994). Far from being entirely absorbed with her on-screen representation, Jero glances at it occasionally but seems more interested in engaging Connor in conversation. Connor, in contrast, fixes her gaze resolutely at the screen, often talking with Jero without looking away. As Asch and Connor note:

> Linda knows the film will only last 30 minutes and that we have very limited footage to record Jero's reactions. There are many topics she wants

Figure 4.5   Frame still from *Jero on Jero*. Jero Tapakan and Linda Connor watch, while Patsy Asch records sound. Bali, 1979. Photographer: Tim Asch

to cover in that time. Linda directs her gaze primarily at the TV and indicates she wants Jero to look at specific bits and to respond to certain questions. But Jero ignores many of Linda's gestural and facial clues. She has never seen the film before, doesn't know how long it will last, and is not used to working within specified time periods. (1994: 17)

Asch and Connor go on to point out that the film viewing does indeed elicit further information concerning spirit mediumship, though they also point out that Jero quickly arrives at her own agenda. Knowing that the viewing session is being filmed and will therefore be seen by others, she takes the opportunity to correct any (mistaken) impression viewers may take away from the earlier film that it is she who is providing advice and help for her clients. That is the work of the deities and spirits, she is just a humble commoner.

In the course of making a later film, concerned with a Balinese cremation ceremony (*Releasing the Spirits*, 1991), Asch, Connor and Asch employ a similar technique. One character, Men Muli, is shown footage of herself – again in possession – while the camera rolls, and the footage of that performance is subsequently incorporated into the finished film. Here there is a marked contrast with the Jero case; Men Muli is absorbed with her representation, but relatively taciturn in response to Connor's questioning. Men Muli, while a neighbour of Jero Tapakan, was not well known to Connor and although they had met before they did not have the intimacy of friendship that Connor and Jero shared; moreover, as Asch and Connor point out, Men Muli's experience of possession was limited and she claimed no particular religious expertise (1994: 19). The implication is that this brief foray into film-elicitation was not a great success.

Film-elicitation, like photo-elicitation, can be a highly productive research tool for the social researcher, yielding insights and understandings that might otherwise be missed or not be discernible by other methods.[11] But even more so than still photography, the moving image – film, video, television broadcast – is a wayward medium, difficult for the researcher to control. Stephanie Krebs's approach, described above, seeks to exert a high degree of control. The film footage was apparently shot solely for the purposes of elicitation and, while the nature of the research demanded a moving image, her use of these images was essentially still-photographic: show a picture, ask informant to describe it; show another picture, ask informant to describe it; and so on. In my own experience of film-elicitation – and that of others such as Melissa Llewelyn-Davies (see Chapter 5.6.2) who have shown completed films to their subjects – issues of viewing practice, engagement with and experience of events depicted, and the politics and ethics of social research more generally, have all been inseparable from and have served to complicate the straightforward task of asking questions and receiving responses. The Balinese example demonstrates that local viewing practice (if any), together with the complexities of the prior relationship between interviewer and interviewee (if any), renders the idea of a straightforward question–answer session mediated by the film highly unlikely.

In Chapter 6.3 I return to these complexities when I consider the presentation of research results through ethnographic film. Before coming to that, we must first consider some issues involved in the creation of documentary film, video and still photographs.

4.5 Working with archival material

I mentioned above (Section 4.4.1) that social researchers sometimes use archival material or other historic images in film- and photo-elicitation exercises. While occasionally such material may be stumbled upon by chance – as in the case of Geffroy, above – more commonly the researcher must actively seek out the material. This normally involves locating suitable archives of material, viewing a selection of images, and then seeking reproduction rights for the selected images or footage. First, however, the researcher needs a clear understanding of why she needs archival material. Apart from film or photographic historians, who by discipline are effectively required to work in archives, most social researchers probably turn to an image archive at a secondary stage in their investigation, often to gain an historical visual perspective on an issue of contemporary research. An educational psychologist researching the layout and design of classroom space as an influence in children's learning behaviour might turn to archival newsreel and documentary footage to gain examples of classroom design from previous decades which could be matched to the findings of contemporary educational studies. An anthropologist acting as a consultant for an Aboriginal group's land rights claim might make copies of photographs of the region and its people from a missionary organization's archive and use these to elicit information about the uses to which the land was put in the past. A medical sociologist interested in the impact of modern disease control programmes in southern Africa might learn valuable lessons from studying colonial health education films from the 1930s and 1940s.

Whatever the case, a viable if provisional set of research questions needs to be formulated in advance of entering the archive. While this is true of all image-based research (as Prosser 1998a calls it), it is especially true in the case of archival images, where the researcher needs to take into consideration the strengths and particularities of historical collections. One common mistake is to assume a comprehensiveness that few if any collections actually have. This was brought home to me when I attempted research on colonial period documentary film in the National Film Archive of India. As the Archive was only founded in the 1960s it is simply good fortune (and assiduous work on the part of the staff) if anything earlier than that date is included. Another mistake is to read back from today's multi-channel, 24-hour news television networks and assume that all events of the twentieth century have a visual record. A cataloguer at the UK's National Film and Television Archive (NFTvA) told me she had received several requests for footage showing the mathematician Alan Turing at work on top secret war-time code-breaking at Bletchley Park.

4.5.1 *Photographic archives and picture libraries*

Numerous differences exist between photographic archives and picture libraries or collections, and it is important for the social researcher to be aware of what kind of institution she is dealing with. For example, while the former will normally have some kind of public access remit and have some sense of the nature of academic research (that is: slow, painstaking, one line of enquiry leading to another in unpredictable fashion), the latter are normally commercial institutions and will expect the researcher to know fairly precisely what it is she is looking for. A related distinction is that each will catalogue their material rather differently: a photographic archive will normally be more interested in documenting details of date, photographer and location, as well as content; most commercial photographic libraries will prioritize content and organize the image catalogue by content categories ('birds', 'Paris: night shots', 'Africa'). It is possible for users to be confused about the difference. One curator of a relatively small ethnographic photographic collection told me that he quite regularly receives requests from fashion magazines seeking photographs of 'tribal beauties' to provide a counterpoint to fashion spreads shot in Africa or Asia. These requests rarely specify an ethnic group, region or even country, and the expectation is that the curator will make a selection of possible shots and send them over. Such requests are normally rejected – as much on practical grounds as ethical grounds.

As with any kind of archive or museum, some basic rules of thumb apply. First, the researcher should check that the institution does in fact have the kind of material in question; second, she should check the conditions of access to the archive – are supporting letters or recommendations required, for example? Third, it helps to inform the archivist, curator or cataloguer in advance of exactly what kind of material is sought or, at least, what the broader context of the research is and hence what parameters will constrain the image research. Most archivists, curators and cataloguers know their collections well and may be able to suggest alternative lines of enquiry. Finally, the researcher must be prepared to conduct her own research and not expect the archive staff to do it for her. All but the last of these are best done by writing exploratory letters. For some archives, especially public ones, an appointment may not be necessary though it can be helpful for an archivist to know when a visitor is coming so that they can prepare a working space or have the materials ready. Specialist and smaller archives often require an appointment to be made.

Like any archival research, photographic research is slow and painstaking, often requiring several visits to an institution to ensure that all the relevant material has been seen. Assuming unlimited resources are not available for having copies made (and if copies are required, to illustrate a book or dissertation, ensure plenty of lead-in time for this), then I have found that as well as a short written description of the image content, a rough outline sketch of the image giving an overview of the composition helps to prompt the memory subsequently. As photographic reproduction is relatively cheap, in many collections researchers work with modern prints which do not require any special care or handling, and which researchers may be allowed to photocopy (the strong light of a photocopier is harmful to older prints). Commercial photographic libraries will commonly use 35mm or larger format colour transparencies, and though a lightbox should be available it is sometimes helpful to have a lupe in one's pocket. Working with older photographs in museums and archives it may on occasion be necessary to examine the original print, in which case the institution should advise on access and handling procedures (access is rarely if ever given to glass plates however). Whether the original is consulted or not, researchers should bear in mind the physical properties of the original – including format and size (see Chapter 3.4) – which ought to be recorded in the catalogue, and to ask themselves a few basic questions concerning both the original (what kind of an image is it?, who made it and why?) and the archive copy (why is this photograph here? does it form part of a collection? is it associated with objects or documents here or elsewhere?). The more remote a photograph's internal narrative is (in both time and space), the more important it is to recover something of its external narrative of historical context and subsequent biography.

4.5.2 Film archives

Conducting research in film archives presents special problems, related to the nature of the medium.[12] The first is time. Allowance must be made not only for the time taken to view any films or footage required, but also for the material to be brought from the vault or storage area and loaded onto an editing table or projector. In most film archives researchers may work only with modern viewing copies of older or unique material, either film reels or videotape. The process of making viewing copies is slow and expensive and I know of few collections (other than film lending libraries) where all the material is automatically available. It is, therefore, possible to identify a film for viewing from the catalogue, only to be told that no viewing copy yet exists. At the UK's National Film and Television Archive there is an ongoing transfer programme, but users may pay to have a viewing copy made of an untransferred film immediately. Typically this is only feasible for television companies with large budgets which wish to incorporate particular archival material into a programme they are making.[13]

Assuming a viewing copy of the desired material is available two visits are usually required, certainly at larger archives: the first to examine the catalogue, order material for viewing and book a viewing slot; the second actually to view the material. Plenty of time should be allowed for this. If a photograph in which a researcher is interested forms part of a collection or sequence, it is important at least to scan the whole collection in order to assess the chosen photograph in its immediate context. With film it is vital to watch the entire film through at least once, before rewinding and beginning to pay close attention to particular sequences. While this is especially true of an edited film, where the juxtaposition and narrative flow of particular sequences is (or should be) as important as the content of any particular scene or image, even unedited amateur footage must be viewed as a whole. Quite apart from the basic shooting chronology that unfolds, one also gains a sense of the filmmaker's priorities and shooting style that allows one to be more confident in the reading of any particular sequence selected for closer observation and study.

The second problem, also encountered in photographic archives but acute in the case of most film archives, is indexing. Worldwide, there is no standardized indexing system for the content of moving images. Even within an archive the principles underlying the cataloguing system, and the conventions surrounding their implementation, may well have changed over the years leading either to a series of overlapping catalogues or, worse, a single inconsistent catalogue. Paper catalogues may be cross-referenced – by title and subject matter, for example – to allow more flexible search access, and computerized catalogues normally permit far more specific searches: by date, director, country of production, and so on. But the choice of keywords for 'subject' is normally arbitrary in the extreme and users must be prepared to make repeated searches, using a variety of synonyms and logical associations, when attempting subject searches.

Secondly, with no standardized cataloguing system universally implemented (though one has been devised: see White-Hensen 1984), and no clear agreement on indexing the content of moving images, even computerized catalogues are of limited use. Locating relevant material can sometimes consist of making optimistic guesses on the basis of a title alone, and then wasting time (and booking fees) watching material that is not in fact what was required. One final point, which is obvious but often forgotten, must be made concerning catalogues. Catalogues contain entries only for what has been catalogued – the absence of an entry for a film is not an indication that the film does not exist, merely that it has not been catalogued (see also Chapter 6.4.2).

Finally, in addition to providing materials for social research formulated and investigated outside the archives, film and photographic archives can and should be subjects of social study in their own right. While academic studies of museums, grand expositions and other repositories of 'heritage' have boomed in recent years,[14] visual archives have been curiously ignored – Houston's social history of the film archival movement being a notable exception (Houston 1994).

Yet although rarely visited by the general public, each archive contains documented anchor points for the ocean of visual imagery that surrounds us – from the relentless flow of television advertising to the quiet domesticity of family holiday snapshots. The decisions as to what material is included in the archives, how it is classified, curated and documented, are as much social decisions as they are fiscal, pragmatic or scholarly ones. An engagement with them is an engagement with our own visual culture, and with the social, political and historical forces that shape and manage that culture on our behalf. Stephen Poliakoff's three-part television drama for the BBC, *Shooting the Past*, gives a vivid and moving account of the life of photographs within one (fictional) photo library in which the social relations between persons are cross-cut by the conversations between photographs (Poliakoff 1999; see Figure 4.6). In an unusual broadcasting move, which further emphasizes the role of visual images and their keepers in society, Poliakoff and the BBC allowed the drama to 'bleed' beyond its frame of three, roughly hour-long parts

Figure 4.6   Frame still from Stephen Poliakoff's *Shooting the Past* (1999). Oswald Bates (Timothy Spall) reveals Christopher Anderson's (Liam Cunningham) family history to him through library photographs. Photographer: Bruno de Keyser

broadcast on consecutive Sunday evenings. At unexpected times of day and night, brief clips of the principal characters discussing the meaning of photographs were inserted between other programmes during the three-week period. The clips were not taken from the drama but the actors addressed the audience in character and directly to camera. The clips – and the drama itself – issued a challenge to the viewers: old photographs have a story to tell: it could be or could come to be your story.

At about the same time as *Shooting the Past* was being broadcast I interviewed a cataloguer at the NFTvA about the types of user the archive attracted. Students and academics make up a large portion of the users, both those interested primarily in content as well as those interested in the media themselves. Researchers from film and television companies form another main constituency, often in search of archival footage to 'quote' in other programmes.[15] But the most interesting category of users in many ways are the non-media, non-academic members of the public who contact the NFTvA in search of decades-old television programmes. While some are on private and personal quests (to watch every episode of *Coronation Street* perhaps) others have desires that are more overtly social. A typical, and apparently common, request is for a copy of a particular episode of *Opportunity Knocks*, an amateur talent show broadcast from 1964 to 1978. The enquirer then explains that their father, or grandmother, or some other relative had his or her five minutes of fame when they sang their song or danced their dance before millions of viewers. Now the enquirer wishes to show the recording at the relative's 80th birthday party, or to the grandchildren who never knew their grandmother in her prime. While sometimes poignant, these stories also tell us something about the social entanglement of television and other visual media in our lives, our understandings of time, memory and personhood, the significance of apparent ephemera.[16]

Notes

1 My interest was initially in non-clothing items, which being flat could be easily displayed. The same embroidery and mirror-work techniques are more commonly used on clothing, particularly women's skirts – see Tarlo 1996: Chapter 7; see also Parker 1996 for an insightful social history of embroidery in Europe.

2 Such aesthetic criteria were by no means confined to students. In an article on the creation and assessment of value at the top end of the ethnic art market – auction house sales of 'ethnographic art' – Jeremy MacClancy notes a similar concern with the patina of wear, denoting that an object has been used in an 'authentic' context (preferably a ritual context) prior to sale (MacClancy 1988:

170). See also Baaré et al.'s 1992 film *In and out of Africa* for more on the construction of authenticity in ethnic art objects.

3 Lull's understanding of the ethnographic method is very different, at least in overview, from what most anthropologists would understand. Typically, an anthropologist would be conducting broad-range ethnographic enquiries in a town or village over the course of many months, during which time she could choose to spend some time observing television viewing practice. Such observation might be unstructured, the anthropologist simply taking notes whenever their visit to a home coincided with television viewing and then ameliorating the results later, or she could adopt a standard sampling method, visiting a random or stratified sample of homes in the community at set times over a period of a month or more. Either way, the trust and familiarity that Lull speaks of would already have been established through the course of ongoing residence in the community and normal techniques of participant-observation, and wouldn't be tied specifically into the television viewing practice study.

4 'Market forces' are, however, by no means a simple factor for the television researcher to consider. In August 1999 a journalist and broadcaster estimated the current costs of British television production (per hour) as follows:

daytime game shows	£10–15,000
soaps (early evening)	£45–90,000
investigative documentaries	£140,000
primetime quiz shows	£170,000
primetime drama	£600–700,000
period costume drama	£1m plus

(Brian Park, 'It'll cost *how much?*', The *Guardian* G2, 3.8.99)

The following week another television producer challenged these figures, pointing out first that these were estimated figures for terrestrial broadcasting, and that cable and satellite broadcasting production costs were generally far lower – £10–15,000 per hour for a cable leisure and lifestyle show compared to the terrestrial norm of £80,000, for example – and secondly that size of spend is no guarantee of quality or audience popularity, citing the BBC's 1998 'expensive flop' costume drama *Rhodes* as an example (Andrew Lowrie, 'Cheap and cheerful', The *Guardian* G2, 11.8.99). Unfortunately, the tendency of some media studies and cultural studies writing on television towards a focus on the internal narrative fails to consider even basic issues of external narrative context such as production cost, scheduling decisions and audience composition and numbers, leading to largely ungrounded claims concerning the meaning of programmes.

5 Abu-Lughod does not indicate whether she actually watched episodes of the serial with her informants, nor how informants were selected for the sample. The implication is that her information derives from unstructured or semi-structured conversations with people who were the subject of ongoing ethnographic research, as is normal for participant-observation techniques in

anthropology. One advantage of this, although qualitative investigation of this kind needs no defence, is that Abu-Lughod does not appear to have prejudged television and its viewership to be a privileged source of socio-logical information. It seems banal, but perhaps necessary, to point out that any sociological investigation that takes television as its prime object of study is almost duty-bound to end up justifying itself by confirming that television is indeed extremely important. Abu-Lughod, unfettered by such an agenda, is free to conclude that *Hilmiyya Nights*, while undoubtedly popular, was hardly a key factor in introducing Egyptian peasants to modernity.

6 This distinction between 'adaptation' and 'integration' reveals a sociological distinction that partly reflects different attitudes in the USA and Europe towards the perceived 'problem' that ethnicity, and particularly minority immigrant ethnicity, poses for nation states. See Banks 1996b, especially Chapters 3 and 4, for more details.

7 I am fully conscious of a point a colleague of mine stresses in his own work and when teaching research methods: that the process of research, including the unforeseen, unexpected, difficult and even tiresome aspects, can all yield fruitful research results (Pieke 2000). To that extent, there is no such thing as bad research practice, simply bad analysis that ignores the 'failures' and preambles, and concentrates only on the high points of the 'successes'. Bad research practice, for example, would involve ignoring some informant comments in the course of an interview, while recording and taking further only those that appear congruent with some previously concocted hypothesis. Nonetheless, within the tightly bounded parameters of a training exercise it would make sense to devise and achieve clearly defined goals.

8 In fact, from my experience of setting photo-elicitations as a brief student exercise, disengaged from any wider research project and other forms of social enquiry on a topic, the danger to be constantly avoided is to focus too narrowly on the purely biographical. I urge the students to consider the autobiographical narrative of interview subjects as a starting point, not an end in itself.

9 Some teachers of both film and visual anthropology occasionally use the same technique with students: playing a sequence of film without sound to a class, or playing a sound track but no picture, and asking students to describe what they understand – where in the world are we? what are they doing? what kind of sound track might help to structure the images? what kind of pictures might accompany these sounds? and so on. However, the point of this exercise is not so much to conduct any kind of experiment with the students, but rather to use it as the starting point for developing their visual literacy, helping them to make explicit and self-conscious their tacit film reading skills (see also Martinez 1990: 46).

10 The film's primary intended audience would seem to be anthropology students and academics, not Balinese villagers, though this is not intended as a criticism. The film is not, however, constructed to act as a full visual ethnography of Bali or even Balinese trance mediums; like Asch's well-known

films on the Yanomamö, it takes a single slice of action – a consultation and ensuing seance – and presents it in something not too far removed from real-time. As with the Yanomamö films, a solid written ethnography accompanies the series of Balinese films (Connor, Asch and Asch 1986); see also Chapter 6.3.1, and Chapter 6.5.1.

11 Zeitlyn and Fischer (n.d.) describe the use of sequences of digitized video to elicit information about the structure of a ritual held in a West African village. The Mambila informants, despite participating in the ritual, were unable to place the sequences in the correct chronological order, leading Zeitlyn and Fischer to rethink conventional theories of ritual and cognition.

12 This section is based largely on my own experiences during earlier research projects and interviews I conducted while writing this book, but is by no means comprehensive. Anyone planning a serious and sustained piece of work in a film archive should consult Paolo Cherchi Usai's eminently practical guide, *Burning Passions* (1994), while Houston's *Keepers of the Frame* (1994) provides a general historical account of the film archiving movement and gives valuable insight into the social as well as intellectual factors that influence archiving decisions.

13 I was also told that repeated requests from users to see untransferred material could cause it to be moved up in the notional queue, but this could not be guaranteed.

14 Ames (1992), Harvey (1996), Karp and Levine (1991), MacDonald and Fyfe (1996), and Price (1989) represent just a small part of this recent output.

15 'History' begins five minutes ago, and 'archival' here should be understood in a very broad sense. The NFTvA records the entire output of the BBC, on commission to provide a public viewing service, and records approximately 25 per cent of the ITV and Channel 4 output for the ITC (which in fact covers most if not all of the UK-originated material screened, the remainder being imported programming, films and adverts). The Archive also schedules occasional 'snapshot' days when the entire output of terrestrial programming is recorded.

16 There is an added poignancy in the fact that the NFTvA often cannot satisfy such requests. Like its film collection, the television collection grows increasingly patchy as one goes back and in the early years of broadcasting much material was broadcast live and not taped. Granada Television is the only surviving company from the original group set up when commercial broadcasting began in the UK, in 1955 (*Opportunity Knocks* was made initially by ABC Television and subsequently by Thames Television; both companies are now defunct). As the original commercial companies went out of business they rarely had time to worry about disposing of the material they held, a situation that still holds true in some cases: one eminent and highly respected documentary filmmaker I know was distraught when he learned that all the prints and negatives of a series of films he had made for a commercial company in the 1970s had been sent for landfill. Material can still come to light, however, including tapes of early television shows illicitly made by

studio technicians and gratefully accepted by archives, no questions asked. The British Film Institute – which has produced a volume itemizing early film material known to have existed, *Missing Believed Lost* (Eyles and Meeker 1992) – holds annual 'Missing believed wiped' events at the National Film Theatre in London, and is planning a companion volume to *Missing Believed Lost* to itemize early television material.

5

Making images

Figure 5.1 Oxford city centre, overseen by closed circuit TV camera; the camera itself is inside the dark bubble (right foreground) and shielded from public view. Late 1990s. Photographer: Richard White

5.1 Observing

If tape recorder, camera, or video is set up and left in place, large batches of material can be collected without the intervention of the filmmaker or ethnographer and without the continuous self-consciousness of those who are being observed. (Margaret Mead 1995: 9, first published in 1975)

The Panopticon is a machine for dissociating the see/being seen dyad: in the peripheric ring, one is totally seen, without ever seeing; in the central tower, one sees everything without ever being seen. (Michel Foucault 1977: 201–2)

Two views about the power and utility of observing – silently and passively. The first is a vision of a possible future, intended to be

positive, where technology aids the social researcher in providing a
continual stream of high-quality data. The second is an observation of
the past, of how those in power devised 'scopic regimes' to control the
socially unruly – the bad, the mad, and the diseased. Mead's view now
seems hopelessly dated, locked within a paradigm of positivistic social
science. Foucault's view – while still very popular in some areas of the
social sciences – now seems hopelessly bleak, a vision of total social
control in which a mysterious force, 'power', holds absolute sway. But
while there are many differences, Mead and Foucault share a basic
premise that simply to watch someone is to learn something about them,
knowledge that can be later analysed and converted into intellectual
capital for Mead, knowledge that can be used to exert control for
Foucault.[1]

In this chapter I argue for a rather different position from that of Mead
(and cite others who argue that the Foucauldian position is weak and
does not invalidate the creation of images of some by others) and devote
most of my discussion to a series of examples and arguments that see
visual research as an actively, and perhaps inherently, collaborative
project between image maker and image subjects. There are two justifica-
tions for this. One is simply humanistic: it seems more morally laudable
to recognize the co-humanity of those we work with than to treat them as
experimental subjects. The second reason is analytical: away from some
behaviourist social science endeavours, such as ethology, most anthropologists and sociologists today recognize that social knowledge is a
processual aspect of human social relations, not a static thing to be discovered and seized. In order to do good social research, a researcher has
to enter into that process self-consciously, not pretend that they can
somehow transcend their humanity and stand outside, merely observing.

5.2 Creating images for research

The discussions of Chapter 4 concentrated on visual research conducted
largely with 'found' visual artefacts: images with which the subjects
of research might already be engaged independently of any social
researcher's academic agenda, such as family photographs or television
soap opera. In this chapter I move on to images that the social researcher
creates in the course of research – film, video recordings, and photographs. This is not, however, intended to be primarily a technical
discussion: as I outlined in the Preface, there are many technical manuals
available, plus a number of more sociologically oriented works that
discuss the practicalities of image-creation in social contexts, and it

seems pointless to cover the same ground. Instead, this chapter addresses some of the issues that lie behind image-creation and some of the reasons that social researchers might have in making images.[2]

By creating images of persons and their actions, the social researcher is intervening in the lives of those she works with, forging representations in which they have a variable degree of interest and over which they may have little control. Her exercise of agency is more obvious – literally so as she lifts a camera to her eye – and, as with all social research, she should take steps to ensure that people understand what she is doing and why. In some contexts people will actively encourage the researcher to create images, in others they will appear indifferent, and in others they will more or less politely tell her to stop or evade the lens. In the course of making a documentary film in India (Banks 1988b), with people I had known well for several years, I encountered a constantly shifting terrain of attitudes towards my filmmaking: this had not merely an ethical dimension (see Section 5.6 below) but a practical one.

The first problem was simply explaining to people what I was doing, and why. The idea of making a film was relatively straightforward, even a documentary film. What was problematic was the subject matter. From my point of view, I wished to make a loosely-structured film in the observational style about a friend and informant, an unmarried man with a close family and a set of unusual and interesting friends. My aim in making the film wasn't terribly clear, even to myself, but I knew I wanted to show something of the value of friendship in Indian urban society, and also to show the fluidity of social interaction in daily practice in contrast to the presentation of rigid social categories in the anthropological literature (for example, Dumont 1980). Although I tried to explain this to my friend and others who would feature in the film, I could tell it didn't make a great deal of sense to them. Friendship seemed a rather flimsy topic, and they weren't familiar with the specialist anthropological literature on caste. Eventually, they created their own external narrative for the film: I was making a film about the everyday life of a middle-class shopkeeper in order to demonstrate to my students back in England that ordinary Indian citizens were neither starving beggars nor ex-princes living in fading splendour (both types, the subject of endless visual representations in Euro-American media, were familiar to them as stereotypes of India).

While for the most part our divergent understandings of the film's subject matter were not in conflict, I did face a number of situations early on in the shoot where people wanted to know what they should do next. In other words, they wished to be directed, so that I would have the most

appropriate images to show to my students according to their understanding of the film's purpose. At the time I found this frustrating and,
unhelpfully, told them to act naturally or just to carry on with whatever
they were doing. As the shoot progressed, we learned more of each
other's motivations and responses to the shooting, and the main character and I had many discussions in between shooting periods about where
the film was going and what we might shoot next. By the end, he had
taken partial control of the locations and characters, setting up trips,
meetings and events. The film was never truly a joint venture, but the
informal and unplanned collaboration between us in creating the film's
content was in many ways inevitable (see also Banks 1988a; 1989b).

Collaborations, planned and spontaneous, are the subject for later discussions in this chapter. First, however, I wish to consider an apparently
more objective form of image making, one where the social researcher
sets the agenda and retains a high degree of control.

5.3 Documentation

Most fieldworking social anthropologists and sociologists take still photographs during the course of their fieldwork. Stills cameras are generally
light, cheap and relatively sturdy, their technical operations familiar. I
would suspect that in many cases few people other than the social
researcher, a few colleagues, their family and friends and possibly a few
of their informants ever see these photographs. If the researcher has any
self-conscious agenda in their fieldwork photography it is probably some
aspect of documentation: to remember the experience, to show others
how things looked, to record things that were too complex to be
described in a notebook.

The major argument of this book is to emphasize the importance of the
external narrative when incorporating images into social research and
analysis. This is especially the case when working with 'found' images or
images that the social researcher has not produced herself. Researchers
must ask themselves questions to elucidate the external narrative (why
does this image exist? who created it? what is its biography?) as well as
considering the internal narrative (what is this image of?). However, it is
easy to overstress the importance of the external narrative and there are
contexts in which the internal narrative is equally if not more important.
When a researcher produces her own images for her own consumption,
many of the questions concerning the external narrative are unproblematic
and have known answers (though these will still need to be communicated
to anyone who later views the work: see Chapter 6.1). In the case of

documentation, the internal narrative of the image – its content – is paramount.

In a famous article on ethnographic 'thick description', Clifford Geertz draws on an idea of Gilbert Ryle's and discusses the distinction between an eye twitch and a wink (Geertz 1975: 6–7). The first is involuntary – a spasm of the muscles around the eye – and is intended to convey no social message, while the second is laden with social significance, at least in some societies; yet an 'objective' video camera, passively recording the moment of twitch/wink cannot distinguish between the two. For Geertz, the distinction is an argument against mute, passive observation and against mute 'objective' description presented to others: simply to describe an eye movement (as he imagines a camera might) cannot communicate what it means.[3] But for the anthropologist who has worked in a society that recognizes winking as a form of social communication, and who has captured a 'wink' on videotape, then her off-camera awareness of the social significance of the wink in that society is sufficient for her to use that piece of videotape in her own analysis. It is not 'evidence' of anything in particular, but it can be represented as data that she plans to use. Her reading of the internal narrative of the videotape – who winked at whom, when – will help her towards an understanding of why people in that society wink, and for what purpose.

Plenty of people, not just social scientists, create visual images for the purpose of 'mere' documentation. Real estate agents, for example, take photographs to illustrate the printed details of property they wish to sell; museum curators take photographs of the objects in their collections; doctors take photographs against measuring charts to show the profile of noses destined for plastic surgery. The *use* of photography in these and many other instances is clearly a social act (what persuades people to buy houses? why do people have nose jobs?) and amenable to social analysis, but the *intention* on the part of the photographer is largely or wholly documentary. So too, a social researcher can have purely documentary intentions when creating images, and while these intentions may be subject to the scrutiny of later social researchers this does not invalidate the original intentionality.

Like many anthropologists, in order to fund my original field research on Jain religious and social organization in India I obtained a number of grants from various organizations. One of these came from a university museum, which commissioned me to make a collection of distinctive textiles from the region where I was working, and to document the productive process. The textiles, known as *bandhani*, are produced by a form of intricate tie-dyeing, repeated several times to produce a pattern of tiny dots. The main use is as saris, though lengths suitable for scarves, shawls and turbans are also made. As several of my Jain research informants were cloth merchants and sold locally-made *bandhani*, it was relatively easy to obtain access to the workshops and to interview producers about the technicalities of production. I was also able to photograph as much as I wanted (see Figure 5.2). However, although I

Figure 5.2   Muslim outworker knotting *bandhani* ready for first dyeing. Jamnagar, India, 1983

was interested in Indian textiles in a general way (see Chapter 4.1) and enjoyed learning about *bandhani* production, it was not my primary research interest; I suspect my photographs were rather superficial, revealing what I perceived then to be principles of good composition as much as the specific details of the technical processes as they were understood by the producers.[4] A similar point is made more strongly by John Collier in discussing a series of photographs he took to document the weaving of raw wool into finished textile by Otavalo Indians in Ecuador in the 1940s (Collier and Collier 1986: 71–4). After he had photographed the first stages of the process (washing, drying and carding of the wool) he developed the film, printed contacts and showed the results to the weaver. The weaver was not pleased and considered that the photographs had shown him to be a poor weaver. He insisted that Collier re-photograph the same stages, while he indicated when and precisely what Collier should photograph.

5.3.1 *Documentary exploration*

More than one social researcher has highlighted the need to be aware of and to overcome unconscious or taken-for-granted approaches towards the use of still photography, even in 'mere' documentation. Victor Caldarola, an experienced photographer accompanying his anthropologist wife on a research trip to South Kalimentan, Indonesia, consciously rejected a closed reading approach to the internal narrative, one that presumes that the meaning of a photograph (aesthetic or informational) inheres within the image itself (Caldarola 1985). Instead, he adopted three guiding premises that made his own understanding explicit. First, that photographic images are event-specific representations (a denial, at least in the documentary research context, of a photographic representation to make generalizing claims); second, that any meaning in the image is dependent upon the context in which it was produced (not merely the narrative or content it portrays); and third, that the production of photographic images is a social event, involving communication and mutual understanding on the part of both image-maker and image-subject. The consequences of this approach are many and include, not least, the assumption that any images shown to a third party without any other information are considered meaningless. Caldarola's methodology was to take copious notes as he photographed the duck rearing and egg production that formed the chief sector of the local economy. In these notes he described not only what he thought was taking place before the camera, but also indications of his own intentions in taking the images, and the circumstances – social and technical – of their production.

Caldarola's methodology was also iterative: he took photographs, interviewed subjects with the photographs, took more photographs in response to their comments, and so on. This iterative process is similar to that of van der Does and her Dutch colleagues, described in Chapter 4.4.2, but while they apparently employed the images they had produced as *generalizing* representations, the basis for a discussion of how things were in the neighbourhood, Caldarola seems to have employed his images as *specific* representations, depictions of unique events in space-time. Part of the difference lies in the 'things' photographed or thought to be photographed in both cases: intangible social relations in the Dutch case, concrete productive action in the Indonesian case. In fact, the indexical properties of mechanical visual representation mean that the Dutch photographs clearly show unique, space-time bound events and material objects, while the Indonesian photographs could be used as the basis for discussions of social relations more generally. The important point is that both Caldarola and van der Does and her colleagues appear to have had a clear understanding of their own intentions in taking the photographs in the first place, and were thus able to develop their analysis accordingly. Within the parameters of their respective research frames, each was aware of the degree of control they exerted over the photographic process and what this meant for their research.

5.3.2   Documentary control

In Chapter 4.4.3 I noted that the ability of the social researcher to retain control over the work done by photographs in interviews was at least in part related to the amount of control (if any) the researcher had exercised in the creation and selection of the images. Yannick Geffroy for example, at least initially, had no control whatsoever – the images were presented to him. Paolo Chiozzi similarly had very limited control initially, relying on the serendipity of the photographs he initially had to hand. Patricia van der Does and her Dutch colleagues consciously and deliberately decided to share that control with their informants (an issue discussed in more detail below, Section 5.4), while in other cases – such as Stephen Gold's selection of his own photographs, and even more so in Stephanie Krebs's creation and selection of film clips – a great deal of control was consciously retained by the researcher.

While this degree of control – effectively limiting what the photographs can say and how the informants can interact with them – is normally associated with a more positivistic theoretical stance, it does not have to be this way. Gold for example mentions that one of his selected photographs, an apparently rather dull line-up of college students, elicited a high degree of unexpected interest from his informants, though in the article he does not say what his original intention was in including the image in the sequence, nor quite what it was that his informants found so interesting about it (1991: 21).

In yet another photo-elicitation study a Swiss anthropologist, Ricabeth Steiger, adopted Glaser and Strauss's notion of 'grounded theory' to guide her study, reformulating her theoretical stance as the research revealed new findings (1995: 29; Glaser and Strauss 1967). In this research, designed to explore the change in family dynamics of Swiss professional couples upon the arrival of their first child, she took her own photographs specifically for the study and describes in some detail the technical issues she had to consider. This included the fact that her theoretical orientation and working hypotheses were liable to change during the course of the research in response to what her subjects said or did, and thus the criteria for composition, lighting, etc. could never be fixed or absolute. Her basic methodology was to conduct an initial semi-structured interview with subjects, take a series of photographs, and then return for a follow-up photo-elicitation session (1995: 29–30). As she was concerned primarily with mothers, many of Steiger's images were of mothers in their home environments, as well as views of that environment as seen by the mothers (such as the view from their kitchen windows). But as the focus was also on the mothers' relationship with their children, several images were taken from a child's point of view – low down, at a child's eye-level.[5]

5.4 Collaborative projects

In all the cases of 'mere' documentation described above, it is evident that the subjects of the photographs and films must have colluded with the image-maker in the creation of the images, but the extent to which the image-maker sought their opinions or allowed them to intervene more actively was influenced in part by the nature of the project and in part by the extent to which the subjects knew or cared about the project. All image production by social researchers in the field, indeed all first-hand social research of any kind, must be collaborative to some extent. The researcher's very presence among a group of people is the result of a series of social negotiations, some formal (such as obtaining visas and research permits from government agencies), most informal (establishing trust, giving gifts, saying 'please'). At the point at which a camera – stills, cine or video – is produced, even if no explicit permission is sought, the researcher often relies on a tacit agreement between herself and her research subjects formed through their earlier contact.[6]

For the most part, image production of this kind is casual and spontaneous, often unmotivated by any concern beyond documentation as described above. When there is an explicit and self-conscious visual research agenda present, then questions concerning what a researcher should reveal of that agenda come to the fore. Aside from completely covert research, which few researchers would countenance today for ethical reasons, it is difficult to imagine what wilful non-collaborative image-production in the field would look like. Nonetheless, some researchers have adopted strategies of dissimulation, (presumably) explaining the broad parameters of the project to research subjects but on occasion seeking to take photographs or film/video sequences without drawing attention to their activity. Often, the justification for this has been to preserve a presumed unselfconsciousness on the part of the research subjects. Gregory Bateson, for example, sometimes used a stills camera with an angular viewfinder in his quasi-ethological work with Margaret Mead on Balinese body styles, apparently allowing Bateson to identify and frame a shot 'when the subject might be expected to dislike

Figure 5.3   A ceremonial feast. Figure 1, Plate 29 of Bateson and Mead's *Balinese Character* (1942). Bali, 1937. Reproduced by permission of the Annals of the New York Academy of Sciences. Photographer: Gregory Bateson

being photographed at that particular moment' (Bateson and Mead 1942: 49). The example he identifies, Plate 29 of their joint work, is a series of eight photographs entitled 'Eating meals' and is prefaced by the caption that 'The eating of meals is accompanied by considerable shame. Those who are eating usually turn their backs toward anybody who may be present' (Bateson and Mead 1942: 112; see Figure 5.3).

Reversing this strategy, the anthropologist and filmmaker David MacDougall describes how, in his early film work in East Africa, he constructed a shoulder brace that allowed him to carry his camera with him constantly, whether he was planning to film or not (see Figure 5.4). As a result the Jie pastoralists with whom he worked quickly became accustomed to this man-machine combination, speaking to him and each other, going about their daily tasks, without a clear and obvious signal – the lifting of the camera to the eye – that he was filming them. But as he goes on to point out, the aim and effect was not to hide when he was actually filming; rather '[a]s far as they were concerned I was *always* filming, an assumption which no doubt contributed to their confidence that their lives were being seen fully and fairly' (MacDougall 1995: 119,

Figure 5.4   David MacDougall filming with a camera strapped to a brace made from a rucksack frame. Turkana, northern Kenya, 1974. Photographer: Judith MacDougall

emphasis added; note that MacDougall consequently prefers the term 'participatory cinema' to 'observational cinema').[7]

Visual anthropologists and visual sociologists often directly collaborate with their informants or subjects in the production of visual texts of various kinds. This may be done for purely documentary purposes; for example, asking a craftsperson to pause in the process of production at various stages in order to photograph the process. It may be done for some project that is more of interest to the investigator than the subjects; for example, Worth and Adair's extension of the Whorf-Sapir hypothesis concerning language and cognition into the realm of the visual, which involved giving film cameras to cinematographically illiterate Navajo and telling them to film what they liked (Worth and Adair 1972). Or, perhaps most humanistically as well as most interestingly, it may involve working together on a project that simultaneously provides information for the investigator while fulfilling a goal for the subjects. Here a wide range of projects have been accomplished: from encouraging the subjects to discuss their family photographs and in turn learn more about themselves, through helping people to document problematic or contentious areas within their own lives,[8] to full-blown attempts to empower people through visual media. Some researchers have sought to make their subjects so familiar with the technology of image production that they become image makers themselves. This lies at the heart of a wide variety of initiatives grouped loosely under the labels of community video or indigenous media.

5.5 Indigenous media collaborations

Some visual anthropologists have suggested that now that research subjects have access to visual media production, even in the heart of the Amazon rainforest, anthropologists and others should cease trying to make ethnographic films about or even with such subjects and leave them to document themselves (for example, Ruby 1995b). Rather less polemically, Lawrence Babb noted some years ago that handing out cameras to research subjects was not always necessary, at least in India where the local film industry provided a constant stream of indigenous self-representation for anthropologists to study (1981: 391).

Nonetheless, many anthropologists, sociologists, social activists and others continue to see a value in working with research subjects to create collaborative visual products, most typically video films. Leaving the arguments concerning the political and ethical dimensions of this activity to the final section of this chapter, there are still a number of practical issues to be considered and a variety of methodologies implemented. For example, in the early 1970s when Sarah Elder and Leonard Kamerling first began filmmaking with Inupiaq and Yup'ik Eskimo communities in Alaska (see Figure 5.5) video was not a practicable option. As they had to edit back at their base in Fairbanks, far away from the communities they were working with, native participation in the editing process was restricted to villagers visiting Fairbanks for other reasons, and final cuts could not be shown to the entire village (Elder 1995: 95). In contrast, Terence Turner has been able to arrange local video editing facilities for the Brazilian Kayapo and can observe editing decisions on material that has been shot entirely by and for the Kayapo themselves (Turner 1992: 7–8; see also Chapter 2.4.1).

Almost everyone who has written about their involvement with community video projects agrees on the necessity of gaining the agreement of the research subjects from the outset, and ensuring that they comprehend what is involved. Vincent Carelli, a Brazilian indigenous rights activist, has been involved with Indian community video projects for over twenty years (Aufderheide 1995; see also Carelli 1988). Initially concerned with making his own activist videos *about* Brazilian Indian groups (while working *with* them on matters of cultural preservation and territorial protection), his Video in the Villages project now acts as a facilitating organization, enabling groups to make their own video films. While some groups have approached Carelli directly, the majority are those he and his team have worked with and established a relationship with over a number of years. As Terence Turner observed with the Kayapo Indians, many of those Carelli works with have already been exposed to various forms of visual media, primarily television, and have a sophisticated understanding of its power and uses (Aufderheide 1995: 91). To enhance this understanding, Carelli shows videos already produced by or about one group to others. For example, Kokrenum, an ardent fan of Hollywood action movies and the leader of a Gavião group that had undergone near extinction after being first contacted in the 1950s, 'instantly grasped the possibilities' of community activist video after being shown Video in the Villages tapes made about another group's rituals (Aufderheide 1995: 86).

Similarly, Tim Quinlan had a longstanding involvement with a community of animal herders in eastern Lesotho prior to his involvement with community video (Criticos and Quinlan 1991). He had previously been involved with a project to develop a conservation management policy for Lesotho's alpine zone and had become aware of the poor living conditions of the young men who herd sheep, goats, cattle and other animals for stock owners in the region. The conservation policy

Figure 5.5   Sarah Elder with Yup'ik children from Bethel, Alaska during the making of *Every Day Choices*, a community collaborative film on alcohol abuse, 1981. Photographer: Katrina Kassler Waters

threatened to exacerbate these problems and, while Quinlan was aware of this, at the time he felt a greater involvement of the herders in his research would enable him and them to comprehend these problems more clearly. Having already made a video film *about* the herders, he decided to encourage a more active video collaboration *with* them. While some older men had seen both technical training films and feature films during earlier periods of migrant labour in South African mining settlements, the herders' initial discussions about making a video for themselves were limited by their lack of experience of the medium and its capabilities. Consequently, Quinlan and his team made up a short demonstration video, consisting of scenes of themselves travelling, interviews and episodes from earlier field trips, which then acted as a successful focal point for discussion and explanation (Criticos and Quinlan 1991: 47–8).

While the notion of 'community' video has a cosy feel, social researchers involved as mediators or facilitators need to work with specific individuals, whatever role each plays in the project. In common with many others, Carelli's approach has been to work with established political leaders in each Indian group (he refuses, for example, to work in factionalized communities, or where there are challenges to the leadership). The leaders in turn then select young people to be trained and work with the Video in the Villages team. There are potential disadvantages to this approach: first, the people selected may be selected for political reasons rather than for their potential to become competent filmmakers; second, and more seriously to many outsiders, 'women's perspectives virtually disappear, since lowlands Brazilian Indian cultures typically construct complementary spheres of activity for men and women, and . . . men deal with external relations' (Aufderheide 1995: 90). This means not simply that women are not engaged with the video production: Carelli's use of community video is overtly political and, as politics is also an aspect of the men's sphere of activity, so it is men's perspectives that dominate the content as well as the production of the videos.[9]

Sarah Elder, while not as overtly focussed on political activism as Carelli, similarly decided to allow indigenous social and cultural practices to dictate decisions about who collaborated and what the subject matter should be. Again, this also meant dealing with the effects of gendered spheres of activity. In preparing for their second film with an extremely traditional Alaskan Yup'ik community, she and Kamerling introduced the idea for a film to a variety of individuals and then returned to Fairbanks, knowing that 'democratic' notions from the south, such as a public debate or a vote, would get nowhere. In due course the community reached a decision and decided to allow the film to take place. Elder and Kamerling returned and negotiated agreement about permissions, copyright and royalties. The subject matter was still un-decided, other than it should be a film concerned with a significant but commonplace event in the community: 'As a young feminist, I was hoping they might choose family life [very much an activity within the women's sphere]. The village chose whale and walrus hunting [an exclusively male activity, women being considered unlucky on the hunt]' (Elder 1995: 99).

In contrast, Costas Criticos working in the late 1980s with a fishing community of indentured Indian descent in Durban Bay, South Africa, did hold a community meeting to discuss the production of a video of oral history testimony. The possibility of the video had been raised by a social geographer already working in the community, who then invited Criticos to participate. At the meeting, the researchers – like Carelli and his team – showed examples of earlier community videos they had facilitated and discussed their working methods. In turn, members of the community brought along photographs, letters and other documents relating to their forebears to act as the basis of discussion. The meeting then elected a number of people to work directly with Criticos, and agreed upon an explicit list of aims to be achieved by the video, such as raising money through video sales to erect a monument (Criticos and Quinlan 1993: 42). Criticos goes on to note that these aims shifted over the duration of the project, indicating if nothing else, that ventures such as these are subject to the fluidity and constant renegotiation of any social process (Criticos and Quinlan 1993: 44–5).

Finally, several commentators on community video have raised the issue of professionalism and conflicting demands. Some, like Elder and Kamerling, see themselves as professional filmmakers who contribute their skills to service the interests and knowledge of their indigenous collaborators, but who do not normally seek to train local people to become technicians. Others, such as Terence Turner, provide the resources and training to allow their indigenous collaborators not only to set the shooting agenda but to execute it. As one of the Kayapo filmmakers states, in a film about his own work: 'Do Whites alone have the under-standing to be able to operate this equipment? Not at all! We Kayapo, all of us, have the intelligence. We all have the hands, the eyes, the heads that it takes to do this work' (cited in Turner 1992: 8). Quinlan by contrast felt it was a 'necessary compromise' that he and his team from Durban retained control of the filming in Lesotho as they had neither the time nor the resources to train the herders. They also desired to maintain the professional standards of their film training, something that was not always in the best interests of the project's more general aims (Criticos and Quinlan 1991: 48).

From all the above, and from many other reports, it would seem that community video projects work best when the researcher has had an extensive engagement with the community prior to the video project, when she has a thorough understanding of processes of decision making within the community, and most of all when she is prepared to relinquish control. Elder describes the personal as well as the intellectual rewards that come from 'relocating the daily work of filmmaking to a shared space', one where 'boundaries between image maker and subject, between scholar and ordinary men and women dissolve or become permeable' (Elder 1995: 101), while Turner uses – as Lawrence Babb advocated – the products of indigenous media production as further material for his ongoing analysis of Kayapo society and culture.

5.5.1 Collaborative after-effects

While collaborations between social researchers and indigenous subjects in media projects are (presumably) satisfying for both parties for their duration, the phenomenon is so recent that there is little in the published literature concerning the long-term after-effects. Furthermore, the complexity of social processes is such that it would be difficult to claim with confidence that community video was the single decisive factor in bringing about some positive or desired social change. Turner's work on the Kayapo indicates that this is perhaps to miss the point. While some community video projects are unabashedly activist,[10] many are not or have a more modest goal to help promote cultural pride or resilience. Either way, it would seem churlish to withhold video technology from local groups on the grounds that it could not be proven to help them in some way, even if some claims about the 'empowerment' that is supposed to ensue can occasionally be naive. An argument against celebrating the introduction of video, especially to fragile societies such as Amazonian Indian groups, has nonetheless been put forward by James Faris (1992; 1993). He argues that to do so is further to lock such groups into the inevitably unequal relations of global capitalism and that they would perhaps be better off being left alone (Faris 1992: 176). But Turner counters this by pointing out that the Kayapo at least seem to be well in control, both of their visual media and of their relations with outsiders that video mediates. Furthermore, he states that although his initial intention was politically motivated (video could be empowering for the Kayapo), he has subsequently come to realize that the study of how the Kayapo use video has provided him with much more general theoretical insights (Turner 1992: 16).

Pulling back from considering only the after-effects of collaborative video projects, visual research more generally can sometimes produce unexpected results. In Chapter 4.4.1 I discussed Yannick Geffroy's photo-elicitation work in France. A further aspect of his research in the villages of the *arrière-pays*, the 'backlands' behind the Côte d'Azur, is worth mentioning here. After his initial discovery of the treasure trove of photographs kept by the unnamed old women in a cardboard box, Geffroy and his colleague began to collect and copy all the old photographs they could lay their hands on. This was not always an easy task – some did not want their old photographs reproduced, others rightly expected the students to exercise care when taking them away for copying. But a collaborative project was developing, one that had two main aspects. First, Geffroy noticed that an old custom of *veillées* – evening social gatherings in people's homes, that had withered away, replaced by private domestic evenings in front of the television – began to be revived as people came to each other's homes to examine one another's family photographs. These meetings took place both when Geffroy and his colleague were conducting interviews, but also without them, as people began to explore for themselves what Geffroy calls their 'visual heritage'. Secondly, Geffroy and his colleague mounted an exhibition one winter in one of the villages of all the photographs they had so far gathered. As they had not yet been able to gather information on all the photographs and the people, places and events depicted, they placed an outline drawing of each photograph side by side with the photographic copy, in the hope that visitors to the exhibition would supply names and other details. Not only did this happen, still more photographs were given to them, either for their research or to be included in the exhibition. Moreover, the exhibition 'created an atmosphere of excitement in Utelle: new meetings, intergenerational exchanges, discussions, and *veillées* took place. During the exhibition, it was not unusual to see people, photographs in hand, either meeting in the street or crossing the village to a friend or relative's house' (1990: 376).

5.6 Ethics

I opened this chapter with a reference to Foucault's vision of the Pan-opticon, the instrument of surveillance and social control that grants power to those observing, subordination to those observed. Its spectre raises a fundamental ethical point in relation to all visual research, but particularly that in which the social researcher creates visual representations of her research subjects: what right do we have to film, photograph or videotape those we work with? The question is not novel, nor is it confined solely to visual representations: what right do we have to make – and subsequently publish or disseminate through lectures, dissertations and so forth – *any* representations of others? If the answer to this question is 'none' then all social research should cease, immediately, and this book – and all other social science publications – should be consigned to the bonfire forthwith. But so too should many other endeavours: journalism, television broadcasting, even casual chat. Taken to extremes, all human sociality should cease, as all humans continually construct and disseminate representations of others.

So let us pull back a little and examine the proposition more closely. The question is not so much whether social researchers have the right in the abstract, but how and under what conditions do they negotiate that right with those who are represented? (The specific issue of copyright is addressed in the next chapter [Chapter 6.6] with particular reference to publication and other forms of image dissemination; in this section I wish to focus on more general ethical issues.) As Turner notes, the misuse of representations – visual or otherwise – is not a 'natural' or inherent quality of representation, and to assume that it is is to fall into a Foucauldian trap that fetishizes representation, assigning to it mysterious powers and in effect obscuring any effective analysis (Turner 1995: 102–3). Certainly, some forms of visual representation employed by social researchers and other professionals in the past can, by today's standards, be seen to work in the service of some group's exercise of power over others; Turner cites Tagg's study of Victorian photography and its role in reinforcing class structures (Turner 1995: 102, citing Tagg 1987) and a similar accusatory finger could be pointed at Cesare Lombroso's use of photography to support his theory of 'criminal man' at the end of the nineteenth century (for example, Gould 1996: 152 ff., citing Lombroso 1887). In more recent times, civil liberties groups have raised concerns over the widespread and increasing use of CCTV surveillance cameras in city centres, shopping malls and the like, arguing that while the stated aim of their use – to observe or even prevent street crime – is laudable, the checks on those who operate them may be insufficient to prevent use of the tapes for blackmail or merely for social humiliation.

For the social researcher, generally working in the field with a small number of people and seeking to establish a relationship of trust with them (for the benefit of the quality of their research if nothing else), the ethical issues faced are no less pressing but on a far more manageable scale. Though there are numerous instances of professional documentary filmmakers and photographers breaching the trust of those they have worked with, or unintentionally causing harm to them, this is partly exacerbated if not caused by the insertion of their representations into media of mass communication.[11] Few social researchers are lucky (or unlucky) enough to be taken up by a mass readership, and while having only a small, professional readership or viewership for one's research does not by any means bypass ethical considerations it does mean they can be dealt with to some extent on a case-by-case basis. For example, part of the controversy generated by Colin Turnbull's ethnographic study of the Ik of Uganda (Turnbull 1973) hinged on the fact that Turnbull included photographs in his monograph of named individuals making spears and poaching – illegal activities that could leave the individuals open to action from the state (Barth 1974: 100). This situation seems to have been caused by sheer thoughtlessness, given that names need not have been mentioned in the picture captions at all; moreover, as with so many instances of photographs used in ethnographies, the images seem to serve little overt purpose other than as mere illustrations and could simply have been omitted or replaced with less potentially damaging ones.

Of course, not using names or employing pseudonyms in photographic captions (or in film subtitles and narration) solves only part of the problem. While most social researchers give their subjects pseudonyms when writing or speaking about them and perhaps alter details of locations, events or times in order to prevent the identification of individuals by other means, this option is less open to those who take photographs, films or videotape (I have never seen the 'fuzzy face' effect adopted by television programme makers to disguise identity in any ethnographic or sociological documentary film, and indeed to employ it in the light of its televisual use would be to invoke associations with criminality for Euro-American viewers). Individuals can be seen and recognized by those who know them, or traced by those who wish to find them.[12]

Apart from ceasing to film and photograph altogether, the most useful solution to the problem would seem to be to turn it on its head. Instead of worrying about the power of mechanical visual media inevitably to identify individuals and then seeking ways to curtail this, the answer would seem to be to explore and utilize this property. The collaborative film and video projects described above (Section 5.5), and others like them, rest on an extended period of discussion with the subjects concerning the nature of visual representations and on encouraging subjects to use the media to express their voices (literal and metaphorical). Such an approach is not necessarily limited to visual representations produced for sole or primary consumption within the community itself, but can just as easily be employed for films and photographic projects designed for consumption well away from the local context. The result may be that some voices are not heard – as with the case of the indigenous Brazilian women in the Video in the Villages project – but it may also be that those voices that are heard are projected self-consciously, with permission for their use.

5.6.1 Permissions

'Permission' has to be understood in a socially or culturally appropriate context. Some ethnographic and documentary filmmakers insist on using formal, written release forms or contracts with their subjects before filming. Others do not; I have been told that Frederick Wiseman, whose *vérité* documentary films often include images of people in extreme distress, would begin filming by asking 'is it ok for me to film?' and as soon as assent was given would continue and take the verbal, on-camera permission as a blanket permission for the rest of the shoot. Among the media-literate, and in situations such as the collaborative community video projects described above where a great deal of prior discussion takes place, the use of written release forms may well be possible and effective.[13] Among groups who have little familiarity with either literacy or mechanical image technologies it may not be appropriate; for others who may have good reasons for being suspicious of legalistic processes, the use of such forms may itself create unwarranted suspicion. People harassed by government agencies, caught up in bureaucratic webs of words, forms, checkboxes and the like, may happily give verbal assent on camera in the Wiseman style as a result of trust previously established, but refuse to put their names to documents they do not fully comprehend.

Even when release forms are used, the visual researcher may still face a classic 'letter versus spirit of the law' predicament. Some years ago a friend of mine made a film in a young offenders' institution. He used release forms, partly because he was required to by the institution and partly because he hoped to have the film screened on television one day. He selected and worked with a group of subjects, all of whom co-operated closely with his work. The film was successfully completed, shown at a few film festivals but then laid aside for various reasons. Some years later, however, a television company indicated interest in broadcasting the film. The original release forms still held, but my friend took the trouble to trace all the principal subjects and alert them to the fact that what had once been a dim possibility might now be a certainty. By this time all had moved on from the institution and their reckless pasts, and were settled with jobs, partners and families. They agreed to the television screening, and were in fact rather excited by the idea of appearing on national television – with one exception. This man, who like the others now lived a crime-free life, had concealed his past from his wife and work colleagues and had no desire for it all to be revealed. Although he was still bound by the release form he had signed at the time of shooting, he was extremely unhappy about the past intruding upon his newly created present. While my friend could legally have gone ahead with the television screening, he reluctantly chose to walk away from it instead.

5.6.2   Returning images

Even if the legal ownership of most (but not all) visual images resides with the person who created them (see Chapter 6.6), many would argue that the human subjects of others' images retain some moral ownership. In addition, many Native American and other indigenous groups claim moral (and sometimes legal) ownership of archival images of their ancestors. The most obvious response to this for the social researcher is to seek some way to return copies of images she has created in the course of her research. In the case of photographs this is a relatively straight-forward matter, although issues will need to be resolved concerning where the images should be placed (in a local museum, for example, or by mounting an exhibition in a community centre) and who will subse-quently control access to them. There are also more creative approaches that can be taken. At the conclusion of a project to investigate the social networks surrounding illegal building activity in a Lisbon neighbour-hood, Ruud van Wezel wished to do something to present his results to his poorly-educated informants. His solution was to create a *fotonovella*, a textual/visual form with which they were well-acquainted, which was then distributed for local sale (van Wezel 1988).

In my own case, I have mostly worked with – and taken photographs of – people united by their religion, but scattered across an ever-growing city and belonging to no single organization. They are a minority group, further subdivided by caste and sect, and there is no single place that I could deposit or exhibit a body of photographs that would be equally accessible to all. The simplest solution has been to offer copies of photographs directly to the individuals featured and to have multiple copies of general shots (street scenes and so forth) for those that want them (not everyone does). In some cases, people have been simply pleased that I had not only taken their photograph but published it. This was poignantly so in the case of a family whose father died sometime after I had used his photograph in a publication and who contacted me to request a copy.

Film and videotape can also be relatively easily returned, though technical problems of access can intrude. Today, many communities in the world have some access to a video player and monitor, and it is now relatively common practice for an anthropologist or sociologist who has made a film with a community to return a few months (or even years) later to screen the film, either in a large public gathering or in front of small domestic groups or even for single individuals. Sometimes, screening the film will provide further research opportunities, sometimes not. Asch, Connor and Asch's screening of their film about a Balinese medium to Jero, the main character, became the basis for a further research film (*Jero on Jero*, 1980b) (see Chapter 4.4.4). In a more complex fashion, the Hungarian filmmaker János Tari used the same technique within a single film (one of a series on the Hungarian Jewish diaspora), filming both the principle character Benjamin Weiss 'in the field' and his later reactions to rough cut footage in the editing room (Tari 1991). One early sequence in the film, shot and utilized with the full permission of Benjamin, shows him in some distress, visiting the graves of his parents in Hungary (see Figure 5.6). Benjamin had long since left Hungary to live

Figure 5.6   Frame still from János Tari's film *Benjamin* (1991). Benjamin Weiss watches rough-cut footage of himself on a Steenbeck. Beaconsfield, UK, 1990. Photographer: János Tari

in Jerusalem, and while he visited the cemetery annually as a filial duty, memories of the war and persecution meant that his visits were doubly painful. Viewing the same sequence over Benjamin's shoulder later in the film allows both him and the audience to gain some distance and to think through the reasons for his distress.

Often there may be no specific research aim in showing the film, merely a feeling that the subjects of the film have a right – and may be amused or entertained – to see themselves. For example, the British anthropologist and filmmaker Melissa Llewelyn-Davies made a series of films with a Kenyan Maasai group in the 1970s and 1980s, all of which were initially screened on British television and unlikely to have been seen by the subjects themselves. In the early 1990s she returned to the village where she had worked, after an absence of several years, to make a new film that documented changes in the community. The 1993 film, *Memories and Dreams*, opens with a sequence of Maasai villagers sitting in the dark watching one of the earlier films on a monitor mounted on a high stand. Women giggle and squirm with embarrassment as they

Figure 5.7   Frame still from Melissa Llewelyn-Davies's film *Memories and Dreams* (1993). A Maasai woman watches her younger self in one of Llewelyn-Davies's earlier films. Kenya, 1992. Photographer: Dick Pope

recognize themselves. 'You were a pretty woman in those says', says a man off camera to a woman watching her own representation avidly. 'I was a pretty little fool who knew nothing', she replies (see Figure 5.7). At least as portrayed in *Memories and Dreams*, Llewelyn-Davies does not explicitly question the women on their reactions to seeing their earlier representations, nor is the film particularly concerned to explore such issues. Rather, the sequence serves to establish the filmmaker's previous involvement with the community for the benefit of the (Western) audience, and to suggest that the Maasai recognize and are self-aware of the passage of time and the changes that have occurred.

The return of visual images created or utilized by the social researcher is not entirely without problem, including the creation of further ethical dilemmas (see Barbash and Taylor 1997: 6–9 for some examples), but in general should be seen as a minimum requirement, and a small price to pay for people's co-operation.

Notes

1 I radically over-simplify, of course. A page earlier Mead talks of training local assistants in Bali in the 1940s to act as critics of film material made about them. Foucault's discussion of panopticism (from Jeremy Bentham's model for penal architecture) is placed within a highly specific set of historical contexts; nonetheless, Foucault is sometimes rather vague about the who, how and why of the human agents who benefit from and operate scopic regimes of surveillance, leading to an anti-humanistic reductiveness in the work of some of his champions (see Barry 1995 for some criticisms and a more agent-oriented approach to observation and surveillance).

2 The key work for film and video is undoubtedly Barbash and Taylor 1997, covering as it does a huge range of technical issues as well as more general discussions of film styles, ethics and so forth (see also Asch 1992). Anthropologists and other makers of ethnographic films have also generated a more anecdotal literature: see Rollwagon's edited collection (1988) for a good cross-section of articles, and on film style in particular see Loizos's history of ethnographic film (1993). Apart from Wright's book (1999), the practice of still photography is less well served, but the journals *Visual Sociology* and *Society for Visual Anthropology Newsletter/Visual Anthropology Review* have contained a number of relevant methodological articles over the years, some of which I cite or discuss in this book. Apart from Gell's discussion of diagrams (1999: Introduction and Chapter 1) Tufte's three books (1983, 1990, 1997) contain some clear examples of bad as well as good design that could serve as models. Finally, on digital images and other computer-mediated image use, the bookshop shelves and the pages of the Web are full of technical works and

discussions, though keeping up with changes, developments and rendered obsolescences is a full-time job. Once the basics of image formats have been grasped (.jpg vs .gif files and so forth), my suggestion would be to go on a short training course (most university computer centres run courses on Web design, use of PhotoShop, etc.), consult some of the many 'how to' technical manuals available (and also, perhaps, Fischer's book on computing for social anthropology – 1994), and most importantly look at and learn from actual examples: some are discussed in Chapter 6.5.

3 See Ruby 2000: 243–5 for a discussion of Geertz's visual naivety in this passage.

4 Documenting technical processes visually is quite common, and often a subject for first time film- or videomakers in the field. The anthropologist Karl Heider notes, with reference to a film he made with the Dani in Irian Jaya (West New Guinea) on sweet potato cultivation, that technical and aesthetic considerations – clear focus in this case – should be of secondary consideration to the informational value of the shot in the sequence of which it forms a part (Heider 1976: 47–8).

5 The angle at which a photograph is taken or a film scene shot needs careful thought. Well-fed Euro-American male anthropologists can be considerably taller than those they work among in the field and may take photographs that (literally) look down on their subjects. One anthropologist working with children in a British school went to perhaps rather extreme lengths to lessen the social distance between her and her subjects, including behaving as though she were their height – refusing, for example, to reach up for objects in high cupboards and waiting for a teacher to fetch them instead (Lærke 1998: 3). Similarly, the point of view of the image-maker is not neutral. Returning again to Patricia van der Does and her colleagues' study of a Dutch neighbourhood, several of their informants directed them to take photographs of a horse sculpture in the local park. One wanted it shown head on, to give a nice impression of the park, though all in fact found the park boring and unused as a social space; another wanted it shown from the rear, demonstrating how unpleasant it could be (van der Does et al. 1992: 22, 30, 52).

6 In cases where there is no earlier contact to provide the basis for this tacit understanding – a student researcher descending unannounced and uninvited on a poor urban neighbourhood to photograph social interaction in a decaying landscape, say – it is also difficult to justify this as any kind of sociological endeavour rather than mere voyeurism or photojournalism. It should go without saying that pure, mute observation, unaccompanied by a bare minimum of social interaction between researcher and research subjects, is fundamentally antithetical to a humanistic sociology.

7 Many anthropologists recount in conversation how they have become associated with the tools of their trade – pens, notebooks, cameras, tape-recorders – by those they live among, to the point where some informants feel slighted if their words are not written down or recorded, their actions not filmed or photographed.

8 Steven Lubeck, conducting a photographic study of a mental health centre in Los Angeles, was asked by a man to photograph his teeth, afraid that the dentist would alter them in some way (Lubeck 1990: 16, n. 3).

9 This might seem to be a contradiction in light of the fact that community video is understood by many to be empowering in its effects, as on the surface Brazilian indigenous women would seem to gain little from it. The explanation would seem to be twofold. First, pragmatically, it is unlikely that the indigenous groups would continue to work with Carelli if he demanded women's participation and thus upset their own pattern of gender relations. Secondly, contemporary Euro-American understandings of emancipation and gender relations are not necessarily universal values and, by the arguments of cultural relativism, should not be used to judge the values of others. See also Turner on the local politics of indigenous video production (1992: 7).

10 The Video in the Villages project is a case in point, but there are many examples closer to home. In Britain, America and elsewhere, environmental activists and others – though not always from the 'communities' in whose name they act – increasingly employ video; see Harding 1997. Less politically radical, but with a guarantee of distribution, the Community Programmes Unit of the BBC helps individuals and groups to make short films on disability rights, urban poverty and other subjects of social concern which are then broadcast.

11 The instances of such breaches of trust, and the debate surrounding them, are too numerous and voluminous to go into here: several British television stations run weekly programmes solely to air such grievances (for example, Channel Four's *Right to Reply*). For an introduction to academic perspectives see Rosenthal 1980; 1988: Part Three; Ruby et al. 1988. Barbash and Taylor provide a concise and practical discussion of the issues for would-be film-makers (1997: 48–61).

12 A colleague of mine who has conducted research with child prostitutes in Asia, is critical of well-meaning but poorly informed journalistic accounts and films that seek to 'expose' the horrors of child prostitution. By dwelling on images of the children, identifying their location and sometimes even naming them such accounts are at best salacious – at worst, they provide useful tips and pointers for visiting Euro-American sex tourists (Heather Montgomery, personal communication).

13 Barbash and Taylor provide three release form templates of varying complex-ity but advise consulting a lawyer nonetheless (1997: 485–7).

6

Presenting research results

Figure 6.1 Jero Tapakan (foreground, left) and Linda Connor (foreground, right) watch a film on cremation together with other residents of Jero's hamlet. Bali, 1979. Photographer: Patsy Asch

6.1 Audiences

Perhaps the most important issue to consider when presenting research results – of any kind, not just the results of visual research – is the audience. For much of the time academics normally only have to consider two audiences in their writing and research presentations – their students and their peers. While the nature and context of the presentation may or should cause changes in how the material is presented (writing for a learned journal versus an informal 'work in progress' seminar, for example), the characteristics of the two audiences are generally well-known and presentations to them follow relatively clear and well-established conventions. In other words, while some academics are notoriously poor communicators, in principle they should be able to master the conventions to make clear and effective presentations of their research results to their chosen audiences. Some academics and other social researchers similarly need to learn to master the conventions to present results to other audiences – public policy makers, for example – while part of a student's training should help them to communicate effectively.[1]

The presentation of visual materials introduces some additional complexities. First, there is the 'problem of images' generally, and their poor appreciation as valid research material in some parts of some academic disciplines (MacDougall 1997: 276). Secondly, the multivocality of visual images means they can address different audiences in quite different ways, creating a 'problem of audiences'. In Chapter 4.3.1 I mentioned the reader-response or reception theory literature that developed first in literary studies and was later exported to media studies and cultural studies. When these approaches finally reached anthropology the primary focus of attention was ethnographic film and its reception (for example, Crawford and Hafsteinsson 1996). Much of this literature highlights the fact that audiences, particularly student audiences, do not transparently and naturally read ethnographic films, but bring to them previously formed social and cultural understandings. David MacDougall was probably the first to bring anthropologists' attention to the fact that the 'meaning' of an ethnographic film was not inherent within either the film itself or in the intentions of its author(s), but was a negotiable property that lies within a conceptual triangle formed by the (film) subject, the filmmaker and the audience (MacDougall 1978: 422).

Following on from MacDougall's and others' insights and allying it to a body of reader-response theory, Wilton Martinez, a doctoral student at the University of Southern California, constructed a meticulously-detailed research project that evaluated undergraduate student response to a select number of ethnographic films (Martinez 1990, 1992). The films were shown to the students as part of an introductory anthropology course and Martinez observed the students watching, issued questionnaires, analysed weekly film reports and essay assignments, and even collected narratives of their dreams (Martinez 1990: 38). His findings were disturbing for those involved with ethnographic film. He concludes that certain films could generate an 'aberrant' response, that far from coming to understand or even sympathize with the film's generally exotic subjects (exotic to the students, that is) the students tended to use the subjects' actions and appearance to confirm inaccurate stereotypes they held of 'primitive' and 'tribal' peoples. Some films, specifically intended to be used in student education, were also found to be 'dry' and 'boring' (one example is Asch and Chagnon's *The Ax Fight* [1975] discussed in Section 6.5.1 below). Even where their attention was engaged by a film, typically because it contained a strong central character and clear narrative drive, such as Nairn's 1974 television film *The Kawelka: Ongka's Big Moka*, their enjoyment could be patronizing and confirm stereotypes of the simple-minded 'natives' (Martinez 1990: 43–4).

Taking a further cue from Umberto Eco and notions of 'open' and 'closed' texts, Martinez also concludes that the more didactic a film is, the more clearly it attempts to establish a clear authorial voice through heavy narration, diagrams and so forth, the more likely a film is to be the subject of an aberrant reading. In contrast, semiotically 'open' films, ones that allow or indeed enforce on the viewer a greater interpretative effort, met with more elaborated and reflexive responses from the students (Martinez 1992: 135–6). In such 'open' films, the space in MacDougall's triangle between subject, author and reader is self-consciously presented as an interpretative space.

Martinez's solution to the problem of aberrant readings is thus two-fold. First, certain kinds of films are more likely to promote more critical and self-aware responses from viewers;[2] secondly, those presenting films to students should help students to develop visual literacy skills, to approach ethnographic films not simply as transparently-represented ethnographic knowledge, but as a particular genre of filmmaking that has a history, a changing set of representational conventions, and a changing set of differentially-placed authors (Martinez 1990: 46; 1992: 152–6). In other words and in my terms, to alert viewers to the external narratives surrounding the films, rather than assuming an unproblematic and automatic transmission of the internal narrative or content.

While Martinez is one of the few to have examined the pedagogic value of ethnographic film empirically (indeed, as far as I know he is the only one to have done so), he is not alone in seeking criteria by which the communicative power of visual materials can be assessed. To conclude this section I want briefly to refer to two such assessment models which, while very different in their underlying aims and objectives, have a superficial similarity. Karl Heider's 1976 book on ethnographic film, while now quite elderly, was for a long time influential simply because no other comparative text existed. Like many subsequent authors, Heider deals at length with the problem of defining 'ethnographic film' (1976: 3 ff.). He settles finally on a multi-faceted property of 'ethnographic-ness' – the degree to which a film successfully conveys an ethnographic understanding of the people and activities represented. This he subsequently formalizes into what he calls an 'attribute dimension grid' – a graphic rendering by which fourteen properties or facets can be charted

(1976: 97–117). These range from technical and production aspects of the finished film itself (basic technical competence, goodness of fit between narration and image), to its relation with external written sources such as study guides and related ethnography. A film which scores highly on all or many of the fourteen analogue scales is overall a 'more' ethnographic film than one which gains low scores for many of the attributes (see Figure 6.2). Heider is well aware of the dangers of over-specifying in this way and indeed the whole model is open to criticism. Nonetheless, his approach has the virtue of defining clearly (if subjectively) what it is he thinks is important about a visual ethnographic presentation, and then using that model to assess specific examples. In this he rather surprisingly shares ground with a very different approach towards evaluating

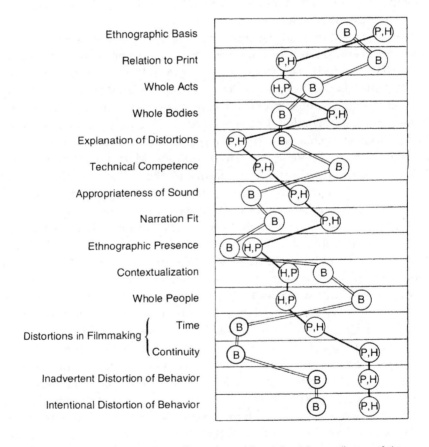

Figure 6.2   Karl Heider's attribute dimension grid, used to plot attributes of three ethnographic films (identified as 'B', 'H' and 'P') (from Heider 1976: 115, Diagram 3)

films. The ChildCare Action Project (CAP) is an American Christian organization that has a declared objective to 'scientifically prove a symbiosis between the entertainment media preferences of youth and the relationship of youth with fair authority' (CAP Website: index.htm). In other words, to demonstrate that (morally) 'unacceptable material' has an impact on the observer (CAP Website: method.htm).

So far, CAP has developed a methodology to evaluate the moral content of mainstream feature films according to seven criteria ('wanton violence/crime', 'impunity/hate', 'sex/homosexuality', and so on). Each criterion is assigned a notional 100 points, which are then deducted, one to three at a time, for each instance of the named behaviour in the film, and represented diagrammatically by a series of seven thermometers (see Figure 6.3). Like Heider, the CAP group has a clear starting point – a vision of morality appropriate to American youth derived from a particular Christian perspective – which is used to create a model by which specific visual narratives can be assessed.

Most qualitative social researchers would be unhappy with the use of formalist assessment criteria such as these, but like all formal models they can serve to clarify an otherwise loose and formless discussion. Martinez's work, and the two models above, all seek to assess the textual encounter between reader-viewer, author and subject, that is, the three points of MacDougall's triangle; in doing so such approaches can be

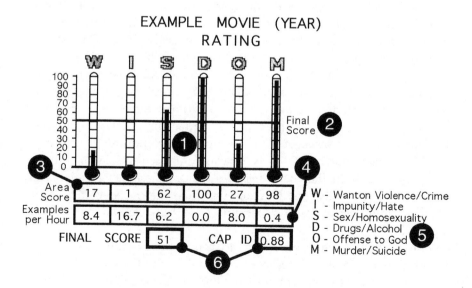

Figure 6.3   ChildCare Action Project (CAP) Graphic Data Display (for *Armageddon*, 1988). Image creator: Thomas Carder

useful in helping a social researcher consider why she is using visual media, what she hopes to achieve by doing so, and whether in fact she has achieved it.

6.2 Presenting photographs

As mentioned above, the multivocality of photographs renders their use in social research problematic. For this reason, away from highly self-conscious uses of photographs such as the visual essay form discussed below (Section 6.2.1), there is a tendency in some academic publications to constrain the multiple voices, allowing only one weakly to remain. The one allowed to speak is normally the voice of 'mere illustration', a largely redundant visual representation of something already described in the text. A variant on this is what in film would be known as an establishing shot – a general overview of the location or the people, not intended to be illustrative of anything in particular except a confirmation of presence (cf. Marcus and Fischer 1986: 55). This appeal to an empiricist truth-claim ('I was there, I heard and saw these things, you can trust my account') has a relatively long genealogy in the descriptive reporting of social research. The silencing of the photographic multivocality is usually accomplished through text, particularly the constraining caption which allows a channel for only one voice to emerge clearly. But over time or in other contexts, the constraints may become looser, as contextual shifts destabilize the original narrative that framed the photograph. Lombroso's mugshots of criminal types (1887; see Chapter 5.6) now look like ordinary men or women: whatever their criminal acts, their faces reveal nothing of them.[3] In a similar vein one reviewer of a 1974 ethnographic film on an Andean peasant group (Harris 1975 on Pasini 1974) pointed out that the number of imported objects present in the footage, plus of course the depth of contact since Columbus, belied the film's narrative insistence on the group's isolation and remoteness (cited in Loizos 1980: 580–1). A quarter of a century later, with an intellectual stress in the social sciences on transnationalism, globalism and cultural hybridity, the sight of 'imported' artefacts would not be taken as mournful tokens of a lost innocence, but celebrated as cultural appropriations.

Photographs, when used in an academic publication, term paper, dissertation or seminar presentation should not, therefore, be taken lightly, included as an afterthought, or thought to be self-evident – communicating their internal narrative transparently and naturally. Conventionally in academic publications, photographs are tied to the main body of text in two ways – through captions and through in-text references. Thinking carefully about the image and the text, and the work that each is doing individually and in tandem to advance the argument, should encourage the author to think about the best way – if at all – to use captions and in-text references. In this book many of the photographs are used as visual quotations from the work of others and I decided that both captions and in-text references were appropriate, but elsewhere I have tried to experiment with other forms. In a monograph on Jain social organization in India and England (Banks 1992), I used no in-text references at all for the 20 photographs included and I also separated the captions from the photographs: the photographs were simply numbered and a separate page of captions was keyed to the numbers. The captions varied from the simply descriptive ('street scene') to brief personal memories and were intended to allow the images some autonomy, to work with the text in presenting a more experiential view of Jain social life. The photographs were placed in the text at what I considered to be a suitable juncture, rather than gathered together as a free standing section of 'Plates', but there was intended to be a narrative relationship between them – for example, the first photograph is of a group of men negotiating, opening discussions, while the last is of a ceremony concluding, wrapping up.[4]

6.2.1 The photographic essay

While a handful of images in a published text must inevitably play something of a supporting role to the main argument, some social researchers have experimented with making the images dominant in conveying the argument or analysis, reducing the written text to an introductory statement and a number of captions. Drawing in part on film as a model, the photographic essay is normally driven by a strong narrative which links one image to the next in sequence, either in a more or less strict chronological fashion or through a more abstract association of ideas. The narrative derives from but transcends the internal narrative of the individual images.

Photographic essays originated as a form of journalism, and though perhaps less common today they can still be found occasionally in the Sunday supplements; thought to be a more direct way of addressing a readership than a dry textual account, there is a particular bias towards matters of social policy and social concern. From the 1960s the art critic/social critic John Berger and photographer Jean Mohr collaborated on a series of projects that effectively transcended the boundaries between serious journalism, social criticism and sociology (1967 – on the British middle classes; 1975 – on migrants in Europe; 1982 – on European peasants), thus perhaps rendering the form more acceptable to an academic readership. For a period of around five years (1985–1990) the journal *Critique of Anthropology* featured a photographic essay in each issue, often on a topic of social concern or allied to an explicitly political stance within the discipline.

Critique was the only non-specialist journal in the social sciences to publish photo essays, as far as I am aware but, by the late 1980s, journals such as *Visual Anthropology* and *Visual Sociology* were regularly printing substantial pieces of visual analysis and narrative. In the debut issue of *Visual Anthropology* Douglas Harper, the author of a number of primarily visual sociological texts (for example Harper 1982, 1987b), outlines four typologies or categories by which photographs can be used in sociological enterprises, two of which are presentational and rest on a working relationship between images in a sequence: the phenomenological mode and the narrative mode (Harper 1987a).[5] In the phenomenological mode, an attempt is made to present the subjective experience of some social phenomenon from both researcher's and insiders' perspectives. Harper does not devote much discussion to this mode, though it would seem evident that the parallels with ethnographic film (which he associates with his final, narrative mode) are strong, and that in part the functioning of the mode must depend upon sequences of images organized by some guiding principle.

The narrative mode, for which he identifies a large number of photographic essays and ethnographic films, is more concerned with telling a story, a story in which the researcher may have participated, but which nonetheless is primarily the story of the research subjects. Another visual sociologist, John Grady, is well aware that some (non-visual) sociologists will immediately counter that the job of empirical sociology is not to tell stories but, for example, to employ survey and other methods to demonstrate that social differences and patterns of organization are not merely a matter of chance; once the research work has been conducted – data collected and analysed – it needs to be written up in the most straightforward fashion, not presented photographically (Grady 1991). Grady's counter argument rests on two premises: first, that objective quantitative sociological approaches do not completely master all they survey (the problem of residual indeterminacy – the figures that don't fit after all the rest have been neatly categorized) and, secondly, that all textual accounts of research are inevitably narrativized anyway (1991: 29, 34). Add in an argument in favour of qualitative ethnographic approaches towards at least some social research topics, and there seems little reason why a narrativized visual essay (in photographic or filmic form) should not be as valid as a purely written account. Certainly such visual essays have the potential to be more appealing to students and to a wider, lay audience.[6]

Good academic writing is a skill – a craft skill in fact – that can be developed and honed, almost independently of the ideas conveyed. The same is true of good visual presentation. For filmmakers, the process of editing and the skills necessary are a familiar part of their work, and audiences appreciate them when displayed well. The sequencing of still photographs into a satisfying narrative demands perhaps fewer technical skills, but a similar depth of judgement and imagination, allied for the social researcher with a clearly developed analytical perspective. A greater degree of presentational control is also required of the researcher – publishers may not understand what is required or may be unable to format image size, text placement and so on in the desired way. This is why researcher-authored films (and multimedia products – see Section 6.5 below) can hold truer to authorial intention and why, on occasion, a live 'performance' of a photographic narrative can be superior to a published version.

For example, the architect and art-historian Sunil Prasad has used a sequence of photographs and spoken text to present two contrasting narratives or journeys: one through the houses and narrow streets of old Delhi, the other through a modern suburb of the same city. Through the images, and in a way that language alone could not accomplish, Prasad was able to demonstrate subtle gradations in the social use of space in the old city. Platforms, steps, stepped doorways, canopies and other features allow for an unfolding and retracting of domestic space for example. The published version of this presentation (Prasad 1998) includes fewer images and obviously cannot key them to specific moments in the text to achieve a simultaneity of word and image. While still communicating something of the original argument, a dynamism and sense of discovery has been lost (at least in my opinion).

6.3 Presenting ethnographic and other films

The French anthropologist and celebrated ethnographic filmmaker Jean Rouch once said that he made films first of all for himself, secondly for the people who participated in the films, and finally for 'the greatest number of people, for everyone' (Eaton 1979: 44–6). The answer is not as glib, or as touch-all-bases as it might seem. Many of Rouch's West African films (for example, *Moi, un Noir* 1957, *Jaguar* 1967) contain fictionalized sequences, improvised by the characters, and in due course

Rouch formed a film production company with some of his regular film participants (MacDougall 1998a: 57, n. 16). In *Chronique d'un Été* (Rouch and Morin 1960), filmed on the streets of Paris, the film participants become their own audience when they settle down to watch the penultimate cut of the film in a screening room. Rouch is fully aware of the space formed between the author, the reader and the (film) text, and exploits it to allow the film subjects to adopt a variety of positions (including authorship and readership), which are in turn communicated to what one might call the secondary audience.

While some ethnographic and other documentary films of sociological interest are made with a specific audience in mind, however, many are not. Although many amateur or independent filmmakers express a hope that their films may one day be screened on television, many also tend to have a rather vague conception of the audience for their films, claiming in treatments and the like that there will be something for everyone in what they plan to make. While this is probably true up to a point, a loose scatter-gun approach to the audience runs the risk of making a film that is ultimately satisfying to no one. Unfortunately, targeting a film too specifically to a particular audience runs the risk of shortening a film's screening life. The Asch and Chagnon films on the Yanomamö, for example, were tailored specifically to be used in teaching anthropology to North American college students of the day. Whatever their reception then, a later generation found them 'boring and repetitious' and 'didn't understand what was happening' (Martinez 1990: 41). I remember being shown Robert Flaherty's 1922 *Nanook of the North* as a student in the 1970s, not as an example of early documentary film style, or even to raise issues of other-cultural representation, but as an apparently unmediated window into native Alaskan culture. In that context I was not Flaherty's intended audience (the film was given a commercial movie house release originally) and it is no surprise that I found it inaccessible.

On the other hand, films made with a specific television audience in mind, while they can be well-received and enjoyed by students (Martinez 1990: 45), can also be castigated by professional researchers for their superficiality and oversimplification of complex social processes (Loizos 1980: 588–9; see also Houtman 1988). At the opposite extreme, research footage created in the field by a researcher for her own consumption, while valuable for her own analysis, can be extremely dull or uninformative for most general viewers, whether academics or not (see Chapter 5.3).[7]

Once completed, most independent documentary productions – if properly advertised and distributed (see Barbash and Taylor 1997: Chapter 9) – are destined for use in the classroom but can also be self-promoted at the large number of documentary and ethnographic film festivals that take place around the world. Both the classroom and the film festival give a contextual shape to the external narrative that surrounds these films, leading to questions of what additional information should also be injected into that narrative.

6.3.1 Study guides and other contextualization

Some contemporary visual artists are unable or unwilling to elaborate on the 'meaning' of an art work when questioned by critics or other viewers, on the grounds that the art work needs no additional interpretation: it stands for itself. Some documentary filmmakers adopt a similar line – what is the point of spending months if not years carefully shooting and thoughtfully editing a film if it needs to be supported by something external to itself?[8]

Yet some writers on ethnographic film in particular argue that study guides are a necessity (for example, Asch 1992: 203; Heider 1976: 127 and passim). The most commonly cited reason is that for many viewers the sheer unfamiliarity with non-Euro-American social forms means that a great deal of basic explanation and description is necessary to appreciate the significance of what is depicted in the film, and that this is better kept out of the film itself to prevent it turning into an illustrated lecture. In some ways, this is back to Geertz's eye-twitch versus wink distinction (Chapter 5.3). While a British viewer of a British television docu-soap may be presumed to utilize a high degree of passive cultural familiarity to make sense of what she is seeing (though in fact such docu-soaps often contain a great deal of additional voice-over narration), the same viewer – this time as a student in a classroom – is unlikely to know a great deal about non-market spheres of exchange in the New Guinea highlands and will need help to understand that, for example, a bundle of currency notes given as part of an agonistic *moka* exchange is not 'payment' for some commodity (see Nairn 1974; also Wason 1990). For a television film, issuing a study guide to several million viewers is not a viable option, but for a film intended for classroom use it might be.[9]

Others are not wholly convinced. Ruby argues, for example, that to insist as Heider does upon supporting written materials devalues the film itself, treating it as little more than an audio-visual aid for teaching purposes (Ruby 2000: 3). In doing so, the power of film to communicate in a unique fashion is devalued, rendered subordinate to the primacy of the written text. Ruby and others have proposed a variety of filmic strategies which seek to insert analysis into the film text itself. In Ruby's case, he advocates what he calls *'trompe l'oeil'* realism: a strategy that exploits documentary film's potential to present an apparently realist view of the world and then to subvert it by reflexively drawing attention to the film's own creation. In this way audiences are forced to confront the (inherently analytical) construction of knowledge that the internal narrative conveys (Ruby 2000: Chapters 6 and 10). Coming from very different analytical perspectives, Peter Biella (1988) and Don Rundstrom (1988) both claim to have inserted anthropological analysis directly into the internal narrative of the film in quite formalist ways, through consciously adopting particular camera angles and editing styles. Rundstrom et al.'s film *The Path* (1971), for example, is a highly constructed film about a Japanese tea ceremony which uses colour, camera angle and frame to convey an aesthetic sensibility rather than a realist representation.

Yet another approach, one adopted by a variety of ethnographic filmmakers working broadly within an observational film paradigm, or as MacDougall more accurately calls it 'participatory cinema' (MacDougall 1995), is to encourage the film subjects to speak for themselves, to convey – or be prompted to convey – a broad spread of background information necessary as context for the film's main narrative. Typically this involves asking a film participant to 'show us around' – to describe the immediate physical environment. In a sequence at the start of *To Live With Herds* (1972) David MacDougall asks the main character to 'describe the extent of Jie territory' which he does by pointing out features on the horizon and naming the various other pastoralist groups who live in this arid area of Uganda; similarly in the MacDougalls' *Lorang's Way* (1977), Lorang (a Kenyan Turkana elder) shows the filmmakers around his compound, explaining features as he goes along. The same technique is adopted by John Baily when he asks Amir, a refugee Afghani musician in Pakistan to show him around the single room house he shares with his wife, parents-in-law and children (in *Amir*, 1985). In my own case, I took the principal character of *Raju and His Friends* (1988b) up on to a rooftop and asked him to describe the buildings around us. In all these cases, what is elicited is not merely a catalogue of physical features, but a narrative that uses those buildings and objects as containers for biographical and social knowledge. Amir's itemization of his possessions allows him to reflect on his refugee experience; Raju's geography of the town's religious buildings provides the basis for a discussion of intercommunal relations. Such approaches, while valuable and much used, do not completely obviate the need for additional contextualization, external to the film. For one thing, the social knowledge that forms the bedrock of people's lives, the most taken-for-granted aspects of existence, are by definition the very things that people rarely if ever discuss, even when prompted (see also Holy 1984).

In the end, the argument for and against accompanying study guides is a false one, for several reasons. First, whether a specially prepared study guide exists or not, all documentary films exist in an intertextual relationship with other films and with written literature. It is difficult to conceive of a group of people or a subject of sociological interest that has not received attention from other social researchers. If a film viewer wishes to, or is instructed to, she can find an academic literature that does not necessarily 'support' the film, but which can provide an alternative representation. Film and written text can thus be brought into an analytically constructive dialogue, rather than one passively support- ing the other.[10]

Following on from this, films that are produced by social researchers in the course of their work are inevitably only part of the presentation of their research findings, albeit the major part in some instances. The social researcher will also produce books, papers, dissertations or other written materials which will be directly linked to the film's narrative. Films made by professional filmmakers in the course of their work may undoubtedly contain material of potential sociological interest but that is probably their limit. Social researchers who make films but do no other research on the topic and present no other research findings are behaving as filmmakers, not as social researchers, and their films should be judged in that light. Films presented as the products of social research that are unrelated to any written materials indicate a weakness or aberration in the social research process itself, not a weakness in the medium of film.

A final bypassing of the film and study guide issue, one that addresses the physical separation between the two (which has the consequence that one may be easily available and the other not) is to combine film, study guide, and a whole variety of other textual, audio and visual materials into a single multimedia package. This is the subject of Section 6.4 below. First, however, the issue of image digitization needs to be addressed.

6.4 Databases and digital images

One advantage of image digitization is that it facilitates quick and easy access to copies of visual materials, allowing a researcher to share her results with other researchers and – in some cases – with her research subjects. A researcher studying Javanese classical dance can digitize sequences of her video research footage and email them to an expert on Labanotation (a form of dance and movement notation) on the other side of the world to check that her transcription of movements is correct. A researcher using still photography to explore children's playground

interaction in schools across the European Union can digitize the photographs and press a Photo-CD for each school, allowing the children to
see and comment not only on themselves, but on their European counterparts. Such uses of digital media are strategic and pragmatic, not intended
to deny the materiality of the originals (Chapter 3), nor pretending that
the circulation of images in this way transcends their social embedded-
ness (Chapter 2). It is up to the researcher to choose whether or not to
incorporate these factors self-reflexively in her work (she must also
consider the ethical and copyright issues involved where appropriate –
see Chapter 5.6 and Section 6.5 below).

Beyond these specific and limited forms of presentation, a researcher
may decide to make a wide range of her visual materials available. To
facilitate easy access a catalogue is necessary, and preferably some means
by which a subset of material can be isolated for further study. This is
most effectively accomplished using a computerized database, regardless
of whether the visual materials exist in digital form or not; if they are,
they can be incorporated into the catalogue itself, if not the catalogue can
reference an external source.

I have constructed two such catalogues in recent years, and consulted
many more: the following section rests largely on my experiences. The
more recent catalogue is a database containing digitized copies of my
fieldwork and other photographs. This is intended as a private database
for my own use, to sort and select images for publication or for teaching.
A simple off-the-shelf database package stores low-resolution scans of
the photographs and associated textual information; the high resolution
scans – suitable for sending to publishers – are stored on CD with back-
up archive copies kept on a secure server. As I am the only intended user
and the database is relatively small I can tailor the text entry fields in the
way I find most convenient and implement as many search routines as I
wish. The earlier catalogue, discussed in more detail below (Section
6.4.2), does not contain digital copies of the material but instead references external sources.

6.4.1   *Can computers see?*

With the advent of relatively cheap and powerful personal computing,
more and more scholars in the social sciences are turning to computers to
store and present visual research results. Even if, as is still common,
visual materials are originated on non-digital media – 16mm movie film,
analogue videotape, 35mm still photographic film – all can be transferred
by more or less complex processes to a digital format. Anything that can
be done to analogue media to prepare it for presentation can equally well

be accomplished using digital media, often more easily and cheaply. Still photographs can be cropped or have the contrast enhanced or the exposure corrected, to bring out important detail. Digital video can be edited and subtitled, maps and diagrams can be inserted, and variant versions can be produced for different target audiences. However, the ease with which such mechanical tasks can be accomplished should not hide the fact that all the conceptual issues surrounding image use in the social sciences remain. Indeed, new conceptual problems may be introduced (see Section 6.5 below). Some mechanical tasks associated with analogue media also remain with digital media, chief among them the task of indexing and retrieving images.

While computers provide easy and convenient storage for digitized photographs, movies and other images they do not really understand them. Of course, computers do not understand text either, but language translated into digital text exhibits regularities and patterns that computers can be instructed to recognize and process. Strictly speaking, while a word processor or text editor cannot search an electronic text for the word 'butterfly', it can be instructed to search for a pattern of code. If the human user creates a pattern of code that she understands as the word 'butterfly', typically by typing it on a keyboard, then the computer can attempt to match it. Lacking a mind, a computer correspondingly lacks the concept of 'a butterfly'. A photograph of a butterfly can be scanned into a computer as many times as is wished, but the computer will still understand it only as a disorganized jumble of shapes and colours (actually, it won't even do this – it will recognize only histograms of colour frequency and the like). This presents serious difficulties when attempting to use computers to organize and sort collections of digital images.

Considering only still photographs for the moment, there are two basic approaches that can be taken towards this problem. The first and most simple, though laborious, is to add textual meta-data manually to all images – labels, captions, keywords. Here the computer, and the digital nature of the image and its textual meta-data, merely expedite what can be and is accomplished with a straightforward card index catalogue of photographic prints and negatives. These data are of course external to the image, part of the external narrative that influences the reading of the image. A great deal of forethought must thus be given to how the meta-data are constructed. Some categories of factual information are relatively straightforward – assigning the image a unique reference number, providing details of the date of production, the name of the photographer, and so forth. The problems occur when trying to describe the content,

translating the jumble of colours and shapes into language-coded concepts – a task of which the computer is incapable. I have explored this
issue at length in Chapters 1 and 2 and there is no need to repeat the
arguments here. Suffice it to say that the degree of abstraction and
interpretation encoded in the textual meta-data associated with an image
will constrain later readings of the image.

The second approach to sorting catalogues of visual materials on a
computer is far more direct, and apparently more objective in that the
external narrative of the image is effectively ignored. Although well
beyond the skill of most social researchers, computer vision scientists can
create algorithms that analyse the formal properties of digitized images
in terms of colour, shape, line, texture and brightness (similar algorithms
lie behind the filters used in off-the-shelf image manipulation software,
such as Adobe PhotoShop). Once properties have been assigned a
numerical value – a code pattern – the computer can then search for
similar values in other images, sorting the complete catalogue into
predefined categories or matching one image against another to find
duplicates. These techniques work best with restricted and often false-
colour data (for example, star maps, where visual and non-visual data
such as X-ray radiation are converted into visual form, colour being used
to mark variation in signal intensity) or where the range of variation
between images is extremely narrow (such as iris-recognition scanners
on security devices). Beyond these narrow parameters such systems
have extremely limited autonomy: as the manufacturer of one image-
recognition toolkit states '[the software] can be used to build seemingly
smart programs . . . [but these] do not understand the concepts of an
image in the way a human being does – there are no built-in functions
that "find all images that have butterflies in them" . . . they do not
automatically understand what's important about your data' (Excalibur
Visual RetrievalWare Web site: FAQ). The process of 'understanding
what is important about your data' is, of course, part of the external
narrative surrounding an image, a process that for the social researcher
can only be derived from a social research agenda. Most computer vision
research is driven by mathematical and natural science agendas, which
currently renders it of limited utility, although some art historians are
now becoming involved.[11]

Software also exists to aid in the indexing and classification of digitized
and analogue moving images – the first route discussed above. Meta-
data tags can be attached to sequences or frames of digitized movies to
aid classification and identification. Alternatively, the software can drive
a video playback machine, helping the user to create an index of the tape,
but one which is stored on the computer not the tape. While obviously

slower, as there is only linear not random access to the tape, there is a saving on the large amounts of storage required for digitized movies. The balance of speed against storage cost is insignificant for a few minutes of material, but becomes important when several hours of video footage has been produced in the course of a research project. While some research work in robotics is concerned with the autonomous recognition of moving images – the second route above – the computing power required is still far beyond that available to most qualitative social researchers and the results still far too crude. Even when a computer can automatically scan hours of digitized footage in search of a particular individual, or a sequence of movement, the motivation and intellectual justification for performing such a task will still lie beyond the capabilities of the machine.

6.4.2 The HADDON Catalogue

The HADDON Catalogue of archival ethnographic film and film footage is a Web-based meta catalogue, incorporating information from the catalogues of other institutions, but it contains no actual digitized film footage and only a very small number of digitized frame stills.[12] It brings together information about approximately 1600 films and lengths of film footage located in archives and film museums from around the world (some of this information was sent electronically on request and merely had to be reformatted, but in most cases I and an assistant visited the institutions and transcribed all the relevant records). My overall objective in designing and disseminating the catalogue was to alert scholars and others to the research potential of historical film footage shot by largely amateur filmmakers in the first decades of the twentieth century. For years, visual anthropologists have bemoaned the fact that visual resources are rarely if ever incorporated into the studies of their non-visual colleagues. My hypothesis was that in part this was down to the fact that many scholars – anthropologists, sociologists, historians and others – were simply unaware of the material, particularly the early material, and that even if they suspected its existence it was extremely difficult to locate.

The amount of material which could be documented by the catalogue was potentially vast, and so my first task was to impose some criteria for selection. Although I will return to the issue of potential users (that is the 'audience' for the catalogue) below, a general rule of thumb is that users get greater utility from something that is tightly delineated and where the criteria of inclusiveness are readily apparent. It is better for some users to know immediately that this is exactly the resource they require and for other users to know that it is not, rather than for all users to waste their time discovering this for themselves.

I settled on two selection criteria: one quite specific, if arbitrary, the other far looser. The specific criterion was date: all the material had to have been produced in the 50-year period from 1895 to 1945 (though a few later films were allowed to creep in if they formed part of a series commencing in the specified period). The start date precedes the earliest 'ethnographic' film footage by a year or so, just to be on the safe side;[13] the end date is arbitrary but gives a neat 50-year span, and takes into account a large amount of footage produced as an indirect result of the Second World War.

The second selection criterion was far more open-ended: the material had to be 'ethnographic'. Somewhat to my surprise I found myself setting aside current debates surrounding the nature of ethnographic film and adopting an old-fashioned definition: the film footage should contain a significant number of shots devoted to 'exotic', non-European people, preferably involved in 'exotic' activities. There are several reasons for this choice. Most importantly, this essentially colonialist view of ethnography is contemporaneous with the material I wished to cata- logue. It was shot from this perspective and has to be understood within this perspective. Secondly, I specifically wished to exclude as much European and metropolitan material as possible (an exception was made for East and Central European folkloristic films). While undoubtedly of interest to many anthropologists and sociologists, this material is gen- erally better catalogued and more accessible; for example, in the next few years, the entire British Pathé newsreel will be online. Moreover, there is a vast amount of this material – the Pathé footage alone constitutes some 3000 hours. As the original aim of the HADDON Catalogue was to highlight and make visible obscure amateur footage shot in parts of the world generally regarded as remote by metropolitan centres, it would have been self-defeating to bury it again in a morass of information describing films shot in London or Paris or New York. Finally, if I had adhered to a modern definition of ethnographic film – for example, film shot by a professional anthropologist on the basis of a sustained period of field research and underpinned in shooting and editing by an explicitly anthropological analytical agenda – then very few pre-Second World War films would fit the criteria and the HADDON Catalogue would have been exceedingly short. The focus, therefore, was predominantly and self-consciously on the content of the images, the film as a product, and largely ignored the intentions of the filmmaker or the subsequent recep- tion of the images (Ruby 2000: Chapter 7).

At the same time as devising the selection criteria, my assistant and I were also selecting the potential users. We did this in a number of ways: I drew on my own knowledge of some of the material and we made assumptions about who might use it and how; I drew on my own memory of the times I had met people looking for old footage, what their reasons and aims had been; and we drew on the few scholars who had actually sought out and used archival footage of this type (for example, Vaughan 1991: Chapter 8). Principally, however, we solicited opinions by posting messages on electronic bulletin boards and email lists (the selection of these obviously biased the kinds of potential users who responded). Perhaps unsurprisingly, but worth checking anyway, those who expressed an interest in such a catalogue were either academics and students (in anthropology, sociology, development studies and history) or museum staff and librarians (particularly those in charge of image collections) who wished to extend their service provision.

From those who did respond, we then drew up a tester group: a cross-section of respondents who agreed to answer various questionnaires, do some simple Web-based research tasks, and eventually to test pre-release versions of the catalogue. In order to get a sense of how the catalogue should be best constructed, we identified a number of existing image databases and catalogues on the Web, and then asked the testers to perform assigned tasks and report back to us. We were interested in how easy they had found it to make the searches, what they understood the range of the database to be, and other issues relevant to our own cata-logue. All social researchers expose their ideas and research trajectories to testing at regular intervals during the course of a project, gaining feedback from grant-awarding bodies, dissertation committees, seminar audiences, anonymous reviewers for journals and publishing houses, examiners. Web-based projects and other self-directed and self-published ventures should be no different, though a depressingly large number seem to be lacking in scrutiny and constructive feedback, resulting in poorly conceived projects and poorly presented results. Therefore, in addition to constituting the user-tester group, my assistant and I also approached a number of senior academics to act as an expert panel of advisers, to which we submitted regular progress reports.

The feedback and advice we received determined a number of presentational and operational aspects of the catalogue. The most sig-nificant of these was to steer users away from making a subject-based search across the whole catalogue, such as 'find all the films – from anywhere, at any time – that show pottery manufacture'. The reason for this is straightforward, if frustrating. Although we watched a great deal of the material we subsequently catalogued, we could not possibly watch it all in the time available, still less take detailed notes on the contents of each shot. We relied instead on each holding institution's own descriptions of the films or footage. While this ranged from the highly detailed, to the completely inadequate (typically, a paraphrase of the film's given title, so a film entitled 'Arctic Life' would be described as 'A film about life in the Arctic'), more importantly, in almost every case each film description was written without reference to a uniform keyword list, by different people, at different times and with different objectives. The HADDON Catalogue contains entries for a number of films featuring pottery manufacture, but for some it will be described as 'pottery', for others 'clay', for others 'earthenware'. There is a huge gap between the necessity for keywords – and authority lists for keywords – to make a large database work effectively, and the current lack of any agreement on how moving image descriptions should be compiled. We simply did not have the time or the resources to transcend this gap, as indeed neither do the majority of the institutions from where we obtained the original descriptions.[14]

However, our work with the testers also told us that the majority of users were not interested in using the catalogue in this way. Most already had, or predicted they would have, a specific group of people or geographical region in mind for their research and were interested in finding films about those people or featuring people who lived in that place. By the time a subset of films matching these ethnic or geographical criteria are isolated from the whole of the catalogue, the total number of entries is typically quite small. It is then manageable to read each film description in turn, to see if any mention is made of pottery manufacture, however described. We therefore made the catalogue geography led. Users must first select one of three levels of geographical specificity (sub-continental region, country, region within a country) from pull-down lists to isolate a subset of the catalogue, after which they can either read each entry manually, or further narrow the subset with an additional search (see Figure 6.4). By designing the interface to use pull-down lists of geographical areas we achieved a further aim that had been indicated by our user tests: the need for a positive response. On the first search of the catalogue it is impossible not to achieve a hit, as the pull-down lists are automatically generated by the catalogue entries. Even if, by the end of the search, the hoped-for film has not been found – for example, a film from the 1930s about pottery manufacture in the Indian state of Gujarat – at least the user can have a fair degree of confidence that she has searched the catalogue thoroughly and correctly. Of course, a final null result does not mean that the desired film does not exist, simply that the HADDON Catalogue does not contain a record of it: this is true of all

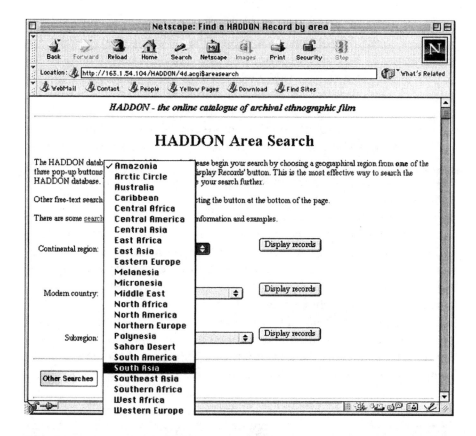

Figure 6.4 Screen shot from HADDON Catalogue Web site, showing selection of geographical area

catalogues, paper and computerized, though the larger a catalogue is – such as a major university library catalogue – the easier it is for users to fall into the representational trap of thinking that it is a perfect and complete index of that which it catalogues.

As I said above, the HADDON Catalogue is a meta-catalogue, drawing together and standardizing subsections of many other catalogues to address a narrow and specific target audience. Its one great weakness is that it does not contain digitized copies of the films themselves. While this is technically possible, it is not practically possible for the simple reason that very few if any film archives have the resources even to contemplate digitizing their collections (and on the budget available to me for the catalogue project, nor could I). Single films and lengths of film footage are, however, increasingly being incorporated into academic and commercial multimedia packages (see Section 6.5.1 below).

Whether digitized copies of their still photographs, movie film and videotape exist or not, the social researcher should also consider the possibility that their own material may one day end up in an archive, for use by future researchers. I said above that my own database of digitized fieldwork photographs was for my own private use and was, therefore, organized and indexed for my own convenience. With an intended audience of one issues of presentation are easy to resolve. The principal problem with archiving visual material is to anticipate the needs of unknown future users, a vast potential audience of unknown interests. The only answer is to provide as much information as possible. A complete account of the external narrative surrounding the images should be provided – when and where they were taken, by whom, with what intention, how they have subsequently been used – together with a grounded reading of the internal narrative, not only covering a description of the image's superficial content but also the basis upon which that reading is founded.

Many of my field photographs, for example, depict aspects of Indian Jain ritual and ceremonial life, but my reading of the content rests in part on my understanding of Jain social organization. Figure 6.5 (a repeat of Figure 2.14, printed at the end of Chapter 2), depicts a woman in a sari leaning over to serve something to a smiling man, seated in a row of

Figure 6.5   A fieldwork photograph. Jamnagar, India, 1983

men. It depicts a particular named woman, serving a particular food item to a particular named man, at a particular named feast held at the conclusion of a named period of fasting, on a particular date, in a particular place. It depicts a Jain laywoman honouring a Jain layman in recognition of an austerity he has performed. It depicts a reversal of status with a woman (not a man) gifting food to a man, rather than preparing it as a domestic duty. It depicts ties between migrant Jains in the UK (the woman is British) and India. At each level, the reading of the image becomes increasingly linked to my own sociological analysis – more interpretative and less reliant purely on the internal narrative, as it were. If intended for archival deposit, I should therefore make the basis of my interpretation clear in my description of the image.[15]

6.5 Multimedia projects

In an oft-cited 1945 article, Vannevar Bush, then President of the Carnegie Institution, envisaged a hypothetical machine – the 'memex', 'a device in which an individual stores all his books, records, and communications, and which is mechanized so that it may be consulted with exceeding speed and flexibility' (Bush 1995: Section 6). Once a user had stored (on microfilm) all the relevant material, and indexed it, he would use a series of mechanical levers and dry photographic processes to create 'trails' through the information, forging links between relevant items. Bush envisaged the 'memex' primarily as a research tool, though he also describes how a researcher could demonstrate a 'trail' to another party – the example he gives is of proving the technological superiority of the short Turkish bow over the English long bow used in the Crusades (1995: Section 7).

Today, despite the claims that Bush's device intellectually prefigured the World Wide Web, users of the Web still have no easy way to link items of 'found' information in the way that Bush envisaged, short of constructing a crude list of 'bookmarks' or 'favorites' in their Web browser. Users can, however, construct their own Web sites (or stand-alone multimedia corpuses written on removable media such as CD-ROMs) which do permit a greater finesse of linkages. Within their own Web site or other corpus, links between sound, text and image files can be constructed at will, although again such links are largely presented as givens to the user. Consequently, although many multimedia applications within the social sciences (Web-based and free-standing) often have a strong orientation towards promoting and facilitating research by users – allowing them access to unedited text, raw video footage, and so on –

they can equally well be seen as presentational applications, presenting materials and interpretation in a form that has already been pre-structured, implicitly or explicitly.

Nevertheless, one of the advantages of computer-based media is the access it provides to images, and the ability to promote research parity between sound, text and image. There is a price to be paid for this: in the digital world of bits-not-atoms, all bits are equal, but at the cost of the loss of the unique materiality of the atoms. The material difficulty (and economic cost) of publishing large numbers of high quality photographs in a written monograph, and the material impossibility of incorporating moving images or sound on the page are transcended, but in doing so an aspect of their unique materiality is lost.[16]

Nevertheless, if creator and user of a product are both aware that they are dealing with copies of images, texts and other original source material and aware that part of the external narrative of these objects has been stripped away, then computer-based multimedia carries a high potential for the presentation of research results to particular kinds of audiences.[17]

In a recent paper, Michael Fischer and David Zeitlyn note that there are several broad models for computer-based multimedia (Fischer and Zeitlyn n.d.). One is strongly time-based and sequential, similar in many ways to a film. For the audience, viewing it is a largely passive experience. A sequence of images, text, graphics and other items follow in predetermined order, although the sequences may be organized into chunks which can be viewed repeatedly or in a variant order. Typical examples would be a marketing presentation to a group of clients using a set of PowerPoint slides or a software 'guide' which uses animation to demonstrate the features of a piece of software. A second model is closer in organization to a book. A series of objects (such as text files) are linked in an overarching sequence, but the user has the opportunity to explore non-sequential links ('hyperlinks'), either to material outside the main body of the text – the equivalent of footnotes – or to other occurrences of similar material – akin to sequentially reading all the page references to a given term in a book's index, without reading the intervening material. Fischer and Zeitlyn point out that this model gives a 'more powerful' book, one which can incorporate moving images and sound. Visual anthropologists have increasingly been attracted to the possibilities this model opens up for adding visual and textual 'footnotes' to ethnographic films. In either case, the model is one of a principal text with associated subtexts.

A third model, and one that perhaps best exploits the medium's potential, is what Fischer and Zeitlyn term the 'layered' model. In this model, no object or set of objects is necessarily primary, nor does the object or object-set necessarily have any definitive organizational structure or predetermined sequencing. Instead, a set of objects are linked to one another in (metaphorical) layers – a group of photographs, a set of fieldnotes – and also linked to objects in other layers: a photograph of an individual in one layer is linked to a genealogical diagram in which the individual features in another layer, and also to half a dozen fieldnotes that concern that individual in yet another layer. The linkages within the layers may be tight and sequential (for example, all the frames in a length of digitized film footage may be viewed randomly but are probably best appreciated in order) or relatively loosely linked (for example photographs of all the inhabitants of a village could be clustered into household or kin groups, but there is probably little to be gained by viewing the photographs in any predetermined order).

This last, the most 'open' model, is potentially the most powerful and useful for the social researcher, but equally the most fraught with potential difficulties – most of which relate to audience and audience use of the final product. In the first 'marketing presentation' model the audience is known or categorizable and their lines of enquiry relatively predictable: how will the launch of a new product affect next quarter's market share? what are the key features of this new version of the operating system? The familiar model of a lecture or talk by an expert aids the audience in making sense of similar material presented in a new medium. The second 'book' model also allows the audience to use familiar concepts, such as footnotes, appendixes and indexes, to navigate an initially unfamiliar product. In contrast, the third layered model makes new demands on the user by presenting a network of information rather than a narrative flow, which places a far greater onus on the user to steer their own course. We may not think serially, as Fischer and Zeitlyn point out, but 'we like to think that we think serially'. Dudley and Petch, who collaborated with Fischer and Zeitlyn on a museum-based multimedia project, recognize in reflecting on their experiences that this type of multimedia is an 'infant forum' for the presentation of material, one whose manipulation is still relatively unfamiliar (Dudley and Petch n.d.).

If the strictures advanced by critics such as Ruby for the production of ethnographic film (for example, Ruby 2000: Chapter 10) have any validity, then they apply equally to the production of computer-based multimedia. Not only should the source materials have been created or selected by a social researcher within the context of a carefully-conceived research project, but they should be assembled into a multimedia product that is as clearly focussed. A difficult line has to be trodden in this respect with regard to freedom and authority. Multimedia, especially of the 'layered' type, offers a great deal of freedom to the user to explore their own lines of enquiry – indeed, this is the medium's strength. On the other hand, if the user has little or no sense of the research frame within which the project lies, nor any sense of the authority of the product's creator to compile the product, then it is difficult for the user to gauge the validity of the choices that she makes in navigating through the materials. If all authority is abrogated or concealed in the name of the freedom of consumer choice, then the user has no incentive to even bother exploring the product. Simply being told that a multimedia CD-ROM will help the user 'find out about' or 'explore' the issue of homelessness, or indigenous rights, or tribal art is akin to being told to go into a library and start reading.[18]

Following Ruby's suggestions (see Section 6.3.1), one clear way forward is the path of reflexivity. If a social researcher has a specific argument to make, one that she considers objective, universal and which will brook no gainsaying, then computer-based multimedia is probably not the best medium. If a social researcher has an argument to put forward, but is aware that there are variant interpretations of what is presented as supporting evidence (almost always the case with visual materials), then she can usefully employ multimedia to state her own case but also to outline the alternative interpretations and provide access to the raw materials to allow the user to test them all. In fact, this is almost always the case as soon as images are involved as an integral part of an argument, rather than merely as redundant illustrations.[19]

6.5.1   *Interacting with the Yanomamö*

A clear example is provided by Peter Biella and colleagues in a stimulating multimedia version of an explicitly visual product, in this case an elderly but renowned ethnographic film extensively used in North American anthropology teaching (Biella, Chagnon and Seaman 1997). The CD-ROM *Yanomamö Interactive* has at its centre Tim Asch and Napolean Chagnon's 1975 film, *The Ax Fight*. The film itself is unusual in a number of ways, not least because as originally constructed it is a self-conscious multimedia piece in its own right. At its core lies around 11 minutes of unedited film footage depicting a fight between two groups of Yanomamö Indians – an Amazonian group living on the Venezuelan-Brazilian border. This footage opens the film, after the opening titles and a brief snatch of narration, and is then followed by four further sequences. First there is a short audio sequence over a blank screen in which the anthropologist and filmmakers discuss what they have just witnessed; then some of the original footage is replayed, but using frame stills and slow motion, as the narration describes the causes and progress of the fight; then there is a series of rostrum camera shots of genealogical diagrams, showing how each of the participants in the fight are related to each other; finally a section entitled 'a final edited version' replays the fight sequence again, without commentary but edited to provide a smooth clean sequence.

The aim of the film is to build up a number of layers, commencing with raw 'reality' as the film crew experienced it (they had no forewarning of the fight and filmed with no preparation from a distant vantage point), which is then overlain with layers of personal and sociological detail and analysis. Viewers of this linear, time-based medium have to carry a great deal in their heads as the film progresses, in order to use it as a basis for reading the 'final edited version'. As Biella notes in the CD-ROM version's introductory essay:

> Despite its effort at precision, to many viewers [the middle] section of the film is unclear. The confusion comes in part from the poor visual quality of the genealogical diagrams and a series of clumsy cuts and pans. More than this, the argument itself is difficult . . . before viewers can even begin to understand the argument they must first associate different faces in the film with genealogical icons, and comprehend the genealogical relationships between the faces. The latter task by itself is difficult to master. (Biella 1997)

In short, the potential of what the film could achieve is hindered by the original medium; the multimedia CD-ROM version by contrast, opens up a non-linear space within which the detail can be absorbed at the user's own pace, and the arguments which rest upon that detail can be fully explored. The CD-ROM contains a complete digital version of the film, which can be played right through but also accessed at a number of cue points. Yanomamö Interactive is not, however, based upon the book model of multimedia described above – the film as a core text with a number of visual and textual footnotes. While the film is central, other materials – textual and visual – are included as additional layers, linked both to the film and to each other. These layers can be read in their own right, partly in order to test a neo-Darwinian hypothesis advanced by Chagnon and Bugos (1979, also contained on the CD-ROM) concerning the role of kin in disputes. Biella presents some variant forms of this hypothesis in his introductory essay and suggests ways of using the filmic, photographic and textual material on the CD-ROM to weigh one up against another. He also suggests ways in which photographs of individuals and their biographical and genealogical data can be used to create a number of internal narratives that interrogate the original film, possibly to the extent of undermining the film's own narrative. For example, a narrative concerning the activities of women in Yanomamö society and their role in disputes can be 'recovered' from the film, despite the fact that the film's narration makes little mention of women in an active capacity, and the camera generally depicts them as reacting to rather than initiating action.

Technically, the construction of these narratives are made possible by embedding a variety of links in the textual and visual materials. While there are a very large number of such links, they inevitably serve to constrain and channel the user's navigation of the product. Within the textual materials – the full narration of the film, additional commentaries, associated essays – the links are embedded in a specific and self-evident way: clicking on an individual's name in a text in one window may cause a photograph of the individual to be displayed in another window, or a genealogical diagram to be redrawn with that individual at its centre. Within the visual materials, the links are less evident. Of the many persons and objects within the film and the associated still photographs, Biella and colleagues have chosen to tag individuals – men, women, children – rather than, say, items of material culture. A click on an individual's name in the narration window cues the film to the appropriate point and identifies the individual on screen with a red cross (see Figure 6.6). A click on the word 'hammock' or 'ax' does not produce the same result. This is not a criticism of the multimedia product, merely a reiteration of the point made above (Section 6.4.1) that while text is easily and automatically transformed into hypertext such that all text strings can be matched to all equivalent text strings, computers have great difficulty in dealing with 'hypervisuality' matching one image to another, or automatically linking text string to visual representation.

There is a great deal more that could be said about the value (and limitations) of computer-based multimedia for the presentation of visual research materials. Briefly, *Yanomamö Interactive* succeeds because the specific visual and textual materials are selected and interlinked with a clear aim and purpose. The authors have also considered their audience: they are explicit in stating what materials were used, and what thought lay behind the project – reflexivity – and in acknowledging that those encountering this 'infant forum' (Dudley and Petch n.d.) need clear and straightforward guidance to aid in their reading.

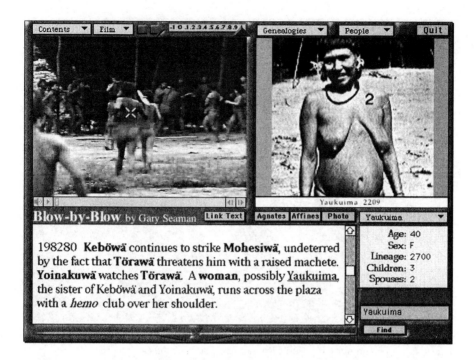

Figure 6.6 Screen shot from *Yanomamö Interactive* (1997); clicking on an individual's name identifies them in the film footage. Reproduced with permission of Harcourt Brace & Company.

6.6 Copyright

> I get very angry when I see some of the products that are advertised . . . they're stealing the Princess's image, they're stealing her dignity. (Trustee of the Diana, Princess of Wales, Memorial Fund quoted in the *Electronic Telegraph*, Issue 1089, 19 May 1998)

For an image to be stolen, it must belong to someone in the first place. Shortly after Diana, Princess of Wales, was killed in a car crash in August 1997 images of her began to appear on thousands of memorial objects for sale – mugs, plates, plaques – as well as in innumerable print publications commemorating her life. These photographic images presumably 'belonged' to the photographers who had created them or to the agencies for which they worked. They did not 'belong' to Diana or her heirs, unless they of course had taken them or legally acquired them. But later in 1997 the Diana, Princess of Wales, Memorial Fund sought to register the image of Diana as a trademark, filing around 50 images as samples of this 'trademark' with the British Trade Marks Registry (the trademark

Figure 6.7   Frame still from Paul Henley's film *Faces in the Crowd* (1994),
showing Diana, Princess of Wales, on a visit to Solihull, West Midlands.
Photographer: Paul Henley

application was later transferred to the executors of Diana's will). While single images of individuals have successfully been registered as trademarks – for example, a distinctive image of the racing driver Damon Hill looking through his visor – the large number of Diana images submitted appeared to be a claim for all and any image of Diana to be covered, preventing almost any use of her image from being used without payment of royalties to her estate (*Electronic Telegraph*, Issue 1329, 14 January 1999). On the back of this, the Fund embarked on legal action against the American manufacturers of a commemorative 'Diana' doll, claiming that the company was 'exploiting her identity' (*Electronic Telegraph*, Issue 1089, 19 May 1998).

The case served to worry many people in the media that merely creating and reproducing an image may not guarantee ownership of that image. It seems relevant largely to representations of celebrities, those deemed likely to have a financial interest in the use of their representations and, with some exceptions, few academics routinely conduct research with such images. More down-to-earth issues of copyright still remain important however. Many images that the social researcher will be using in the course of research will have been created by the researcher herself, and consequently she will normally own the copyright and have relative freedom in her use of the images (although see the earlier discussion in Chapter 5.6 on image ethics). However, any images used that come from other sources may well be subject to copyright and permission will have to be sought for their use in any publication, including 'publication' on a Web site.

Permission generally consists of two aspects: seeking permission from the copyright holder to publish the image or to screen a film, and payment of any reproduction or screening fee. In addition, the copyright holder may request (and be entitled to if it is a condition of the permission) a copy of the publication together with an acknowledgement in the publication, or film programme. Finally, the user normally has to pay whatever reproduction or handling charges are involved in making the image available.

Normally, for educational uses reproduction fees are waived or a purely nominal charge is made. Researchers requesting reproduction rights should make it explicit in their letter of request that the publication (or Web site) is academic not commercial (assuming this is in fact the case). Reproduction costs and handling charges are, however, fixed and inevitable costs incurred by the individual or organization that holds the copyright and are not normally waived.

The normal procedure is to identify the image or footage that is required and then to write to the copyright holder explaining what the image is required for and either requesting a copy of the image or permission to reproduce it from another source (for example, a book plate). A line should be added requesting that reproduction fees, if any, might be waived as the image will be used in a purely academic or educational context. Larger museums and archives normally have their own form to complete, covering much or all of the above.

There are, needless to say, many complications that can arise. Most commonly, the copyright holder may not be the individual or institution holding the image. In cases where book plate reproduction is sought, the first course of action is normally to contact the publisher if no other details are given. Alternatively, the caption for the image (or possibly the acknowledgements page of the book) will indicate the source of the image, such as a museum or art gallery. In the case of some film archives the archive acts as a holding institution for other people's material and does not have copyright in the films (for example, the UK's National Film and Television Archive does not own copyright in the majority of the films it holds).[20] In cases such as these, the reproduction is normally obtained from the holding institution – and appropriate charges paid; the permission to use the image – and again, any rights or reproduction fees – are negotiated with the copyright holder. It is sometimes the case that the copyright holder cannot be located – especially if she or he were an amateur image maker who deposited the material long ago and has since died or moved on. When images such as these are used in academic publications, the publishers may cover themselves with a standard form of words in the book's introductory matter along the lines of 'Every effort has been made to trace all the copyright holders [of the images in this book], but if any have been overlooked, or if any additional information can be given, the publishers will be pleased to make the necessary amendments at the first opportunity' (Evans and Hall 1999: xviii).

Protecting one's own copyright in images is quite a different matter. For example, it is not wise to publish high resolution images on the Web without any form of digital or manual watermarking (see Chapter 3.5.1),[21] although in practice most network operators (the IT specialist who oversees a network of computers) would probably raise objections to this on account of the storage costs for such large files – several megabytes for photographic quality reproduction. Generally, the low resolution of 72 d.p.i. (dots per inch) which is all that is required for on-screen viewing is too poor quality for ink-on-paper publication.

Equally unwise is to loan a photographic print to a friend or colleague for publication without ensuring that appropriate credit will be given (in addition, publishers often have part of a book's production budget set aside for reproduction fees – the front cover image, for example – and it may be worth asking if a reproduction fee is available). Even if an image is not originally published on the Web it may easily find its way there through unauthorized scanning, after which it is extremely difficult both to monitor and to prevent unauthorized reproduction. The best an image maker can do if she sees one of her images used on a Web site without permission is to contact the site's owner and either ask for the image to be removed or for appropriate credit to be made (a request for a fee is unlikely to be met). If that brings no satisfactory result then the researcher should contact the Web host, the company that provides storage for the site's files and access to them. Many Web hosting companies, especially the larger ones with publicly quoted stock, are very sensitive to allegations of Web misuse. Of course, many amateur photographers and film- or videomakers are quite happy to see their work more widely distributed, or are simply not bothered about issues of copyright especially given that there is rarely any financial advantage to be gained. Some anthropologists, however – including myself – are concerned about the ethical implications of allowing images to flow freely through the networks, especially when their content becomes divorced from their context. There is a potential for misuse, for example with images of tribal peoples when unwanted or misleading emphasis could subsequently be placed on their nudity or apparent savagery (see also Chapter 5.6 on ethics).

Notes

1　The extent to which clear communication is effected or to which presenters of research consciously consider their audiences at all is, of course, extremely variable. My argument here is not so much that social researchers should learn to present their results more effectively, simply that whether they are conscious of it or not, there *is* an audience.

2　Martinez cites several 'open text' films as examples; the qualities they share include reflexivity – an acknowledgement within the film that a filmic representation is being constructed (see Section 6.3) – and narrativity (see Section 6.2.1).

3　The Finnish photographer Jorma Puranen has actively sought to liberate the long-silenced voices of archival images. By rephotographing images from the 1880s of Sámi indigenous people, printing them on plexiglass, placing the panels in the northern Finnish landscape and then photographing the resulting installations, Puranen has loosened the constraining narrative of 'races and types' photography of the late nineteenth century, as well as the narrative of 'archival interest', and has effected an 'imaginary homecoming' for these long-dead Sámi (see Edwards 1997: 72–3; Puranen 1999).

4　For another account of selecting images for academic publication, see Harper 1987a: 7–9; see also Wright 1999: 97–105.

5　Harper also stresses that the assignment of images to any of the four categories depends on the overall research frame, not properties inherent in the images themselves. The other two categories, which I do not discuss here and which do not necessarily rely on viewing the images in sequence, are the scientific mode – images treated primarily as evidence or data; and the reflexive mode – images that mediate the relationship between social researcher and subject, as in photo-elicitation (see Chapter 4.4).

6　For Grady, rendering sociology more appealing to students is not a trivial issue. Following Becker (1986) he argues that the reproduction of the discipline is in crisis, producing students – and hence future teachers – who have little appreciation of what he calls the craft of sociology (cf. Epstein 1967) and who are 'insecure, deeply unsure of their work and their voice, and more concerned with justifying their projects than with carrying them out' (Grady 1991: 37, n. 5). Producing visual narratives instead of written essays from secondary sources, Grady argues, would allow students to develop these craft skills and consequently a confident analytical voice.

7　In my experience, some of the least engaging ethnographic films I have seen are those that were edited from research footage by their makers who had not at the time intended to make 'a movie' but were unwisely encouraged to do so afterwards. See also Barbash and Taylor (1997: 287) on planning for the audience in advance of shooting.

8 These debates are also found with regard to the internal narrative or content of the film itself. Proponents of the direct cinema and *cinéma-vérité* movements of the 1960s and 1970s generally eschewed voice-over narration and interviews, claiming that the flow of live action alone should be strong enough to sustain the film and communicate what the filmmaker wished to say; see also the debate surrounding Gardner's *Forest of Bliss* in Chapter 2.2.1.

9 It is one thing for a filmmaker to decide to write a study guide, another to decide what to put in it. Some I have seen are little more than a background ethnographic essay of a largely factual nature – details of economy, habitat, marriage practices and so forth. This approach would seem to indicate that the film is intended as little more than an illustration of these facts. Instead I would suggest that a study guide should include a full transcript of the film's dialogue, camera angles and editing cuts, together with an essay outlining the circumstances of the film shoot. In this way a viewer can appreciate the film as film – as a constructed representation, as well as the film as ethnography – as a representation of particular people.

10 The catalogues for the Royal Anthropological Institute's ethnographic film library (Woodburn 1982; Willson 1990) contain a list of recommended reading for each film.

11 In Britain for example, the Computers and History of Art Group (CHArt) encourages research and discussion in this area and organizes annual conferences. See also Frauenfelder (1997) for an interesting overlap of agendas.

12 The HADDON Catalogue is available through the Web at < www.rsl.ox.ac/isca/haddon/ >.

13 At least for the early footage, my criterion was that material had to be shot on location, in the field, and hence the catalogue includes A.C. Haddon's Torres Strait Island footage (1898). Earlier material of some ethnographic relevance, though shot away from the subjects' normal location, would include Thomas Edison's Sioux 'Ghost Dance' footage (1894), Felix Louis Regnault's Wolof potter footage (1895), and the Lumière brothers' twelve shorts of Asante women dancing (1897); see Jordan 1992 for further details.

14 The current draft of *Archival Moving Image Materials: a Cataloguing Manual* (Balkansky et al. 1999) puts the position well. While devoting an extraordinary amount of detailed discussion to how cataloguers should differentiate between types of production credit, or how they should deal with films released with different titles in different countries, for the 'Summary' field devoted to a description of the film or television show's content it merely says 'Give a summary of the content of a work. The object of a summary is give the viewer a good idea of what to expect when he or she views the work, thus avoiding unnecessary handling of the film or video.' The brief examples given all focus on content, except for one that mentions the film includes

'close-up magnified photography'. While the descriptions of a film's content are at best inadequate at many institutions, and hence in the HADDON Catalogue, descriptions of a film's form and structure are almost entirely absent (see also Usai 1994: 48).

15 It would be hypocritical of me to pretend that this is anything other than a wish list, a statement of good intention. While my photographic collection is relatively well-organized, like many other visual anthropologists, I spend my academic life surrounded by cans of disorganized film footage and cassettes of unindexed videotape. Ideally, when budgeting time and resources for a research project an allocation should be made for archiving the materials at the conclusion of the project. Perhaps funding agencies should even insist on this, as the UK's Economic and Social Research Council currently does for quantitative and qualitative (but essentially textual) datasets.

16 In an article on computer-based music, Georgina Born includes some illustrations that are actually photographs of printed pages of an in-house computer software manual (Born 1997: Figures 7.3–7.7, pages 147, 149). Howard Morphy and I, the editors of the volume in which the article appeared, had some difficulty in persuading one or two readers of the manuscript that these images should not be replaced simply by a retyping of the text of the pages (their manifest content). Born's argument in part concerned the fact that these manuals were fluid and often incomplete documents needing handwritten annotations by those who were learning the programs from them and her photographs of the pages showed such annotations. Moreover, the poor quality of the manuals – dog-eared and blurred from much copying – was another aspect of their materiality, and a manifestation of the gap that she perceived between the supposedly pure and universal logic of the programming code and the highly socially-embedded circumstances of its communication. Mechanically reproducing the unique documents through a photograph was the closest we could come to communicating some of that unique materiality, where the latent content of the pages was foregrounded by Born's sociological analysis.

17 Strictly speaking, 'multimedia' is a misnomer, the computer being the single medium through which a number of sound, text and image files are displayed. The term acts as a useful reminder however of the media-specific objects – photographs, audiotapes, 16mm films – that have been brought together on the computer. The term is so omnipresent and associated so closely with a new physical object, the CD-ROM or DVD, that I shall continue to use it here.

18 I have written about these issues elsewhere, somewhat overstating the arguments against multimedia, particularly for educational use, to stimulate debate. See Banks 1994 and Biella 1994.

19 This variant interpretation reflexivity model is well-demonstrated in 'Ancestors in Africa', a largely text-based multimedia product by David Zeitlyn (Fischer and Zeitlyn 1999). Zeitlyn's project, together with several others, forms part of a package under the title 'Experience-Rich Anthropology', distributed

widely in Britain in 1999–2000 on CD-ROM. Many of the other projects include far more visual materials than the one I discuss here, but this nonetheless provides a good model.

20 By contrast, stock-shot libraries (film clips, normally out-takes from completed productions) and picture or photo libraries, have normally cleared the copyright on everything they hold, enabling the user to make a 'one-stop shop' and pay a single amalgamated fee. However, such libraries are normally commercial and oriented to the needs of commercial customers, making them expensive for the student or academic researcher.

21 Terence Wright raises the interesting point that a photograph taken from one source and subsequently manipulated digitally by another photographer or artist could be considered to be a new image, unconstrained by the original owner's copyright (Wright 1999: 164–5). This situation would be compounded when the 'original' was taken by a digital camera, there being no original source apart from an easily manipulable string of digital code to prove where the altered copy had come from. In fact, software similar to that used for digital watermarking is available that can tag electronic documents of all kinds and then indicate subsequent alterations.

7

Perspectives on visual research

Figure 7.1 'Hide and Seek'. Undated postcard perhaps printed in Germany, from a photograph almost certainly taken in India. Photographer unknown

7.1 The state of visual research

I opened Chapter 1 by mentioning that, despite the claims of some practitioners that they are not sufficiently recognized by their colleagues, visual research in the social sciences seems in quite good shape. The numerous examples mentioned in the chapters that followed bear testimony to that, as does a great deal of second-order analytical literature based upon visual research.[1] Specifically methodological discussions are, as noted, rather more scarce and tend to be confined to specialist journals devoted to visual anthropology or visual sociology – preaching to the converted, as it were. Nevertheless, the production and use of visual images in empirical, field-based research needs to be understood as one and only one of several methods that a social researcher might employ. Typically, this would be in the course of some long-term ethnographic research. Yet a recent book on general ethnographic practice – explicitly subtitled 'a way of seeing' – contains only three short passages related to visual research (Wolcott 1999). The first recounts an early but unfounded fear that visual methods might pose a threat: 'in the 1950s . . . still photography and filmmaking were carving such inroads that it seemed they might *become* forms of ethnography rather than mere tools in fieldwork' (1999: 216, emphasis in original); the second is a passage wondering rhetorically what ethnographic filmmakers do 'when they discover, all too late, that they do not have at hand . . . the film record called for and must make do with whatever is available' (1999: 2247); the third is a warning about collecting too much data: 'Audio- and videotape recording present the same problem [as voice-activated word processors] by making it too easy to record too much, too indiscriminately' (1999: 269).

The authors of another, older but very popular book on ethnographic practice (this time from an educational studies and medical sociology background), devote a little more attention to film and video recording but overall conclude that it is rarely worth the effort. Like Wolcott, Hammersley and Atkinson worry that video can record 'more data than one can ever actually use' and that subsequent transcription will be extremely time consuming. Worse, the 'data' collected may be *too* precise: 'detailed pictures of individual trees are provided but no sense gained of the shape of the forest' (1983: 161). They do admit, however, that 'used selectively' visual recording could aid as a check on fieldnotes or to augment other forms of data collection.

What are we to make of this? None of the passages from Wolcott's book seem terribly positive and it seems as though he considers cameras merely to be recording devices (but be careful not to do too much recording) of rather limited utility (you may not have the shot you want). On the other hand, such casual asides could also indicate that the use of visual media is so well embedded in social research practice (in Wolcott's case, ethnographic studies of schools and schooling) that it is hardly worth comment. Similarly, Hammersley and Atkinson don't appear to think very much needs to be said about visual methodology in social research. To some extent it is normalized, a method that some social researchers use to gather or present 'data', occasionally to good effect. It can cause some problems of a practical, technical nature, but the visual *qua* visual is not inherently problematic in their opinion.

This book takes the opposite stance. The production of images by social researchers cannot be understood apart from the consumption of images by everyone – social researchers, academics more generally and, of course, the subjects of social research themselves. All visual images, whatever their source, are inherently complex and problematic – messages without codes, says Barthes of photographs (cited in MacDougall 1998b: 64) – yet at the same time they are an omnipresent aspect of almost all human social relations. While modern Euro-America may particularly privilege the visual, that – properly understood – would seem grounds to concentrate on the visual rather than avoid it, or relegate its study to the margins of social research.

7.2 The place of visual research

Must then all social research involve a consideration of visual images? Clearly not, though even the most quantitative of research projects will generally present a number of tables, diagrams and other figures in the presentation of results (Chapter 2.3). On the other hand, it is also difficult to imagine how social research could proceed using nothing other than visual methods. The principal academic disciplines that employ field-based research methods are inherently language- and text-based in their construction and execution of research programmes (whether the subjects of research are literate or not). Even within the broad and rather vague category of ethnographic research methods there are many different research practices that can be employed, each providing the opportunity to gain further insight into the field of human social relations and each with its own strengths and weaknesses. Visual research, whether conducted through the creation of images or the study of images, or both, is no different. It has to be seen as only one technique to be employed by social researchers, more appropriate in some contexts, less so in others.

In field research methods courses that I have been involved in teaching, some topics are far more popular than others with the students. The visual methods session – unsurprisingly – is very popular, the ethnomusicological research session far less so. When we have asked students why they failed to attend the ethnomusicological sessions, the standard response is that they don't intend to look at music in the field. Our rejoinder is that when they discover a group of people in the world who have no music and no opinions about the music of others they should let us know. Field-based research is unpredictable in many ways, however carefully a research strategy has been devised, and it seems foolhardy to remain wilfully ignorant of any particular field methodology. Finding a group of people in the world who have no conception of the visual, no use for visual images, and no interest in the visual images of others seems improbable to say the least. The value of visual methods is not confined to studies of overtly visual phenomena, nor is it simply the provenance of those who consider themselves to be good photographers or who would like to make movies. Many of the research projects mentioned in the course of this book could probably have been accomplished without any consideration of the visual at all, although they would have turned out very differently. Researchers such as Lila Abu-Lughod and Veena Das, mentioned in Chapter 4.3.1, are interested in issues of modernity and national identity, not television, yet the study of television soap opera in Egypt and India is one way to get closer to those issues. Visual research methods are, or should be, a step along the way: a means to an end, not an end in themselves.

7.3 The nature of visual research

Throughout this book I have made very little explicit reference to what is often called 'theory', either in the abstract or through discussion of particular theories and their applicability to the study and use of visual images; while I do not intend to begin now, the absence warrants some discussion. As mentioned above, the study and use of visual images is only of value within broader sociological research enterprises, rather than as ends in themselves. To that extent then, the overall theoretical frame of the research project will influence the orientation taken towards any visual images encountered or produced. But it is not simply a question of devising a theoretical frame, and then selecting certain methods to accomplish the objectives set by that frame.

While some social researchers apparently understand the term 'method' and cognates to refer exclusively to practical, hands-on activities (such as different types of interviewing or survey techniques), this is not my understanding. 'Method' is inseparable from 'theory' and 'analysis', and in the human sciences no method that seeks to document or, better, engage with the field of human social relations can be performed in a theoretical vacuum, even taking the term 'theory' very loosely indeed. But that does not give priority to the theoretical or analytical framework. For humanistic reasons if for no other, research that involves human subjects requires their co-operation if not participation and, while they may not be educated or well-informed about the latest intellectual fashions, they know more about their own lives than a visiting researcher can ever hope to. Social research has to be an engagement, not an exercise in data collection. That engagement is bound to be partial and bound to include elements of serendipity: contexts, events and social alignments that could not have been predicted or foreseen (Pieke 2000). Swooping god-like into other people's lives and gathering 'data' (including visual 'data') according to a predetermined theoretical agenda strikes me not simply as morally dubious but intellectually flawed. Following on from this, no 'method' can be applied in a social vacuum. If nothing else, one of the lessons that postmodernism has taught the social sciences is that social research is itself a social activity, necessitating a meta-analysis and hence an understanding of the processes of social research itself (Becker 1998). The first three chapters of this book sought to highlight everyday assumptions within the social research-producing societies of Euro-America about what images are, what they mean, and what we do with them, as a necessary prelude to the field and archival projects discussed in the following chapters.

This is not to advocate a position of crippling self-doubt, of casting the social researcher adrift on a restless sea of uncertainty and contingency. Quite the contrary, my position stems from a resolutely and unabashedly empirical approach to the visual image. Images exist materially in the world, are involved in particular and specific human social relations. Their meanings are historically and socially embedded, told through their internal and external narratives. They have authors and consumers, they are attributed with agency and affect the agency of others. All these features are discernible, documentable, and can be isolated for analysis and comparison. The practitioners of visual social research who bemoan the lack of attention paid to their labours are, in some ways, missing the point. Visual images are ubiquitous in the lives and work of those who study and those who are studied. There is no lack of attention paid to the visual, merely a failure of perspective.

Figure 7.2   Frame still from *Raju and his Friends* (1988). Children from the village of Beraja, Gujarat, India, waving goodbye to the film crew. Photographer: Andy Jillings

Note

1 The contribution from cultural studies is particularly prominent, although this is often not based on empirical field research, nor is it normally concerned with image-making on the part of the analyst: see for example Evans and Hall 1999, Jenks 1995, Mirzoeff 1999.

Further resources

A list of useful addresses, relevant journals and online resources is provided on the Web site that accompanies this book.

Go to: < www.rsl.ox.ac.uk/isca/vismeth >

Bibliography

Abu-Lughod, Lila (1995) 'The objects of soap opera: Egyptian television and the cultural politics of modernity', in D. Miller (ed.), *Worlds Apart: Modernity Through the Prism of the Local*. London: Routledge. pp. 190–210.

Ames, Michael (1992) *Cannibal Tours and Glass Boxes: the Anthropology of Museums*. Vancouver: University of British Columbia Press.

Appignanesi, Richard and Zarate, Oscar (1979) *Freud for Beginners*. London: Writers and Readers Publishing Cooperative.

Asch, Patsy and Connor, Linda (1994) 'Opportunities for "double-voicing" in ethnographic film', *Visual Anthropology Review*, 10 (2): 14–27.

Asch, Timothy (1992) 'The ethics of ethnographic film-making', in P.I. Crawford and D. Turton (eds), *Film as Ethnography*. Manchester: Manchester University Press. pp. 196–204.

Aufderheide, Patricia (1995) 'The Video in the Villages project: videomaking with and by Brazilian Indians', *Visual Anthropology Review*, 11 (2): 83–93.

Babb, Lawrence A. (1981) 'Glancing: visual interaction in Hinduism', *Journal of Anthropological Research*, 37 (4): 387–401.

Balkansky, Arlene et al. (1999 [draft]) *Archival Moving Image Materials: a Cataloging Manual [2nd Edition]*. Washington, DC: Library of Congress, Motion Picture, Broadcasting, and Recorded Sound Division. [Also on the Web at < http://lcweb.loc.gov/catdir/cpso/amimcovr.html >].

Banks, Marcus (1988a) 'Forty-minute fieldwork', *JASO (Journal of the Anthropological Society of Oxford)*, 19 (3): 251–63.

Banks, Marcus (1989a) 'The narrative of lived experience: some Jains of India and England (Photographic essay)', *Critique of Anthropology*, 9 (2): 65–76.

Banks, Marcus (1989b) 'Seeing yourself as others see you', *CVA Review*, (Fall): 33–8.

Banks, Marcus (1992) *Organizing Jainism in India and England*. Oxford: Clarendon Press.

Banks, Marcus (1994) 'Interactive multimedia and anthropology – a sceptical view'. World Wide Web document. Published at < www.rsl.ox.ac.uk/isca/marcus.banks.02.html > .

Banks, Marcus (1995) 'Visual research methods', *Social Research Update*, 11. [Also on the Web at < www.soc.surrey.ac.uk/sru/SRU11/SRU11.html >]

Banks, Marcus (1996a) 'Constructing the audience through ethnography', in P.I.

Crawford and S.B. Hafsteinsson (eds), *The Construction of the Viewer: Proceedings from NAFA 3*. Højbjerg, Denmark: Intervention Press. pp. 118–34.

Banks, Marcus (1996b) *Ethnicity: Anthropological Constructions*. London: Routledge.

Banks, Marcus (1998) 'Visual anthropology: image, object and interpretation', in J. Prosser (ed.), *Image-based Research: a Sourcebook for Qualitative Researchers*. London: Falmer Press. pp. 9–23.

Banks, Marcus (2000) 'Views of Jain history', in P. Dresch, W. James and D. Parkin (eds), *Anthropologists in a Wider World: Essays on Field Research*. Oxford: Berghahn Books. pp. 187–204.

Barbash, Ilisa and Lucien Taylor (1997) *Cross-cultural Filmmaking: a Handbook for Making Documentary and Ethnographic Films and Videos*. Berkeley: University of California Press.

Barry, Andrew (1995) 'Reporting and visualising', in C. Jenks (ed.), *Visual Culture*. London: Routledge. pp. 42–57.

Barth, Frederick (1974) 'On responsibility and humanity: calling a colleague to account', *Current Anthropology*, 15: 99–102.

Bateson, Gregory and Margaret Mead (1942) *Balinese Character: a Photographic Analysis*. New York: New York Academy of Sciences.

Becker, Howard (1982) *Art Worlds*. Berkeley and London: University of California Press.

Becker, Howard (1986) *Writing for Social Scientists*. Chicago: University of Chicago Press.

Becker, Howard (1998) *Tricks of the Trade: How to Think About Your Research While You're Doing It*. Chicago: University of Chicago Press.

Benjamin, Walter (1992 [1968/1936]) 'The work of art in the age of mechanical reproduction', in *Illuminations*. (Ed. Hannah Arendt) London: Fontana. pp. 211–44.

Berger, John and Jean Mohr (1967) *A Fortunate Man: the Story of a Country Doctor*. Harmondsworth: Penguin.

Berger, John and Jean Mohr (1975) *A Seventh Man: a Book of Images and Words About the Experience of Migrant Workers in Europe*. Harmondsworth: Penguin.

Berger, John and Jean Mohr (1982) *Another Way of Telling*. London: Writers and Readers Publishing Cooperative.

Biella, Peter (1988) 'Against reductionism and idealist self-reflexivity: the Ilparakuyo Maasai film project', in J. Rollwagon (ed.), *Anthropological Filmmaking*. Chur: Harwood Academic Press.

Biella, Peter (1994) 'Codifications of ethnography: linear and nonlinear'. World Wide Web document. Published at < www.rsl.ox.ac.uk/isca/marcus.banks.02.html >.

Biella, Peter (1997) 'Introduction', in P. Biella, N. Chagnon and G. Seaman, *Yanomamö Interactive: The Ax Fight* (CD-ROM with User's Guide). Fort Worth: Harcourt Brace and Company.

Biella, Peter, Chagnon, Napoleon and Seaman, Gary (1997) *Yanomamö Interactive: The Ax Fight* (CD-ROM with User's Guide). Fort Worth: Harcourt Brace and Company.

Born, Georgina (1997) 'Computer software as a medium: textuality, orality and sociality in an artificial intelligence research culture', in M. Banks and H. Morphy (eds), *Rethinking Visual Anthropology.* New Haven and London: Yale University Press. pp. 139–69.

Bourdieu, Pierre (1990 [1965]) *Photography: a Middle-brow Art.* Cambridge: Polity Press.

Bourdieu, Pierre, Darbel, Alain with Schnapper, Dominique (1991 [1969]) *The Love of Art: European Art Museums and Their Public.* Cambridge: Polity Press.

Brownstone, Arni (1993) *War Paint: Blackfoot and Sarcee Painted Buffalo Robes in the Royal Ontario Museum.* Toronto: Royal Ontario Museum.

Burns, Stanley (1990) *Sleeping Beauty: Memorial Photography in America.* Altadena, CA: Twelvetrees Press.

Bush, Vannevar (1995 [1945]) 'As we may think'. World Wide Web document. Published at < www.isg.sfu.ca/~duchier/misc/vbush/vbush.shtml > [originally published in *Atlantic Monthly,* June 1945].

Calcutt, Andrew (1995) 'Computer porn panic: fear and control in cyberspace', *Futures,* 27 (7): 749–62.

Caldarola, Victor (1985) 'Visual contexts: a photographic research method in anthropology', *Studies in Visual Communication,* 11 (3): 33–53.

CAP (ChildCare Action Project): Christian Analysis of American Culture. Web site: < www.capalert.com/ >

Carelli, Vincent (1988) 'Vidéo dans les villages: un instrument de réaffirmation ethnique', *CVA Newsletter,* October: 13–19.

Chabria, Suresh (1994) 'Before our eyes: a short history of India's silent cinema', in S. Chabria (ed.), *Light of Asia: Indian Silent Cinema 1912–1934.* Pordenone/Pune: Le Giornate Del Cinema Muto/National Film Archive of India. pp. 3–24.

Chagnon, Napoleon and Bugos, Paul (1979) 'Kin selection and conflict: an analysis of a Yanomamö ax fight', in N. Chagnon and W. Irons (eds), *Evolutionary Biology and Human Social Behavior: an Anthropological Perspective.* North Scituate, MA: Duxbury Press. pp. 217–38.

Chaplin, Elizabeth (1998) 'Making meanings in art worlds: a sociological account of the career of John Constable and his oeuvre, with special reference to "The Cornfield" (homage to Howard Becker)', in J. Prosser (ed.), *Image-based Research: a Sourcebook for Qualitative Researchers.* London: Falmer Press. pp. 284–306.

Chiozzi, Paolo (1989) 'Photography and anthropological research: three case studies', in R. Boonzajer Flaes (ed.), *Eyes Across the Water.* Amsterdam: Het Spinhuis. pp. 43–50.

Classen, Constance (1993) *Worlds of Sense: Exploring the Senses in History and Across Cultures.* London: Routledge.

Collier, John Jn. and Collier, Malcolm (1986) *Visual Anthropology: Photography as a Research Method.* Albuquerque: University of New Mexico Press.

Connor, Linda, Asch, Patsy and Asch, Timothy (1986) *Jero Tapakan: Balinese Healer.* Cambridge: Cambridge University Press.

Coote, Jeremy and Anthony Shelton (eds) (1992) *Anthropology, Art and Aesthetics.* Oxford: Clarendon Press.

Cort, John (1997) 'Art, religion, and material culture: some reflections on method', *Journal of the American Academy of Religion*, 64 (3): 613–32.

Crawford, Peter I. and Hafsteinsson, Sigurjon Baldur (eds) (1996) *The Construction of the Viewer: Proceedings from NAFA 3*. Højbjerg, Denmark: Intervention Press.

Criticos, Costas and Quinlan, Tim (1991) 'Community video: power and process', *Visual Sociology*, 6 (2): 39–52.

Criticos, Costas and Quinlan, Tim (1993) 'Communication that doesn't work? Postmodernism and community video: a reply to Deacon', *Visual Sociology*, 8 (2): 67–9.

Das, Veena (1995) 'On soap opera: what kind of anthropological object is it?', in D. Miller (ed.), *Worlds Apart: Modernity Through the Prism of the Local*. London: Routledge. pp. 169–89.

Davis, John (1992) *Exchange*. Buckingham: Open University Press.

Deacon, Roger (1992) 'Power, knowledge and community video revisited', *Visual Sociology*, 7 (2): 39–48.

Dowmunt, Tony (ed.) (1993) *Channels of Resistance: Global Television and Local Empowerment*. London: BFI Publishing, in association with Channel Four Television.

Dudley, Sandra and Petch, Alison (n.d.) 'Using multi-media tools to teach anthropology: "Pitt Rivers, anthropology and ethnography in the nineteenth century" '. Unpublished paper.

Dumont, Louis (1980 [1966]) *Homo Hierarchicus: the Caste System and its Implications* [Complete revised English edition]. Chicago: University of Chicago Press.

Dundas, Paul (1992) *The Jains*. London: Routledge.

Eaton, Mick (1979) 'The production of cinematic reality', in M. Eaton (ed.), *Anthropology-Reality-Cinema: the Films of Jean Rouch*. London: British Film Institute. pp. 40–53.

Eck, Diana L. (1985 [1981]) *Darsan: seeing the divine image in India*. Chambersburg, PA: Anima Books.

Edwards, Elizabeth (ed.) (1992) *Anthropology and Photography, 1860–1920*. New Haven: Yale University Press in association with The Royal Anthropological Institute, London.

Edwards, Elizabeth (1996) 'Postcards – greetings from another world', in T. Selwyn (ed.), *The Tourist Image*. London: John Wiley. pp. 197–221.

Edwards, Elizabeth (1997) 'Beyond the boundary: a consideration of the expressive in photography and anthropology', in M. Banks and H. Morphy (eds), *Rethinking Visual Anthropology*. London and New Haven: Yale University Press. pp. 53–80.

Elder, Sarah (1995) 'Collaborative filmmaking: an open space for making meaning, a moral ground for ethnographic film', *Visual Anthropology Review*, 11 (2): 94–101.

Epstein, A.L. (ed.) (1967) *The Craft of Social Anthropology*. London: Tavistock.

Evans, Jessica and Stuart Hall (eds) (1999) *Visual Culture: the Reader*. London: Sage, in association with the Open University.

Evans-Pritchard, E.E. (1940) *The Nuer: a Description of the Modes of Livelihood and Political Institutions of a Nilotic People*. Oxford: Clarendon Press.

Excalibur Visual RetrievalWare. Web site: < http://www.excalib.com/products/ vrw/index.shtml >

Eyles, Allen and Meeker, David (1992) *Missing Believed Lost: the Great British Film Search*. London: British Film Institute.

Faris, James C. (1992) 'Anthropological transparency: film, representation and politics', in P.I. Crawford and D. Turton (eds), *Film as Ethnography*. Manchester: Manchester University Press. pp. 171–82.

Faris, James C. (1993) 'A response to Terence Turner', *Anthropology Today*, 9 (1): 12–13.

Fischer, Michael D. (1994) *Applications in Computing for Social Anthropologists*. London: Routledge.

Fischer, Michael and Zeitlyn, David (1999) *Experience-rich Anthropology: Resource Guide and Sampler CD for Teachers and Students*. Canterbury: Centre for Anthropology and Computing, University of Kent at Canterbury. [Also on the Web at www.era.anthropology.ac.uk/]

Fischer, Michael D. and David Zeitlyn (n.d.) 'Visual anthropology in the digital mirror. Part 1: Computer-assisted visual anthropology'. Unpublished paper.

Foucault, Michel (1977) *Discipline and Punish: The Birth of the Prison*. Harmondsworth: Penguin.

Frauenfelder, Mark (1997) 'Content-based image retrieval: in other words, how the Naked People Finder works', *Wired*, 5 (6): 82.

Geertz, Clifford (1975 [1973]) 'Thick description: towards an interpretive theory of culture', in *The Interpretation of Cultures*. London: Hutchinson. pp. 3–30.

Geffroy, Yannick (1990) 'Family photographs: a visual heritage', *Visual Anthropology*, 3 (4): 367–410.

Gell, Alfred (1992) 'The technology of enchantment and the enchantment of technology', in J. Coote and A. Shelton (eds), *Anthropology, Art and Aesthetics*. Oxford: Clarendon Press. pp. 40–63.

Gell, Alfred (1998) *Art and Agency: an Anthropological Theory*. Oxford: Clarendon Press.

Gell, Alfred (1999) *The Art of Anthropology: Essays and Diagrams*. London: Athlone Press.

Ginsburg, Faye (1991) 'Indigenous media: Faustian contract or global village?', *Cultural Anthropology*, 6 (1): 92–112.

Ginsburg, Faye (1994) 'Culture/media: a (mild) polemic', *Anthropology Today*, 10 (2): 5–15.

Glaser, Barney and Strauss, Anselm (1967) *The Discovery of Grounded Theory: Strategies for Qualitative Research*. Chicago: Aldine.

Gold, Stephen (1991) 'Ethnic boundaries and ethnic entrepreneurship: a photo-elicitation study', *Visual Sociology*, 6 (2): 9–22.

Goody, J.R. (1986) *The Logic of Writing and the Organization of Society*. Cambridge: Cambridge University Press.

Gould, Stephen Jay (1996 [1981]) *The Mismeasure of Man* [2nd edition]. Harmondsworth: Penguin.

Grady, John (1991) 'The visual essay and sociology', *Visual sociology*, 6 (2): 23–38.

Grimshaw, Anna (1997) 'The eye in the door: anthropology, film and the exploration of interior space', in M. Banks and H. Morphy (eds), *Rethinking Visual Anthropology*. London and New Haven: Yale University Press. pp. 36–52.

Gutman, Judith (1982) *Through Indian Eyes: 19th and Early 20th Century Photography from India*. New York: Oxford University Press.

Hammersley, Martyn and Atkinson, Paul (1983) *Ethnography: Principles in Practice*. London: Tavistock Publications.

Harding, Thomas (1997) *The Video Activist Handbook*. London: Pluto.

Harper, Douglas (1982) *Good Company*. Chicago: University of Chicago Press.

Harper, Douglas (1987a) 'The visual ethnographic narrative', *Visual Anthropology*, 1 (1): 1–19.

Harper, Douglas (1987b) *Working Knowledge: Skill and Community in a Small Shop*. Chicago: University of Chicago Press.

Harper, Douglas (1998) 'An argument for visual sociology', in J. Prosser (ed.), *Image-based Research: a Sourcebook for Qualitative Researchers*. London: Falmer Press. pp. 24–41.

Harris, Olivia (1975) 'The Quechuas (film review)', *RAIN (Royal Anthropological Institute News)*, 6: 11.

Harvey, Penelope (1996) *Hybrids of Modernity: Anthropology, the Nation State and the Universal Exhibition*. London: Routledge.

Heider, Karl (1976) *Ethnographic Film*. Austin: University of Texas Press.

Hitkari, S.S. (1981) *Ganesha-Sthapana: the Folk Art of Gujarat*. New Delhi: Phulkari Publications.

Holy, Ladislav (1984) 'Theory, methodology and the research process', in R.F. Ellen (ed.), *Ethnographic Research: a Guide to General Conduct*. London: Academic Press. pp. 13–34.

Houston, Penelope (1994) *Keepers of the Frame: the Film Archives*. London: British Film Institute.

Houtman, Gustaaf (1988) 'Interview with Maurice Bloch', *Anthropology Today*, 4 (1): 18–21.

Hughes-Freeland, Felicia (1997) 'Balinese on television: representation and response', in M. Banks and H. Morphy (eds), *Rethinking Visual Anthropology*. New Haven and London: Yale University Press. pp. 120–38.

Jenks, Chris (ed.) (1995) *Visual Culture*. London: Routledge.

Jordan, Pierre-L. (1992) *Cinéma* ('Premier Contact–Premier Regard' series). Marseille: Musées de Marseille.

Karp, Ivan and Levine, Steven (eds) (1991) *Exhibiting Cultures: the Poetics and Politics of Museum Display*. Washington DC: Smithsonian Institution.

King, Jonathan C.H. (1999) *First Peoples, First Contacts: Native Peoples of North America*. London: British Museum Press.

Klaue, Wolfgang (1993) *World Directory of Moving Image and Sound Archives*. Munich: K.G. Saur.

Kottack, Conrad Phillip (2000) *Cultural Anthropology* [8th edition]. Boston: McGraw-Hill.

Krebs, Stephanie (1975) 'The film elicitation technique', in P. Hockings (ed.), *Principles of Visual Anthropology* [1st edition]. Berlin and New York: Mouton de Gruyter. pp. 283–302.

Lærke, Anna (1998) 'By means of remembering: notes on a fieldwork with English children', *Anthropology Today*, 14 (1): 3–7.

Laidlaw, James (1995) *Riches and Renunciation: Religion, Economy and Society Among the Jains*. Oxford: Clarendon Press.

Latour, Bruno (1988) 'Opening one eye while closing the other . . . a note on some religious paintings', in G. Fyfe and J. Law (eds), *Picturing Power: Visual Depiction and Social Relations*. London: Routledge. pp. 15–38.

Leslie, Jacques (1995) 'Digital photopros and photo(shop) realism', *Wired*, 3 (5): 108–113.

Loizos, Peter (1980) 'Granada Television's Disappearing World series: an appraisal', *American Anthropologist*, 82 : 573–94.

Loizos, Peter (1993) *Innovation in Ethnographic film: from Innocence to Self-consciousness, 1955–1985*. Manchester: Manchester University Press.

Lombroso, Cesare (1887) *L'homme Criminel*. Paris: F. Alcan.

Lubeck, Stephen (1990) 'An island of authenticity: documenting community mental health', *Visual Sociology Review*, 5 (1): 6–17.

Lull, James (1990) *Inside Family Viewing: Ethnographic Research on Television's Audiences*. London: Routledge/Comedia.

Lynch, Michael and Edgerton, Samuel (1988) 'Aesthetics and digital image processing: representational craft in contemporary astronomy', in G. Fyfe and J. Law (eds), *Picturing Power: Visual Depiction and Social Relations*. London: Routledge. pp. 184–220.

MacClancy, Jeremy (1988) 'A natural curiosity: the British market in primitive art', *Res*, 15: 163–76.

MacDonald, Sharon and Fyfe, Gordon (eds) (1996) *Theorizing Museums: Representing Identity and Diversity in a Changing World*. Oxford: Blackwell.

MacDougall, David (1978) 'Ethnographic film: failure and promise', *Annual Review of Anthropology*, 7: 405–25.

MacDougall, David (1995 [1975]) 'Beyond observational cinema', in P. Hockings (ed.), *Principles of Visual Anthropology* [2nd edition]. Berlin and New York: Mouton de Gruyter. pp. 115–32.

MacDougall, David (1997) 'The visual in anthropology', in M. Banks and H. Morphy (eds), *Rethinking Visual Anthropology*. London and New Haven: Yale University Press. pp. 276–95.

MacDougall, David (1998a) 'The fate of the cinema subject', in *Transcultural Cinema*. Princeton: Princeton University Press. pp. 25–60.

MacDougall, David (1998b) 'Visual anthropology and the ways of knowing', in *Transcultural Cinema*. Princeton: Princeton University Press. pp. 61–92.

Marcus, George and Fischer, Michael M.J. (1986) *Anthropology as Cultural Critique: an Experimental Moment in the Human Sciences.* Chicago: University of Chicago Press.

Martinez, Wilton (1990) 'Critical studies and visual anthropology: aberrant vs. anticipated readings of ethnographic film', *CVA Review*, Spring: 34–47.

Martinez, Wilton (1992) 'Who constructs anthropological knowledge? Towards a theory of ethnographic film spectatorship', in P.I. Crawford and D. Truton (eds), *Film as Ethnography.* Manchester: Manchester University Press in association with the Granada Centre for Visual Anthropology. pp. 131–61.

Mead, Margaret (1995 [1975]) 'Visual anthropology in a discipline of words', in P. Hockings (ed.), *Principles of Visual Anthropology* [1st edition]. Berlin and New York: Mouton de Gruyter. pp. 3–10.

Michaels, Eric (1986) *The Aboriginal Invention of Television in Central Australia, 1982–1985.* Canberra: Australian Institute of Aboriginal Studies.

Mirzoeff, Nicholas (1999) *An Introduction to Visual Culture.* London: Routledge.

Moore, Alexander (1988) 'The limitations of imagist documentary. A review of Robert Gardner's "Forest of Bliss" ', *SVA Newsletter*, 4 (2): 1–3.

Moore, Alexander (1990) 'Performance battles: progress and mis-steps of a woman warrior', *Society for Visual Anthropology Review*, 6 (2): 73–9.

Morley, David (1992) *Television, Audiences and Cultural Studies.* London and New York: Routledge.

Morley, David (1995) 'Television: not so much a visual medium, more a visible object', in C. Jenks (ed.), *Visual Culture.* London: Rouledge. pp. 170–89.

Morley, David (1996) 'The audience, the ethnographer, the postmodernist and their problems', in P.I. Crawford and S.B. Hafsteinsson (eds), *The Construction of the Viewer: Proceedings from NAFA 3.* Højbjerg, Denmark: Intervention Press. pp. 11–27.

Morphy, Howard and Marcus Banks (1997) 'Introduction: rethinking visual anthropology', in M. Banks and H. Morphy (eds), *Rethinking Visual Anthropology.* London and New Haven: Yale University Press. pp. 1–35.

Negroponte, Nicholas (1997) 'Pay whom per what when [Part one]', *Wired* [UK Edition], 3 (2): 112.

Nichols, Bill (1988 [1983]) 'The voice of documentary', in A. Rosenthal (ed.), *New Challenges for Documentary.* Berkeley: University of California Press. pp. 48–63.

Östör, Ákos (1989) 'Is that what "Forest of Bliss" is all about? A response.', *SVA Newsletter*, 5 (1): 4–8.

Parker, Rozsika (1996 [1984]) *The Subversive Stitch: Embroidery and the Making of the Feminine.* London: The Women's Press.

Parry, Jonathan (1988) 'Comment on Robert Gardner's "Forest of Bliss" ', *SVA Newsletter*, 4 (2): 4–7.

Parry, Jonathan (1994) *Death in Banaras.* Cambridge: Cambridge University Press.

Pieke, Frank (2000) 'Serendipity in anthropology and culture', in P. Dresch, W. James and D. Parkin (eds), *Anthropologists in a Wider World: Essays on Field Research.* Oxford: Berghahn Books. pp. 129–50.

Pinney, Christopher (1992a) 'The parallel histories of anthropology and photography', in E. Edwards (ed.), *Anthropology and Photography, 1860–1920*. New Haven and London: Yale University Press in association with The Royal Anthropological Institute, London. pp. 74–95.

Pinney, Christopher (1992b) 'Underneath the Banyan tree: William Crooke and photographic depictions of caste', in E. Edwards (ed.), *Anthropology and Photography, 1860–1920*. New Haven and London: Yale University Press in association with The Royal Anthropological Institute, London. pp. 165–73.

Pinney, Christopher (1997) *Camera Indica: the Social Life of Indian Photographs*. London: Reaktion.

Prasad, Sunand (1998) 'A tale of two cities: house and town in India today', in G.H.R. Tillotson (ed.), *Paradigms of Indian Architecture: Space and Time in Representation and Design*. Richmond, Surrey: Curzon Press. pp. 176–99.

Price, Sally (1989) *Primitive Art in Civilized Places*. Chicago: University of Chicago Press.

Prosser, Jon (ed.) (1998a) *Image-based Research: a Sourcebook for Qualitative Researchers*. London: Falmer Press.

Prosser, Jon (1998b) 'The status of image-based research', in J. Prosser (ed.), *Image-based Research: a Sourcebook for Qualitative Researchers*. London: Falmer Press. pp. 97–112.

Puranen, Jorma (1999) *Imaginary Homecoming*. Oulu (Finland): Pohjoinen.

Quigley, Declan (1993) *The Interpretation of Caste*. Oxford: Clarendon Press.

Quigley, Declan (1994) 'Is a theory of caste still possible?', in M. Searle-Chatterjee and U. Sharma (eds), *Contextualizing Caste: Post-Dumontian Approaches*. Oxford: Blackwell/The Sociological Review. pp. 25–48.

Rius [Eduardo del Rio] (1976) *Marx for Beginners*. London: Writers and Readers Publishing Cooperative.

Rollwagon, Jack (ed.) (1988) *Anthropological Filmmaking*. Chur: Harwood Academic Publishers.

Root, Jane (1986) *Open the Box*. London: Comedia Publishing Group.

Rosenthal, Alan (ed.) (1980) *The Documentary Conscience: a Casebook in Film Making*. Berkeley: University of California Press.

Rosenthal, Alan (ed.) (1988) *New Challenges for Documentary*. Berkeley: University of California Press.

Rowson, Martin (1990) *The Waste Land*. London: Penguin.

Rowson, Martin (1996) *Tristram Shandy*. Dublin: Lilliput Press.

Ruby, Jay (1991) 'Death and photography: a review essay', *Visual Sociology*, 6 (2): 82–6.

Ruby, Jay (1995a) *Secure the Shadow: Death and Photography in America*. Cambridge, MA: MIT Press.

Ruby, Jay (1995b) 'The moral burden of authorship in ethnographic film', *Visual Anthropology Review*, 11 (2): 77–82.

Ruby, Jay (2000) *Picturing Culture: Explorations of Film and Anthropology*. Chicago: University of Chicago Press.

Ruby, Jay, Gross, Larry and Katz, John (eds) (1988) *Image Ethics: the Moral Rights of Subjects in Photographs, Film and Television*. New York: Oxford University Press.

Rundstrom, Don (1988) 'Imaging anthropology', in J. Rollwagon (ed.), *Anthropological Filmmaking*. Chur: Harwood Academic Press. pp. 317–70.

Salt, Barry (1992 [1983]) *Film Style and Technology: History and Analysis*. London: Starword.

Scherer, Joanna (1992) 'The photographic document: photographs as primary data in anthropological enquiry', in E. Edwards (ed.), *Anthropology and Photography, 1860–1920*. New Haven and London: Yale University Press in association with The Royal Anthropological Institute, London. pp. 32–41.

Sekula, Alan (1982) 'On the invention of photographic meaning', in V. Burgin (ed.), *Thinking Photography*. Basingstoke: Macmillan Education. pp. 84–109.

Sharma, Ursula (1999) *Caste*. Buckingham: Open University Press.

Silverstone, Roger (1985) *Framing Science: the Making of a BBC Documentary*. London: British Film Institute.

Singer, André (1992) 'Anthropology in broadcasting', in P.I. Crawford and D. Truton (eds), *Film as Ethnography*. Manchester: Manchester University Press in association with the Granada Centre for Visual Anthropology. pp. 264–73.

Slater, Don (1983) 'Marketing Mass Photography', in H. Davis and P. Walton (eds), *Language, Image, Media*. Oxford: Basil Blackwell. pp. 245–63.

Spencer, Frank (1992) 'Some notes on the attempt to apply photography to anthropometry during the second half of the nineteenth century', in E. Edwards (ed.), *Anthropology and Photography, 1860–1920*. New Haven and London: Yale University Press in association with The Royal Anthropological Institute, London. pp. 99–107.

Stasz, C. (1979) 'The early history of visual sociology', in J. Wagner (ed.), *Images of Information: Still Photography in the Social Sciences*. Beverly Hills: Sage. pp. 119–36.

Steiger, Ricabeth (1995) 'First children and family dynamics', *Visual Sociology*, 10 (1–2): 28–49.

Tagg, John (1987) *The Burden of Representation: Essays on Photographies and Histories*. London: Macmillan.

Tarlo, Emma (1996) *Clothing Matters: Dress and Identity in India*. London: Hurst and Company.

Tufte, Edward R. (1983) *The Visual Display of Quantitative Information*. Cheshire, CT: Graphics Press.

Tufte, Edward R. (1990) *Envisioning Information*. Cheshire, CT: Graphics Press.

Tufte, Edward R. (1997) *Visual Explanations: Images and Quantities, Evidence and Narrative*. Cheshire, CT: Graphics Press.

Turnbull, Colin M. (1973 [1972]) *The Mountain People*. London: Jonathan Cape.

Turner, Terence (1990) 'Visual media, cultural politics, and anthropological practice: some implications of recent uses of film and video among the Kayapo of Brazil', *CVA Review*, Spring: 8–13.

Turner, Terence (1991) 'The social dynamics of visual media in an indigenous society: the cultural meaning and the personal politics of video-making in Kayapo communities', *Visual Anthropology Review*, 7 (2): 68–76.

Turner, Terence (1992) 'Defiant images: the Kayapo appropriation of video', *Anthropology Today*, 8 (6): 5–16.

Turner, Terence (1995) 'Representation, collaboration and mediation in contemporary ethnographic and indigenous media', *Visual Anthropology Review*, 11 (2): 102–6.

Usai, Paolo Cherchi (1994) *Burning Passions: an Introduction to the Study of Silent Cinema*. London: British Film Institute.

van der Does, Patricia, Edelaar, Sonja, Gooskens, Imke, Liefting, Margreet and van Mierlo, Marije (1992) 'Reading images: a study of a Dutch neighborhood', *Visual Sociology*, 7 (1): 4–67.

van Wezel, Ruud H.J. (1988) 'Reciprocity of research results in Portugal', *Critique of Anthropology*, 8 (2): 63–70.

Vaughan, Megan (1991) *Curing Their Ills. Colonial Power and African Illness*. Cambridge: Polity Press.

White-Hensen, Wendy (1984) *Archival Moving Image Materials: a Cataloging Manual*. Washington, DC: Library of Congress, Motion Picture, Broadcasting, and Recorded Sound Division.

Willson, Margaret (1990) *The Royal Anthropological Institute Film Library Catalogue* [Vol. II]. London: Royal Anthropological Institute.

Wolcott, Harry F. (1999) *Ethnography: a Way of Seeing*. Walnut Creek, CA: AltaMira Press.

Woodburn, James (1982) *The Royal Anthropological Institute Film Library Catalogue* [Vol. I]. London: Royal Anthropological Institute.

Worth, Sol and Adair, John (1972) *Through Navaho Eyes: an Exploration in Film Communication and Anthropology*. Bloomington: Indiana University Press.

Wright, Terence (1999) *The Photography Handbook*. London: Routledge.

Zeitlyn, David and Fischer, Michael D. (n.d.) 'Visual anthropology in the digital mirror. Part 2. A case study of multimedia in anthropological research: the Mambila Nggwun ritual'. Unpublished paper.

Filmography

Note: Where known, current distributors for the films below are listed on the Web site that accompanies this book.

Asch, Timothy and Chagnon, Napoleon (1975) *The Ax Fight* (30 mins). University Park, PA/Watertown, MA: Center for Documentary Anthropology, Pennsylvania State University/Documentary Educational Resources.

Asch, Timothy, Connor, Linda and Asch, Patsy (1980a) *A Balinese Trance Seance* (30 mins). Watertown, MA: Documentary Educational Resources.

Asch, Timothy, Connor, Linda and Asch, Patsy (1980b) *Jero on Jero: 'A Balinese Trance Seance' Observed* (17 mins). Watertown, MA: Documentary Educational Resources.

Asch, Timothy, Connor, Linda and Asch, Patsy (1991) *Releasing the Spirits: A Village Cremation in Bali* (43 mins). Watertown, MA: Documentary Educational Resources.

Baaré, Gabai, Barbash, Ilisa, Steiner, Christian and Taylor, Lucien (1992) *In and Out of Africa* (59 mins). Los Angeles: University of Southern California.

Baily, John (1985) *Amir: an Afghan Refugee Musician's Life in Peshawar, Pakistan* (52 mins). Beaconsfield, UK: NFTS/RAI.

Banks, Marcus (1988b) *Raju and His Friends* (40 mins). Beaconsfield, UK: NFTS/RAI.

Beckham, Michael (1987) *The Kayapo* (52 mins). Manchester: Granada Television.

Beckham, Michael (1989) *The Kayapo: Out of the Forest* (52 mins). Manchester: Granada Television.

Burum, Ivo (1991) *Satellite Dreaming* (60 mins). Australia: CAAMA, in association with Channel Four and APT Film and Television.

Flaherty, Robert (1922) *Nanook of the North* (55 mins). USA: Revillon Frères.

Gardner, Robert (1985) *Forest of Bliss* (80 mins). Boston, USA: Film Studies Centre, Harvard University.

Harris, Paul (1994) *Scenes from a Museum* (22 mins). Manchester: Granada Centre for Visual Anthropology, University of Manchester.

Henley, Paul (1994) *Faces in the Crowd* (39 mins). Manchester: Granada Centre for Visual Anthropology.

Hitchcock, Alfred (1948) *Rope* (80 mins). Los Angeles: Warner Brothers.

Llewelyn-Davies, Melissa (1993) *Memories and Dreams* (90 mins). London: Allegra Productions.

MacDougall, David and MacDougall, Judith (1972) *To Live With Herds: a Dry Season Among the Jie* (90 mins). Los Angeles: University of California Ethnographic Film Program.

MacDougall, David and MacDougall, Judith (1977) *Lorang's Way* (69 mins). Los Angeles: University of California Ethnographic Film Program.

MacDougall, David and MacDougall, Judith (1991) *Photo Wallahs: an Encounter with Photography in Mussoorie, a North Indian Hill Station* (60 mins). Canberra: Oxnard Film Productions.

Montgomery, Robert (1947) *The Lady in the Lake* (105 mins). Los Angeles: Metro-Goldwyn-Mayer.

Nairn, Charlie (1974) *The Kawelka: Ongka's Big Moka* (50 mins). Manchester: Granada Television.

Pasini, Carlos (1974) *The Quechua* (50 mins). Manchester: Granada Television.

Poliakoff, Stephen (1999) *Shooting the Past* [3 part television drama] (75 + 55 + 55 mins). London: Talkback, for BBC Television.

Rouch, Jean (1957) *Moi, un Noir* (80 mins). Paris: Films de la Pleïade.

Rouch, Jean (1967) *Jaguar* (110 mins). Paris: Films de la Pleïade.

Rouch, Jean and Morin, Edgar (1960) *Chronique d'un Été* (90 mins). Paris: Argos Films.

Rundstrom, Don, Rundstrom, Ron and Bergum, Clinton (1971) *The Path* (34 mins). Santa Fe: The Sumai Film Company.

Tarantino, Quentin (1994) *Pulp Fiction* (154 mins). New York: Miramax.

Tari, János (1991) *Benjamin* (27 mins). London: NFTS/Hungarian Academy of Drama and Film/Jerusalem Film School.

Wason, David (1990) *The Trobriand Islanders of Papua New Guinea* (50 mins). Manchester: Granada Television.

Index